POSTSTRUCTURALIST GEOGRAPHIES

Poststructuralist Geographies

The Diabolical Art of Spatial Science

Marcus Doel

ROWMAN & LITTLEFIELD PUBLISHERS, INC.
Lanham • Boulder • New York

ROWMAN & LITTLEFIELD PUBLISHERS, INC.

First published in the United States of America
by Rowman & Littlefield Publishers, Inc.
4720 Boston Way, Lanham, Maryland 20706

ISBN 0-8476-9818-1 (cloth: alk. paper)
ISBN 0-8476-9819-X (pbk.: alk. paper)

Printed in Great Britain

Let us space. The art of this text is the air it causes to circulate between its screens. The chainings are invisible, everything seems improvised or juxtaposed. This text induces by agglutinating rather than demonstrating, by coupling and decoupling, gluing and ungluing [*en accolant et en décollant*] rather than by exhibiting the continuous, and analogical, instructive, suffocating necessity of a discursive rhetoric.

Jacques Derrida, *Glas*

For a hinge-logic, a hinge-style.

Jean-François Lyotard, *Duchamp's* TRANS/*formers*

... an infernal machine is being assembled.

Gilles Deleuze and Félix Guattari, *A Thousand Plateaus*

Contents

Acknowledgements

I would like to thank Keith Bassett and Nigel Thrift for their remarkable guidance and long-lasting inspiration that dates back to the mid-1980s. Not only did they nurture in me a taste for the theoretical, they also gave me a passion for geography. What I cherish even more than that, however, is the fact that they allowed me to take great pleasure in reading, writing, and thinking, even though such *jouissance* often took me far from the customary habits and *habitus* of academic geography. I hope that this book expresses sufficient taste, passion, and pleasure for their own liking. I am only sorry that it took such a long time in coming. Ian Cook and David McEvoy were kind enough to open up considerable swathes of time within which I could think and write, and for that I am truly grateful. In formulating and writing this book I have been privileged to have spent my time in three wonderful and supportive contexts: the Departments of Geography at the University of Bristol and Loughborough University, and the School of Social Science at Liverpool John Moores University. I am especially indebted to David Clarke, with whom I have collaborated for many years (many of the ideas and trajectories laid out here are as much his as my own), and to journals such as *Society and Space* and *Transactions of the Institute of British Geographers* that have been receptive to my kind of experimentation in spatial science. I would also like to thank those people who were kind enough to comment on one or more of the various chapters: Ed Brown, Mike Gane, Martin Gren, David Matless, Chris Philo, George Revill, Richard Smith, and Ulf Strohmayer. I am also grateful to Peter Wissoker who helped me to launch this project, and to John Davey who saw it to fruition. I would like to express my appreciation to all those who have affected my work without explicit reference in the text. What remains dearest to me is often too close and too imperceptible to be adequately unfolded. Finally, apologies to Anne, James, and Beanie who were 'tortured for years by this bloody thing.' Such is life in the slow lane ...

Introduction –
opening poststructuralist geography

Speaking always as geographers. (Deleuze, 1983a, p. 83)

It is not only time that is 'out of joint,' but space, space in time, spacing.
(Derrida, 1994b, p. 83)

The ethic of geography

You are a slow little stream. You will be passed by fast little streams ...
She tells herself that thought takes time and there's nothing you can do
about it ... That doesn't much resemble streams. Ponds, rather. You
flounder in them ...

Conclusion: the true streams are subterranean, they stream slowly beneath
the ground, they make headwaters and springs: You can't know where
they'll surface. And their speed is unknown. I would like to be an underground cavity full of black, cold, and still water. (Lyotard, 1997, p. 5)

It is much easier to become swept up by a powerful current than it is
to be the origin of a great effort. In the present conjuncture, many
human geographers have become swept up by currents loosely referred
to as poststructuralist, deconstructive, or postmodern; currents which
braid in innumerable ways with others within critical human geography,
such as Marxism, feminism, and postcolonialism. Despite their manifold
nature, signified most clearly in the recent pluralization and hybridization
of what were often considered to be broadly unitary perspectives, these
currents can be said to flow through the dissolution of the postpositivist
closure of theoretical debates within the frame of reference staked out
by humanism and structuralism; often streaming through channels first
carved out by structuration theory and critical realism in the wake of a
rejuvenated time-geographical insistence on the indissociability of space
and time, as both contexts and outcomes of human practice (see, for
example: Carlstein, Parkes and Thrift, 1978a, 1978b; Cloke, Philo and
Sadler, 1991; Gregory and Urry, 1985; Kobayashi and MacKenzie, 1989;
Peet, 1998; Thrift, 1983, 1996b).

It is not my intention to chart either these currents or the dissolution of the closure of human geography between the pincer movement of structure and agency. Interesting though both of these are, they barely tap into the enormous, subterranean revolution in the art of spatial science that has been taking place in fields as diverse as quantum physics, sociology, and philosophy. And it is this revolution that I have been swept up by. So, for strategic reasons, rather than dwell on the contemporary nature and practice of critical human geography, or detail the various ways in which geography and geographers have taken up the postmodern, poststructural, and deconstructive currents, I will attempt a much more modest task that will, in spite of my desire, entail a great effort on our part: to outline my take on poststructuralist geography. From the outset I should say that this is not the correct version. It is just a version – a pop-philosophical remix – , which affects you or not, which is becoming or unbecoming, fitting or ill-mannered. Such an evaluation is always contextual and determined by the manifold ways in which the work is taken up, the paths by which it goes off and becomes otherwise. Here we are close to Deleuze and Guattari's (1984) *schizoanalysis* – a discordant mode of existence that is perpetually breaking down and in flight from itself; an insatiable deterritorialization evoked by the excessive force of what happens to us (cf. Baudrillard, 1988c; Guattari, 1996; Jameson, 1984). Such a schizoanalysis should not be confused with Lefebvre's (1991, 1996) *rhythmanalysis* – whose employment in the putting of "the finishing touches to the exposition of the production of space" is put in the service of "the necessary and inevitable restoration of the total body" (Lefebvre, 1991, p. 405). The space of the work, along with its libidinal economy and affective machinery, is always in process and never totalizable. Its mode of existence is becoming-otherwise than what it will have been (*post modo*). So while I sympathize with the need for a "rhythm analysis" that would demonstrate how "The repetitions and redundancies of rhythms, their symmetries and asymmetries, interact in ways that cannot be reduced to the discrete and fixed determinants of analytic thought" and how "the body ... is traversed by rhythms rather as the 'ether' is traversed by waves" I hesitate before the expectation of a "general rhythmology" whose "preferred spheres of experiment" would be "the sphere of 'rhythmic cells' and their effects" (Lefebvre, 1991, pp. 205–6).

Accordingly, to be worthy of the events that have effected this work is not to confine them to a total corpus; to bind them in a veritable straight-jacket bearing the tag 'Poststructuralist Geography,' for example. It is rather to affirm and enact their own becoming-otherwise. Everything is in a state of becoming. There are only events that affect you or not, with all of the necessary couplings and redistributions of energy, cast adrift in an "open 'space-time' in which there are no more identities but only transformations" (Lyotard, 1988b, p. 31). It is always a matter of how to plug oneself into a milieu without choking off the infinite array of other modes of existence that could have been drawn out of its event horizon. This is why even the most minimal of events can be unfolded, recomposed, and interpreted in innumerable ways. One will never be finished with the task of doing justice to the event: of reading and re-reading, of thinking and re-thinking, of repeating and differing. Therefore, my paracitation and close reading of others will not be in an attempt to pin things down to a fundamental or essential kernel of absolute meaning. One reads closely in order to differentiate and discriminate: to give rise to new events, "to give space for singular events" (Derrida, 1994c, p. 55). If there is a law of space, the expression of which remains the dream of spatial science, then it is a *harsh* law, as Derrida (1976) once put it. For geography degree zero is infinitely dense: it takes place along what Deleuze and Guattari (1988) called 'a hundred thousand lines of flight.' There are infinite infinities folded into each event of space and spacing. The minimal element is always already maximal in its disjointure: it is not a *point* (a mere given), but a *singularity* – in the mathematical sense of infinite disjointure or infinite density. If poststructuralist geography proves irritating and unsettling to established and sedentary ways of spatial science, then it is because of this insistence and affirmation of the iterability of the event in its insatiable becoming-otherwise than what it will have been. Supporting poststructuralist geography is neither a foundation nor an ontology. Rather, it is carried by an immanent vibration and solicitation: Pefanis (1991, p. 85) aptly refers to his "narration of the heterodoxical tradition of French thought" – Bataille, Baudrillard, Lyotard, etc. – as a "cartography of a ruptured and abyssal territory." The notion of a single narration and cartography is problematic, however, since every portion of the terrain is out of joint. This is why a schizoanalytic and cancerous proliferation of 'minor-languages' (Deleuze and Guattari) and 'little narratives' (Lyotard) surges through "the space of the fallen idols, in the demise of transhistorical and transcendental values" (Pefanis, 1991, p. 90). What we need is "a delirious cartography of thousands of plateaux, each one a shifting ice flow [*sic*]" (Fuller, 1992, p. 169). Poststructuralist geography is a driftwork, a wanton abandonment, an active nihilism.

"Events are fluvia," suggests Deleuze (1993b, p. 79). Everything is in perpetual motion, even if that vibration is often turned back on itself to simulate a constancy, consistency, or rhythmic cell. Insofar as this work takes place, it is a conductor and a vibrator. In consequence, my take on poststructuralist geography entails letting myself get taken up by such a vibration. And insofar as the whole exercise is to affirm the becoming-otherwise of spatial science, to make space for new events and moves in the geographical tradition, neither its trajectory nor its effects can be prefigured and rehearsed in advance. One can never know beforehand how an event will play out, spin out, and splay out, or with what other currents it will become swept up. It is the destiny of every work to be given over to chance (cf. Botting and Wilson, 1998). Yet even though a work is fated to adestination, dissemination, and undecidability, there will nevertheless be innumerable ways in which it is taken up, plugged in, and transformed along the way.

If, then, the work never finally takes place, its interminable and labyrinthine peregrination is nevertheless an occasion for new moves in spatial science. Something will happen to us – or not. You will take it up – or leave it. You will plug yourself in and get swept up by it – or not. Either way, neither you nor I will have exhausted what is in the process of coming into geography. And doing justice to that is the ethic specific to poststructuralist geography: opening oneself to "the dizziness that can take hold of thinking" (Lyotard, 1988b, p. 13). So, "If something can be said about the work that has not yet been said, then it is because it is listened to otherwise," writes Lyotard (1997, p. 139). "In this other *écoute* resides the respect one owes to writing and to thought." Another way of putting this is to say that one has a duty to be worthy of the events that happen to us, to borrow a Deleuzean formulation. What matters, then, are the events and affects that the work gives rise to, events and affects that will only have taken place in relation to a constitutive outside, of which your reading is a necessary and absolutely singular component. "There is, therefore, in the work of writing and thought a pragmatic indeterminacy or an indeterminacy of destination," says Lyotard (1997, p. 139).

In their becoming–other, the schizoid figures that compose this book – Baudrillard, Deleuze, Derrida, Foucault, Guattari, Harvey, Irigaray, Lyotard, and Olsson, amongst others – are symptoms of poststructuralist geography. These names are neither personal nor authorial, and still less do they index a total body of work. Rather, they lend consistency to particular configurations of signs and symptoms, each composing a particular way of existing in the world. If one gives a body of signs a proper name, such as 'Baudrillard' or 'Deleuze,' it is because of the new symptomatology that they propose.

A sign is a symptom of the adestination that accompanies the other *écoutes* for the work. It is symptomatic of the deforming force that is felt in the flesh of the work insofar as it is affected by what is other than what it will have been. This is why a body of signs is never integral, but differential. Every sign is split and given over to dissimilation: cracked-words and cracked-bodies, no less than cracked-I's. In the libidinal economy of psychoanalysis, this splaying force is a return of the repressed, of what has been occluded and 'occulted' in the folding (interiorization) of consciousness – the collective (i.e. impersonal) un-conscious. In the libidinal economy of schizoanalysis, it is the force of the open. "Open the so-called body and spread out all its surfaces," suggests Lyotard:

> perform the dissection of polymorphous perversion, spread out the im-mense membrane of the libidinal 'body' ... made from the most heterogeneous textures, bone, epithelium, sheets to write on, charged atmospheres, swords, glass cases, peoples, grasses, canvases to paint. All these zones are joined end to end in a band which has no back to it, a Moebius band which interests us not because it is closed, but because it is one-sided, a Moebius skin. (Lyotard, 1993, pp. 1–2)

On the 'great ephemeral sk(e)in' of the libidinal band, a symptom is metamorphotic: it redistributes force and affect. "If the symptom is a metaphor, it is not a metaphor to say so," writes Lacan (1977, p. 175). "For the symptom *is* a metaphor whether one likes it or not." In his explication of this passage, Ferrell (1996, p. 83) rightly notes:

> To read the symptom as metaphor is not to believe that it is 'merely metaphoric.' *The symbolic has being; better, the symbolic produces being.* If there is a strength in Lacan's account it is that he makes it impossible to have a sign divorced from its material because the symptom is a material event, its pain has meaning and an experience of life is bound up to it ... a representation is not true, rather, it *is*, it has being.

Now, despite the hostility between schizoanalysis and psychoanalysis, they at least have this in common: a symptom is a material event; it takes place. In short, the fabrication of a poststructuralist geography necessitates a symptomatological approach. One reworks the symptoms of spatial science and redistributes the play of forces composing them (cf. Olsson, 1980, 1991). But the symptomatology that 'isolates' post-structuralist geography as a specific syndrome is no ordinary clinical or critical practice of discrimination. For the immanent mode of existence that it implies is schizophrenic, as sketched in Deleuze and Guattari's *Anti-Oedipus* (1984). As Daniel Smith (1997, p. xx–xxi) writes in his introduction to Deleuze's *Essays Critical and Clinical*:

> Schizophrenia is an acute phenomenon that poses numerous problems to the clinical method: not only is there no agreement as to the etiology of schizophrenia, but even its symptomatology remains uncertain. In most psychiatric accounts of schizophrenia (Kraepelin, Bleuler), the diagnostic criteria are given in purely *negative* terms, that is, in terms of the destruc-tion the disorder engenders in the subject: dissociation, autism, detachment from reality ... The problem with both psychiatry and psychoanalysis is that these negative symptoms are dispersed and scattered, and are difficult

to totalize or unify in a coherent clinical entity, or even a localizable "mode of existence": "schizophrenia is a discordant syndrome, always in flight from itself". (Embedded quotations from Deleuze, 1972, p. 735)

The symptomatology of poststructuralist geography is therefore an affirmation of schizophrenia *as a process*, rather than that process as it is 'arrested,' 'interrupted,' or 'isolated' in a mode of life. One frequently hears complaints that postmodernism, poststructuralism, and deconstruction are dissociated, autistic, and detached from reality, complaints that betray the inability of those clinicians to become attuned to schizophrenia as process. Becoming. Symptomatology. Schizophrenia. Such are the components of an ethic of the event. One traverses a field of non-totalizable fragments, which affect you or not. The ethical task is to become worthy of one's encounter with these forces of affectation: not to force constancy on them, but to lend them consistency. To let them hold together without wounding their disjointure and their becoming otherwise. (This is how the 'good' book runs alongside its bibliography.) Poststructuralist geography affirms what is still coming. This is the good way of engaging with the geographical tradition, an intensive reading that is open to the differential forces traversing and deforming the field, rendering it otherwise. Engagement is the key word here. Drawing on its mechanical senses, one could say that reading and writing are machinic before they are communicative. What matters is not primarily their 'truth' or 'sense' content (the work reduced to its real-world referents, transcendental signifieds, or master signifiers, for example), but their relations of speed and slowness, their circulation and redistribution of energy, and how they affect and are in turn affected.

> Thoughts are not the fruits of the earth. They are not registered by areas, except out of human commodity. Thoughts are clouds. The periphery of thoughts is as immeasurable as the fractal lines of Benoit Mandlebrot. Thoughts are pushed and pulled at variable speeds. They are deep, although core and skin are of the same grain. Thoughts never stop changing their location one with another ... One cloud casts its shadow on another, the shape of clouds varies with the angle from which they are approached. (Lyotard, 1988b, p. 5)

Such an image of thought calls not only for a schizoanalysis, but also for a 'liminal materialism' and a 'libidinal economy' (Doel, 1994a; Lyotard, 1993). "The 'bad' or sickly life is an exhausted and degenerated mode of existence, one that judges life from the perspective of its sickness, that devaluates [*sic*] life in the name of 'higher' values," such as truth, writes Daniel Smith (1997, p. xv). "The 'good' or healthy life, by contrast, is an overflowing and ascending form of existence, a mode of life that is able to transform itself depending on the forces it encounters, always increasing the power to live, always opening up new possibilities for life."

Streaming. Braiding. Becoming. Schizophrenia. Deterritorialization. This is indeed a beautiful milieu for geographers, engendering remarkable events for those prepared to launch themselves into the flux. Learning to let go, to become alert to difference and differentiation, is the task of critical human geography. An openness to the event of space is the ethic specific to geography. From the off, then, I am declining the traditional ethic of geography: the ethic of place, an ethic especially associated with humanistic currents in geography (see for example Buttimer, 1993; Relph, 1976; Tuan, 1977). It is not so much the particularity, nor even the undercurrent of authenticity, that troubles me (everything in *its* place), but rather its adherence to integral formations and pointillism (everything *in* place).

For example, Entrikin (1991, p. 134) concludes his *Betweenness of Place* by suggesting that "The closest we can come to addressing both sides of th[e] divide" between the humanistic–subjective pole of understanding on the one hand (an empathetic and singular knowing-from-the-inside), and the scientific–objective pole of exactitude on the other hand (an affectless and reproducible knowing-from-the-outside), "is from a point in between ... We gain a sense both of being 'in a place' and 'at a location,' of being at the centre and being at a point in a centerless world." *From, in, at*: such a prepositional and sedentary fixation never gets us any closer to recognizing the essential element – that place is an event: it is verbal rather than nounal, a becoming rather than a being. As Revill (1993) demonstrates so wonderfully in his consideration of multi-ethnic life in postcolonial, inner-city Derby, what *takes place* is neither situated nor contained within a particular location, but is instead splayed out and unfolded across a myriad of vectors. In these portraits of Derby, conventionally (mis)placed in the East Midlands region of England, Pakistan, Jamaica, and Bollywood are infinitely closer than its apparently 'nearest neighbours' of Nottingham and Leicester, which, along with London, fold into the darkness (cf. Bhabha, 1993; Chambers, 1994; Massey, 1991). These vectors of disjointure and dislocation may conjugate and reverberate, but there is no necessity for them to converge on a particular experiential or physical location. Such are the mis-meetings consequent upon events sliding past each other in absolute proximity. This is why I emphasize that what takes place *un*folds and splays *out*, rather than give succour to more sedentary images of thought like fusion, hybridization, or glocalization. Such a recognition is the degree-zero of geography: place is nothing if it is not *in process*. This is not to separate pattern from process or events from process. For the event is itself processive.

Now, Marxist geographers and urbanists have made many of us acutely aware of the processive nature of the social production of place and space (see for example Harvey, 1982, 1985a, 1985b, 1989; Lefebvre, 1991, 1996; Massey, 1984, 1995; Soja, 1980, 1989a), although it is important to underscore the fact that this processive quality is carried through the realm of meaning no less than that of matter (see for example Olsson, 1991, 1993; Pred, 1983, 1984, 1986; Thrift, 1983). This emphasis on process is in stark contrast to the study of place in terms of character, meaning, awareness or consciousness where it is these latter that are in process and subject to contestation, rather than (the) place itself (see for example Daniels, 1992; Entrikin, 1997; Taylor, forthcoming). The event of place opens onto metamorphosis, polymorphous perversion, and the redistribution of energy. By contrast, the illicit immobilization of such an event to context, setting, milieu, location, etc. opens onto representation, the crisis of representation, and all manner of imaginative geographies. And despite the innumerable points of convergence between the verbal and nounal engagements with place, they are nevertheless polarized in terms of speed and slowness. Sedentary thought enforces a difference in kind, whilst nomad thought affirms a mere difference of degree. In keeping with sedentary thought, Tuan (1977, p. 6) tells us that "if we think of space as that which allows movement, then place is pause." Place is rest. Place to place is movement. Space is abstract speed – the speed of abstraction. Or again: "when space feels thoroughly familiar to us, it has become place" (Tuan, 1977, p. 73). For sedentary thought, then, *place* may be open or closed, extroverted or introverted, homogeneous or heterogeneous, homely or eerie, totalized or fragmented, univocal or equivocal – but it is always slower, more earthly, more concrete, more grounded, and more real than space. For *space* lends itself to speed, immateriality, abstractness, floatation, and relational disjointure. Hence the tendency for many humanistically-inclined geographers to associate the folding back of space onto place with the quashing of authenticity and specificity, and the advent of alienation, placelessness, and non-places – or as Benko (1997, p. 23) puts it: "dequalification, derealization, and virtualization;" "Never before in the history of the world have non-places occupied so much space" (see also Augé, 1995; Gottdiener, 1995; Relph, 1976). In a symptomatic list of those things "responsible for the production of interchangeable places, identical throughout the world, through which people move without stopping," it is *speed* that heads Benko's (1997, p. 24) list (cf. Mugerauer, 1994). Likewise, the disavowal of the speed of place can be seen in Sack's (1997) framework of *thick* and *thin* places. This solidification of place is echoed in Massey's (1978, 1984) stratification of the emergent spatial structure of an economic space in terms of (overdetermined) 'layers of investment.' Such a sedimentary and sedentary fixation extends into many of the images of thought supporting geography, wherein movement is geared around a moment of rest (e.g. a place for the accumulation of stock or for expanded reproduction); it also lends itself to striation and segmentation (cf. Dixon and Jones, 1996, 1998). Consequently, Harvey (1996) is right to be incredulous towards the absurdity of treating space "as the dead, the fixed, the undialectical, the immobile," whilst treating time as "richness, fecundity, life, dialectic," as Foucault (1980, p. 70) famously phrased it (cf. Foucault, 1986). But one must also be incredulous about the polarization of place and space, which hinges on the glaciation of events in perpetual process. If it were not such an inelegant neologism, I would be tempted to say that there is nothing but *splace*, taking splace – *splacing*. And there would be nothing negative about this: no possibility of a catastrophic or negatory displacement insofar as splacement would always already be disjoined, disadjusted, and unhinged; both place and space would be special – illusory? – effects of splacement's inaugural duplicity (cf. Derrida, 1989f; Lacoue-Labarthe, 1989). It is the same with deconstruction and schizoanalysis. Not dis-placement. Just di-splacement: the prefix 'di-' signifying the double register in which the splacement takes splace; or else the prefix 'di-' or 'dis-' signifying the intensification and thoroughgoingness of the splacement. As Derrida (1995, p. 28) usefully reminds us in his consideration of the suggestion that Deconstruction is/in America: "'in' can indicate inclusion as well as provisional passage, the being-in-transit of the visitor ... If D is in A, it is not A; if D is A, it is not in, etc. The slash indeed inscribes or incises a disjunction in the copula 'is.'" Such a disjointure recurs throughout the chapters that follow.

Place is what takes place: "Producing, a product," say Deleuze and Guattari (1984, p. 7) during their machinic introduction to schizoanalysis. By failing to recognize this minimal dislocation, which splays out the nounal sense of place from the off, 'betweenness' is positioned by Entrikin (1991) as a privileged point of view that proffers an experience of both the interiority and exteriority of place. 'Betweenness,' like 'embedment' and 'situatedness,' does nothing to disrupt the partition between what is inside and what is outside. It seeks to occupy the threshold without realizing that what has been put into question is the threshold itself. Nevertheless, there is much to be valued in many of the more nuanced renditions of the ethic of place, such as those of Mugerauer (1994, 1995), and from very a different direction, Thrift's delineation of a 'new regional geography' (1990, 1991, 1993). Even what Massey (1991, 1993) aptly calls 'a progressive sense of place' that is extroverted rather than introverted, networked rather than isolated, bears the trace of pointillism: discreteness and discreetness. Be that as it may, my own concern with space is not dissociated from place. I am certainly not advocating space in the abstract, but nor am I simply moving towards space as it is lived and practised by human bodies over and against the crushing force of spatial abstractions such as money, clock-time, and calculation (cf. Lefebvre, 1991; Sennett, 1994; Soja, 1989a, 1989b, 1993, 1996). For strictly speaking, place never takes place – here, there or anywhere, least of all *in* time. At best, place *takes* place: and this is why I decline Thrift's (1996b, p. 47) insistence that "being is never out of place," whilst agreeing with him that "all space is practised." Were being to be 'em-placed' or 'contextualized,' as he suggests, then it would simply be unbecoming. And as Thrift (1996b, p. 1) headlines in the title to his introductory essay in *Spatial Formations*, what is at stake here is the 'style' of non-representational theory.

The event of place (is what) deconstructs (cf. Strohmayer, 1998). Hereinafter, there are only events of spacing. Geography is spaced out and splayed out (cf. Strohmayer, 1997a). Hence my decision to parenthesize splay – (s)play: the disjunctive synthesis of play and splay, remarked by the disjointure of the disseminating letter *par excellence*, 's,' and underscored by the incision of the unity of the word by the parentheses themselves as marks of an irreducible interlude or interval in the event itself, and not merely around it. An event is (s)played out: the interval takes all. In what follows I will have occasion to employ some other parenthesized neologisms in order that the text might resonate in several registers at once, and I hope that they do not adversely affect your reading pleasure.

Letting space take place: that is the ambition of geography, when it is radical. For myself, then, geography is simply an inclination towards the event of spacing. This is not spacing in the paranoiac sense of dissociating one position from another, of forcing distanciated identities onto space – a tendency that I have dubbed 'pointillism.' Rather than there being a poststructuralism that could get taken up by geography and geographers, I want to demonstrate that poststructuralism is always already spatial: that it attends from the off to the 'difference that space makes.' It is the event of space, of spacing, that deconstructs. Speaking always as geographers, poststructuralists strain to become sensitive to what it is to space – to what happens when space takes place. Shamefully, spatial scientists steeped in the geographical tradition know very little about what it is to space and to take place. Contrary to popular opinion, neither space nor place are given, least of all as ready-mades or loci of authenticity. Rather, they must be lent consistency: a task that is both contextual and inexhaustible. Hitherto, the spaces and places within which geographers have worked have been ill-mannered and unbecoming. Quite simply, they have invariably lacked consistency, owing in large measure to the predilection for pointillism in geography. In the nick of time, poststructuralism may come to lend relief. Why? It is because poststructuralism affirms the fact that there are no points of constancy in this or any other universe. There are just folds of consistency – and nothing more. Everything is manifold. Even points vibrate.

By turning towards poststructuralism I will therefore be opening and affirming what is always already in play within geography, and not merely around it. If the reader can be dragged away from the negatory myths that have tended to envelop and deaden the joyful force and insatiable passion of poststructuralism, then something both remarkable and important may come into view. New geography may once again become possible. For when all is said and done, geography, like any other activity, has nothing whatsoever to do with representation, least of all the so-called 'crisis' of representation. Geography is an act, an event, a happening. It is evaluated not according to its degree of correspondence, coherence, or integrity, but according to how it affects and is affected by other events. Far from being idealist, textualist or nihilistic, poststructuralism affirms an immanent expression of the material forces lending consistency to an event. It affirms the differential and manifold spacing according to which the event goes off (cf. Barthes, 1984). The ethical and political question therefore becomes what to do with this excess, which, to borrow a phrase from Bataille (1988), could justifiably be called the 'accursed share.' Such excess goes by many names – including difference, alterity, heterogeneity, otherness, contradiction, complementarity, incompossibility, and undecidability. For the time being, however, I will dwell on chaos – if only to shake things up before they have the chance of settling into place. Cast of the die

Flow

> Chaos makes chaotic and undoes every consistency in the infinite. (Deleuze and Guattari, 1994, p. 42)

> fluidifying solidified thinking (Malabou, 1996, p. 117)

Chaos can be (un)folded in many ways. So let me admit it right from the off: there is no possibility of resolution or climax; there is no chance of escaping from the interminable foreplay that is coming; and there is no holding formation that can contain and solidify the whirling vapour that is the world. There is nothing beyond the event horizon of chaosmosis (Guattari, 1992). Consequently, what I long for are concepts that express this infinitely disadjusted chaos. "I would like to plead that if I am unable to take a position," says Lyotard (1988b, p. 5), "this is due not to a bent toward confusion – at least I hope not – but to the lightness of thoughts" (cf. Derrida, 1981a). Going against the grain of common sense and good sense, I want to assemble utterly *chaotic abstractions* – but only on condition that such abstractions do not take thought-and-action away from the chaos (for there is no other), only away from the apparent concretions that dissimulate and disavow the chaos.

For me, there is nothing outside the chaosmos. However, that does not mean that the chaosmos is unified, totalized, or complete. It is infinitely disadjusted, differentiated, and disjoined. Without origin or end, the chaosmos only has a middle, a milieu, a meantime, in which it is (s)played out. One cannot know in advance how the folds will pan out and snap shut. Yet in the swirling that envelops me, like a thick fog, I can sense innumerable shape-shifters starting to stir. Through a certain immanent rhythm in any particular milieu these shape-shifters may take on some recognizable form – a concept, an idea, a person, a thing, a place, a time, etc. – , but they invariably strike me as being insubstantial and immaterial, shimmering on the surface of the particulate mass that is forever in circulation. Through some sort of animism or sorcery, or perhaps through fortuity and happenstance alone, something seems to coalesce amidst the vapour clouds: a 'something-or-other $= x$' takes (the) place (of indiscernibility). Whatever it is, it strikes me that it is only ever a special effect of relations of movement and rest, of speed and slowness, of lighting and texture, and of rhythm and consistency. No thing is there: just effects of differential spacing. One's world is suspended in milieux of chaos, whilst a certain differential and web-like texturing lends 'something-or-other $= x$' a limited consistency – but always from a particular point of view. Yet unlike a spider's web, which orders and regulates a block of space-time as an apparatus of capture, there can be no chaosmotic web-master. If a web is an archetypal network, which endures through connection, capture, filtering, channelling, and extension, then the chaosmos exemplifies the unrelenting scission of irrational cuts and folds. Fortunately, however, each of us has our own way of living with the chaosmos, of conjuring some recognizable forms and discernible things on the screen of a swirling mass, and of dissolving others into the vaporous body that engulfs us.

So: chaos amid chaos. Folds amidst folds. That is all I ever really wanted to say. Rather than write a book, it might therefore have been better to have constructed a quasi-Rorschach test: cast your eyes up from this page, and when you gaze into the chaosmos, what do you see? Or the other way: can you look at some region of the chaosmos *without* seeing some integral things? And if I were to be reckless enough to risk an ambition for this book, then it might be to enable one to glimpse the indiscernible chaosmos *in* the place of everything that seems so effortlessly to hold together, rather than merely *around* it. For the free-form, or metamorphotic perversity, of the infinitely (un)folded chaosmos does not subsist in the interstices between discernible forms and given things, it supersaturates every pore of their becoming-only-to-fade. To lose one's suspension of disbelief with regard to forms, things, places, times, events – and even with regard to numbers: integers and fractions, real and imaginary numbers, etc. If this sounds like a crazy, futile, dangerous, and pointless exercise, which has nothing what-soever to do with geography, then that is unfortunate (cf. Morris, 1996). For me, the irresistible force of poststructuralism is precisely that it is pointless – literally. It promises the possibility of a geographical thought-and-practice that does not revolve around *points*. And anyone familiar with the difficulties, aporias, and paradoxes of conventional forms of *pointillism* in geography should take that promise seriously.

In geography and urban studies, there is much talk of a deterritor-ializing and increasingly borderless 'world of flows' – of capital, commodities, information, taste, culture, value, etc. Were it the case, such fluidity may or may not signal a new epoch in the historical geography of capitalism, with a qualitative shift from, say, industrial to postindustrial society or modernity to postmodernity (cf. Bell, 1973; Castells, 1996, 1997; Harvey, 1989; Jameson, 1984). Likewise, it remains unclear whether or not the rising permeability of established social, cultural, economic, and political boundaries will render state apparatuses of governance increasingly ineffectual, at whatever resolution: local, regional, national, international, global, universal (see for example Tay-lor, 1994, 1995). One should recall, with Deleuze and Guattari (1988), that deterritorialization is always coupled to a correlative reterritoriali-zation. For example, the deterritorialized earth reinscribed on the body of the despot; the deterritorialized body of the despot reinscribed on the inorganic body of capital; the deterritorialized body of capital rein-scribed on the incorporeal body of the code; the deterritorialized body of the code reinscribed on universal schizophrenia. In addition, the 'world of flows' lends itself to a reconsideration of the asymptotic an-nihilation of space through time, which has caught the imagination of writers from the mass uptake of the bicycle in nineteenth-century Europe – as an expression of the first major instalment in the democratization of speed – to the routinization of satellite communication on the eve of the twenty-first century (Thrift, 1994, 1996a; Wark, 1994). But it is not just the disappearance of the drag of space that is up for consider-ation, since there is also the matter of the extermination of time through real-time – the virtual-cum-actual realization and exhaustion of the world's possibilities in the present (cf. Baudrillard, 1995, 1996b; Doel and Clarke, 1998b; Virilio, 1994).

For all of the hyperbole surrounding the 'end of geography' and the emergence of a 'perpetual present,' space-time continues to drag. Indeed, the friction of distanciation is felt even in the control nodes of what Thrift (1995, 1997) aptly refers to as the 'hyperactive world' of 'soft capitalism.' Such friction affects the bodies of the cleaners, caterers, and security staff, no less than those of the foreign-exchange dealers and traders (Allen and Pryke, 1994). It is never simply a matter of *speed* – of time-space convergence, acceleration, and compression (Harvey, 1989, 1996; Leyshon, 1995) – but of speed *and slowness*. There can be no acceleration without a parallel deceleration, no convergence without divergence, and no compression without decompression. For ours is a scrumpled universe of general relativity (Doel, 1996). This is why I applaud Lefebvre's (1991, p. 416) insistence that "nothing and no one can avoid *trial by space*," whilst remaining sceptical about his anthropocentric yearning for the human body to be disclosed as the proper measure of space: "the yardstick of space – or, more precisely, the yardstick of spatial practice" (Lefebvre, 1991, p. 54). It is on the basis of this anthropocentrism that Lefebvre discerns an ongoing historical and geographical conflict between *lived space* and *abstract space* (cf. Blum and Nast, 1996). Lived space belongs to the flesh, to spatial practices, bodily gestures, and sensuous activity. Here, "space ... still held up to all members of society an image and a living reflection of their own bodies" (Lefebvre, 1991, p. 111). By contrast, abstract space is conceived before it is lived. It may appear to serve "those forces which make a *tabula rasa* of whatever stands in their way ... with space performing the function of a plane, a bulldozer or a tank," says Lefebvre. But it "*is not* homogeneous; it simply *has* homogeneity as its goal, its orientation, its 'lens'" (Lefebvre, 1991, pp. 285 and 287, respectively). Abstract space is the enemy of the fully sensuous and organic body. Its objectivation and decorporealization work to dequalify social space, shifting it from an *analogical* to a *metaphorical* register (Gregory, 1994a, 1997; cf. Sennett, 1994). The space that was once isomorphic with the comportment and habits of bodies has given way to a space composed according to the disembodied logic and cold calculation of signs and symbols. Exemplified in the Phallus, Logos, number, geometry, and capital, abstract space strives to dissociate itself from the practices, rhythms, and textures of the body. The contradictions of this disavowal necessitates the dialectical promise of a sublime *differential space* that will restore the body as the proper yardstick of a reappropriated social space: "The body, at the very heart of space and of the discourse of power, is irreducible and subversive. It is the body which is the point of return" (Lefebvre, 1976, p. 89). Or again: "the body takes its revenge – or at least calls for revenge. It seeks to make itself known – to gain recognition – as *generative*. (Of what? Of practice, of use, hence of space – and, by extension, of the human species" (Lefebvre, 1991, p. 384).

Despite my scepticism with regard to his humanism, what I love about Lefebvre's analysis is that he does not simply oppose lived space and abstract space. Rather, abstract space is a certain folding of lived space. It is lived space folded back on itself, not in order to affirm life (what Lefebvre refers to as 'appropriation' and 'reappropriation'), but in order to crush it (what he refers to as 'domination'). "The shift, which is so hard to grasp, from the space of the body to the body-in-space ... somehow facilitates the spiriting-away or scotomization of the body. How did this magic ever become possible"? asks Lefebvre (1991, p. 201). He answers by reference to 'splits,' 'interstices,' and 'intervals' that open up a zone into which something might slip and thereby dislocate itself. Nevertheless, Lefebvre overlooks the fact that lived space *puts itself out of joint* in order to lay the blame squarely on that which slips *into* these lesions in the Order of Things.

Folding, unfolding, refolding. Such is the schizoanalytic potential of Lefebvre's rhythmanalysis. What holds him back? What prevents him from seeing that the scission goes all the way down? The unbecoming illusion of a full body that precedes such a split, an illusion that Derrida (1994b) deconstructs in relation to Marx's spooky story about the fetishism of commodities, and that Lyotard (1993) deconstructs in relation to Marx's prosecution of the inorganic and fragmented body of capital.

> In some circumstances a split occurs, and an interstice or interval is created – a very specific space which is at once magical and real ... But what is it exactly that slips into the interstice in question? The answer is: language, signs, abstractions – all necessary yet fateful, indispensable yet dangerous. This is a lethal zone thickly strewn with dusty, mouldering words. What slips into it is what allows meaning to escape the embrace of lived experience, to detach itself from the fleshy body. (Lefebvre, 1991, pp. 202–3)

If neither place nor the body can serve as an origin or yardstick for an appropriate(d) social space, this is because they are always already given over to the (s)play of polymorphous perversion. However, whether there is anything impervious to the force of polymorphous perversion remains a moot point.

Interruption

> If things aren't going well in contemporary thought, it's because ... analysis in terms of movement or vectors is blocked. (Deleuze, 1992a, p. 281)

Having briefly let myself get swept up by place, the body, and what slips between a body and its space, I now want to hold on for a moment to the motif of a 'world of flows.' Such a motif pervades much of contemporary human geography and urban studies. Surely it is self evident that these flows invariably turn out to be composed of some solid or particulate mass. One need only think of the flows of resources, commodities, capital, and people. As for immaterial flows of number, information, discourse, and money, these are always inseparable from their material supports: infrastructures, phenomenal forms, epistemic communities, actor-networks, etc. (see, for example: Barnes, 1998). Additionally, it should be self-evident that all such flows are never free-flowing: they are directed, channelled, organized, and stockpiled, usually with obvious sources and sink-holes. In short, there can be no fluidity without ground and solidity: no streaming without banks or bed, gravitational mass or slope. And were there to be no such ground or solidity, there would still need to be flow against flow, such that one flow would reterritorialize another flow as its 'baseless ground' or border. There are only relative deterritorializations – even when they are run to infinity. Absolute deterritorialization is always relative. More modestly, even the hyperactive web-masters of the world of soft capitalism, ensconced in the corporate citadels of London, New York, and Tokyo, require their endo- and exoskeletons, their infra- and superstructures. The upshot of this example is simply that the image of a vaporous world of utter chaos is illusory. It is self-evident that innumerable entities are more or less insoluble, whilst others actively resist and marshal liquescence in order to enhance, precisely, their stability and solidity. Things endure.

Harvey (1996, pp. 7–8) puts it beautifully: "While I accept the general argument that process, flux, and flow should be given a certain ontological priority in understanding the world, I also want to insist that this is precisely the reason why we should pay so much more careful attention to ... the 'permanences' that surround us and which we also construct to help solidify and give meaning to our lives." Specifically, 'permanence' (causal structure) amounts to "relatively stable configurations of matter and things," which are 'practically indestructible' (Harvey, 1996, pp. 51 and 50, respectively). It is at this juncture that I depart from Harvey's image of thought. The emphasis on permanency and indestructibility seems to me to occlude the regulation of fluids that is the condition of possibility of rigidity and turgidity, an occlusion that resurfaces in the slippage between "how 'things' crystallize out of processes" and how permanences 'successfully internalize' flows (Harvey, 1996, p. 81). Ontology has always been figured on the basis of sexual difference, especially in terms of Phallus and Logos – that which is given to standing against the flow (Derrida, 1995b; Krell, 1997). Yet there is no Phallus that is not worked over by fluidity, that is not lent turgidity through a certain constriction of fluidity, just as there is no Logos that is not worked over by variation and dissemination. Hence my incredulity towards Harvey's insistence on the necessity for a certain phallogocentric fixation, specifically on the world-wide trial by capital. (The formula 'phallus plus Logos' is perhaps no better expressed than by capital, a would-be transcendental signifier whose current degree of flotation draws everything into its own calculus of difference.) This is what he says:

> While it is formally true that everything can be reduced to flows ... we are in daily practice surrounded by things, institutions, discourses, and even states of mind of such relative permanence and power that it would be foolish not to acknowledge those evident qualities. There is, I believe, little point in asserting some sort of 'dissolution of all fixity and permanence' in the famous 'last instance' if, as far as we human beings are concerned, that last instance is nowhere in sight. The 'solid rock' of historical-geographical materialism ... (Harvey, 1996, p. 8)

My incredulity is sparked by a threefold qualification of Harvey's opening image of thought concerning ontological fluxion. First, it is not a question of 'reducing' something afluvial to flows. One does not have some afluvial substance, which may or may not be dissolvable, on the one side, and some dissolving or corroding fluids on the other, any more than one has a material World over there and an ideal Language over here, or a firm masculinity and a soft femininity. If there is something, then it is only ever as a confluence, interruption, and coagulation of flows. Second, and as a consequence, there is no 'last instance' of ultimate dissolution, wherein permanency and solidity would finally give way to a pure flux. Nor is there any 'first instance' or 'meantime' of (relative) permanence and solidity. There is just a general relativity of flows – with all of the relations of speed and slowness, movement and rest, etc. In this regard it is odd that Harvey (1996, p. 93) should take "The famous 'last instance' of the material practice of production and reproduction ... as both the *starting point* and the *measuring point* of achievement," when he rejects out of hand the infamous 'last instance' of the 'dissolution of all fixity and permanence.' Moreover, the consistency and viscosity of some degree of 'fluidity' and 'solidity' not only depend upon a certain milieu, but also on a certain point of view. On occasion, Harvey seems to equate fluidity in a free state with the microscopic, such as the wave-like flux of atomic particles amidst the solidity of some material substance. But this is to occlude the fact that even a densely-structured macroscopic portion of matter is traversed by innumerable movements. Finally, and most importantly, it is not that solidity can be set off against fluidity, or microscopic fluxion from macroscopic coagula, but that they are all the special effects of folding. Vapoury and fluidity can neither be opposed to, nor separated from, solidity, except through relations of movement and rest, speed and slowness, turgidity and flaccidity, and rhythm and consistency. Permanence is a special effect of fluidics. Harvey seems to repeatedly acknowledge such a state of affairs. For example, capital is capital only insofar as it is in *a certain kind of* motion. And if capital petrifies it is because of the regularity of its orbit and the monotony of its immutable motility. One cannot overcome the sickly affects of 'permanency' by creating another kind of permanency, as Harvey insists is the case. Rather, one can only overcome such a blockage in polymorphous perversion by effecting *another kind of motion*: from restricted to general mobility. Hereinafter, resistance is no longer opposed to power, as one solid construct facing-off another. It just unfolds and refolds. Resistance does not come from outside: it is literally an action re(s)play – a difference-producing repetition. Accordingly, Deleuze and Guattari (1988) do not oppose the speed and mobility of capital to the integrity of the labouring body. They do not oppose a fast, inorganic, and vampiric body against the slow creatures that we humans are. To the contrary, they push for absolute deterritorialization – for the re-release of polymorphous perversion.

Accordingly, while I would agree that relational "Dialectics forces us always to ask the question of every 'thing' or event that we encounter: by what process was it constituted and how is it sustained?" (Harvey, 1996, p. 50), one will not arrive at an answer that is not worked over by disjointure and other *écoutes*. This is why I prefer Deleuze's (1993b) notion of origami: the world can be (un)folded in countless ways, with innumerable folds over folds, and folds within folds, but such a disfiguration never permits one (or more) of those folds to become redundant, nor for one (or more) of them to seize power as a master-fold. Every fold plays its part in lending consistency to the thing that is folded, and since every fold participates in the lending of consistency to 'something $= x$' without ever belonging to it (hence the empiricist principle of the irreducible externality of relations to their relata), folds cannot be distinguished in terms of the essential and the inessential, the necessary and the contingent, or the structural and the ornamental. Every fold plays its part: every fold splays 'it' apart. The event of origami is in the (un)folding, just as the gift is in the wrapping: not as content, but as process.

Despite the almost absolute proximity of Harvey's text and my own, there is something ambivalent in his milieu that is forever falling back on the process in order to arrest it. Three prominent motifs are symptomatic of this attempt to block a return of the repressed: *permanence*, *integration*, and *embedment*. They are invoked at moments of difficulty in order to constrain the disarranging force of the chaosmotic excess of undetermined and unformed matter in a free state. Harvey does not wish to let himself go with the flow. "We all know what Heraclitus meant when he said that we cannot step into the same river twice," notes Harvey (1996, p. 61); "but we also know that there is a sense in which we can return again and again to the banks of the same river."

This serves as a suitable refrain for the whole of Harvey's book. On the one hand, *flow* is given a 'certain' ontological priority: the scare quotes suggesting that this certainty is somewhat uncertain, an ambivalence that is partly unfolded by Natter and Jones (1997). This is simply because every 'thing,' 'event,' 'moment,' 'system,' 'element,' etc., is perpetually *in process* for the duration of its existence: nothing can endure without a life-giving flow from the 'outside' to sustain its turgidity (the life of the fleshy human body, no less than the non-organic life of vampiric capital). On this basis Harvey (1996, p. 54) tells us "that change and instability are the norm and that the appearance of stability of 'things' or systems is what has to be explained." On the other hand, these enduring 'permanences' – as Harvey is fond of calling them – that 'crystallize' out of the flux are given a certain ontological – and ethico-political – priority (the absence of scare quotes suggesting that this is indeed certain). Harvey can be so certain because permanences stratify, constrict, and regulate the flows; an inhibition that can *only* be overcome through the creation of other permanences – permanences that ready the given constriction for a 'dissolution into a flow,' for a release of other possibilities. Yet as Marx noted in relation to the crystallization of value in commodities, such a solidification is both retroflex (untimely) and virtual (incorporeal): a certain calculus of exteriorized, differential relations *falls back on* the surface of bodies, lending them a certain form, consistency, and duration qua body. Value, form, consistency, duration, etc. are all special effects of the (s)play of differential relations.

If (relative) permanence and crystallization fail to block a return of the repressed, perhaps 'embedment' can – a term that appears to play a role akin to superglue: as a universal bonding agent. Embedment secures events into place, and space (and time) into place. It is also called upon to secure the bond between theory and world, and to concretize abstractions into the quotidian. "Theory cannot be brought to bear upon the world of daily political practices without finding ways to embed in it the materialities of place, space, and environment," insists Harvey (1996, pp. 44–5). This presupposes a separation between theory and world, language/discourse and reality, a separation underscored in the claim that "If spatiality disrupts received theory and dominant metanarratives ..." (Harvey, 1996, p. 9). What Harvey challenges, then, is not the gulf between the world and language, but how that gulf is to be bridged: ineffectual 'spatial metaphors' or effective 'material embedment'? In fact, he seeks to *entrench* the expulsion of theory, discourse, and language from the world of lived materiality, as the schematic 'moments' of his 'Cognitive Map of the Social Process' makes plain.

> I am here reducing a vast array of activities to six fundamental moments of social life. The social process ... flows in, through and around all of

these moments and the activities of each and every individual embrace all
of the moments simultaneously ... Each moment is constituted as an
internal relation of the others within the flow of social and material life.
Discourses internalize in some sense everything that occurs at other
moments (thus giving credence to Derrida's foundational statement that
'there is nothing outside of the text' or Foucault's foundational view that
discourse *is* power) ... Errors arise when examination of one 'moment' is
held sufficient to understand the totality of the social process. Again and
again we will find slippages of the sort that convert a dialectically correct
statement like "there is nothing outside of the text" into false statements
that "everything can be understood through texts" (or, worse still, "everything *is* a text and can be understood as such") ... Internal relations are
shaped through an activity of *translation* from one moment to another ...
A gap always exists between the different moments so that slippage,
ambiguity and unintended consequences inevitably occur. (Harvey, 1996,
pp. 79–80)

In this dense passage Harvey is very close to poststructuralism, as
can be seen by his insistence on the irreducibility of material translation,
slippage, ambiguity, adestination, etc. Nevertheless, the passage still
maintains an unblemished distinction between what is *inside* – a 'moment'
of pure 'activity,' such as 'power,' 'material practice,' 'discourse,' or
'desire' – and what is *outside* – other moments irreducible to the first.
What shatters the 'Leibnizian conceit' of *turning inwards* in the belief
that one can thereby recover the whole is the fact that the internalization
of the One-All process into each and every moment is an imperfect
translation: there is always some residue, which Harvey, quite rightly,
calls "metamorphosis" – "each moment internalizes forces from all of
the others" (Harvey, 1996, p. 80). And it is amidst the flows *between*
'moments' that 'things,' 'elements,' 'domains,' and 'systems' "crystallize
out" (Harvey, 1996, p. 81). But crucially for Harvey (1996, p. 106), the
metamorphotic excess that moves, deforms, and transforms bodies is
not located "*outside of* the overall flow of determination within social
relations." He rightly eschews the romanticization and essentialization
of the 'margin.' Yet by disavowing the force of the outside the patchwork
of moments and permanences swells up to fill the whole field. Its logic
of internalization permits of no outside. This is the dialectical ruse *par
excellence* – internalization becomes totalization. One could be easily
seduced by Harvey's *openness* to other *écoutes*, were it not for this eating
disorder, this insatiable compulsion to internalize. "Misconstrued,
treated lightly, Hegelianism only extends its historical domination, finally
unfolding its immense enveloping resources without obstacle. Hegelian
self-evidence seems lighter than ever at the moment when it finally
bears down with its full weight" (Derrida, 1978, p. 251). And it is

precisely at such a moment of sublime lightness that Harvey's 'perma-nences' take on their infinite density: "Because of the contradictions," he says – contradictions that are strictly *internal affairs*, wrought by the *pressure* and *force* of internalization – "there are innumerable leverage points *within* the system that can be seized upon by dissident groups or individuals to try to redirect social change down this or that path" (Harvey, 1996, p. 106). Revolutionary currents and their suppression are, then, strictly internal affairs, as a Minister of the Interior might say. The 'weak links' recognize no outside agency, since the outside *is* the inside. Little wonder, then, that Harvey (1996, p. 71) should be so damning of Derrida's attempt at "rendering delirious that interior voice that is the voice of the other in us" (quoted in Spivak, 1988, p. 294). In his text for Blanchot, *The Thought from Outside*, Foucault (1990, pp. 27–8) puts it superbly:

> To be attracted is not to be beckoned by the allure of the outside; rather, it is to experience in emptiness and destitution the presence of the outside and, tied to that presence, the fact that one is irremediably outside the outside. Far from calling on one interiority to draw close to another, attraction makes it imperiously manifest that the outside is there, open, without intimacy, without protection or retention . . ., but that one cannot gain access to that opening because the outside never yields its essence. The outside cannot offer itself as a positive presence – as something inwardly illuminated by the certainty of its own existence – but only as an absence that pulls as far away from itself as possible, receding into the sign it makes to draw one toward it.

Such is the driftwork that carries one from *production* – embedment, internalization, crystallization, and permanence – , towards *seduction* (cf. Baudrillard, 1990a).

So, one can applaud the implication that each translation or meta-morphosis has nothing whatsoever to do with representation: there is simply a redistribution of energy and affects. However, the boundary maintenance between one moment and another does not hold, since the internal milieu of each is not given in advance of the differential relations that inscribe it as an effect of the play of folding that traverses, halves together, and disjoins the inside–outside in one and the same duplicitous operation. Once one recognizes this, the trifidic mapping of '*flow*' (with its un/certain priority), '*moment*' (the locus where the One-All is internalized through an imperfect translation and material transforma-tion), and '*permanence*' (as an enduring causal structure crystallized between the various moments) deconstructs. One can no longer decide where things fall (apart). So, the topology of the 'windowless world' in which the One-All is traversed by a singularity without totalization is more like a Möbius band than a map – the (s)playing out of differential relations engenders an invaginating torque that turns the inside out and the outside in. In sum, embedment does not hold. So while it is good that Harvey insists on the perpetual 'heterogeneity' of things, that they can be endlessly decomposed into smaller and smaller packets of heterogeneity, he fails to acknowledge the most radical gesture – that relations traverse and deconstruct both the inside and the outside. To speak of 'internal relations' and 'internalization,' no matter how heterogeneous, is to miss the deconstructive force of differential spacing. I will return to this force throughout the chapters that follow.

It is both ironic and deeply symptomatic of his difficulties that Harvey should so badly misconstrue the work of Deleuze, Derrida, and Foucault, insofar as their entire project is not to transport (embed) matter into concepts – and still less to quarantine themselves in a 'windowless world' of sheer idealism (to embed themselves in the discursive moment alone, for example, refusing internal relations with other such moments) – but to affirm the *materiality* of language, thought, signs, etc. Strictly speaking, there is nothing 'merely metaphorical' about the spatialization of signs. When Harvey (1996, p. 92) writes that Derrida argues "(correctly, in my view) that the text internalizes all," he could not be further from the case. After Hegel, the dialectical machinations strive to internalize all. Derrida, by contrast, deconstructs not only internalization, but also the distinction between inside and outside upon which it rests. What Harvey forgets is that everything is always already spatialized. Without it, nothing would take place. Consider Harvey's (1996, p. 57) eleventh and final proposition on the principles of dialectics: "It is ... always an embedded search for possibilities that lies at the very heart of dialectical argumentation." In laying dialectics to rest so that he might arrive at at least one certainty, Harvey invokes the figure of *embedment* – a figure that is gaining almost universal currency amongst those who think that it resolves the tension between the universal and the particular, space and place, the global and the local, text and context, outside and inside, flow and permanence, etc. Sadly, embedment is counterfeit money. In fixing on embedment Harvey makes crystal clear what others try to let slip between the sheets: that to embed is to fix firmly in a surrounding mass and to surround so as to fix firmly (cf. Entrikin, 1991, on 'situatedness,' 'betweenness,' and 'emplotment'). Recall that moment when he writes that "while I accept the general argument that process, flux, and flow should be given a certain ontological priority in understanding the world" – note the general and uncertain qualifiers – "I also want to insist that this is precisely the reason why we should pay so much more careful attention to what I will later call the 'permanences' that surround us and which we also construct to help solidify and give meaning to our lives" (Harvey, 1996, pp. 7–8). On the basis of his more or less certain acceptance of flux as pivotal to a logic of internal relations, Harvey absolutely insists – that is to say, without qualification – on the need for the "'solid rock' of historical-geographical materialism." From an original moment of privilege, the "dissolution of all fixity and permanence" becomes not only the "famous 'last instance'," but one that "is nowhere in sight" (Harvey, 1996, p. 8). The judgement is swift: although there are "certain truths" that we need not go into, "those who reject" the 'solid rocks' – and here Harvey is thinking of "Marx's political commitment and the notion of class agency" – "in effect turn their backs on" all kinds of horrors "and become complicitous as historical agents with the reproduction of the particular set of permanences that capitalism has tightly fashioned out of otherwise open, fluid, and dynamic social processes" (Harvey, 1996, p. 108). In the last instance, then, Harvey wants to be first in affirming flux, but one can only affirm it by endlessly deferring it. One must attend to the permanences – first, and last, and always. I am not so certain for the reasons outlined above and because of what is still to come.

These notions of flow and interruption bring me back to Harvey's (1996, p. 61) suggestion that "We all know what Heraclitus meant when he said that we cannot step into the same river twice, but we also know that there is a sense in which we can return again and again to the banks of the same river." What holds for Harvey is precisely that which borders on the flux, hemming it in, constricting it, and inhibiting its current. Like all good 'permanences' that are made from solid rock or pressurized flows, one can return to them over and over again: capital, Logos, Phallus. Although embedded in change – or rather: precisely because of their embedment – they resist change. They are the condition for the return of the same and the condition of impossibility for the return of difference. This is why one must attend to solidity in the name of fluidity, and why one must work for change through the creation of other permanences. In this schema, flows are passive: it is they that are internalized in moments and embedments; and it is between internalizations that permanences crystallize out. I am not so certain. Whereas Harvey affirms through negation – the dialectical trait *par excellence* – I would rather affirm affirmation: flow against flow, flow interrupting flow, that is all. I am never able to return again and again to the banks of the same river. I know only differential repetition, of difference-producing repetitions. For the banks themselves vary in relation to the flows, not least becomes it is always already and everywhere flows that border against flows. Resistance is a matter of flow, not solidity. This is why I cannot plug myself in. I cannot locate the border, the limit, the event horizon, or the running order, that would allow me to embed this book in a place, a time, a discourse, a practice, a theory, a discipline, etc. Such is "a stream without beginning or end, gnawing away at its two banks and picking up speed in the middle" (Deleuze and Guattari, 1983, p. 58).

Accordingly, I think that Harvey is wrong to tarnish the Deleuzean art of folding with what he refers to as the 'Liebnizian conceit.' This is the conceit of a windowless monad who believes that s/he internalizes everything, such that to "understand the universe" one need only, *can only*, "contemplate [one's] own inner self" (Harvey, 1996, p. 70). Moreover, it is not so much the world of internal relations that troubles Harvey, it is monadic entities understood as permanences – seamless points – rather than "as continuous transformations and internalizations of different 'moments' (events, things, entities)" (Harvey, 1996, p. 74). Rather than look for *the* moment, one should look for *a* moment *in process* – a moment that is in the process of internalizing an outside. (Such is the digestive philosophy of dialectical materialism.) Yet this is to forget that for Deleuze, the windowless chaosmos of the infinitely (un)folded fold does not close in on itself to form a secure interior – in the manner of a homely living room or an asylum cell. To the contrary, it is seamless only to the extent that a fold can be opened up to (an experience of) infinity. Running betwixt and between the four-dimensional universe of solid ground, land masses, fluvia, people, things, etc., is a supplementary universe of *n* dimensions: the seamless fold that is taken to infinity. This is why in the chapters that follow I have sought neither to dissolve, nor to crystallize, nor to embed, nor to solidify. I have sought only to lend a little chaotic consistency to the infinite (s)play of the fold. Programmatically, this has amounted to: *opening up* a certain poststructuralist experience of space and spacing; *opening up* a certain take on geography and geographers; and *opening up* the fold in and of its (differential) self. For the sake of convenience, I have labelled this threefold programme thus: the first opening, *The space of poststructuralism*, which cuts a perverse dash through some of the work of Baudrillard, Deleuze, Derrida, Foucault, Irigaray, and Lyotard; the second opening, *Schizoanalysis of the geographical tradition*, which seeks to unhinge and (s)play out a number of attempts to constrict geography to various pointillistic configurations of thought-and-action; and the third opening, *Poststructuralist geography*, which sets out a certain rhythm and chor(e)ography for deconstruction, nomadology, rhizomatics, and schizoanalysis. If it is not (s)played out to your liking, then take comfort from the fact that the book can be folded, unfolded, and refolded in many ways. Such is the world.

Part I

The space of poststructuralism

The figure is never *one*.
Jacques Derrida, 'Introduction' to *Typography*

It's a question of dissimilating the givens.
Jean-François Lyotard, *Duchamp's* TRANS/*formers*

There's nothing more unsettling than the continual movement of
something that seems fixed.
Gilles Deleuze, *Negotiations*

CHAPTER I

Spaces of perversion in Deleuze and Derrida

> *One cannot assume a position* on the twisted, shock-ridden, electrified labyrinthine band. One's got to get this into one's head.
> (Lyotard, 1993, p. 11)

> Walk not perverted, walk with religious language.
> (The Fall, *Perverted by Language*)

What could possibly connect geography and perversion? Many obscene possibilities spring to mind, but in the chapters that comprise this book I hope to unfold the connection in a more modest way: a love for differential (s)pacing. For my interest is not in all of those things that hold together, and that could be accorded the status of whole Ones, but with the 'calculi of difference' that lend them an apparent integrity. What I want to pursue is spacing: not the points and relata, not this or that, but the bonds and relations that come between. I want to dwell on the spacing of space, and how *this* holds together. And I should add immediately that this concern has little to do with extant spatial science. An apt image of thought for my own diabolical art of spatial science would be origami – folding, unfolding, refolding. Everything that presents itself as a whole One is a special effect of a certain regulated (s)play of folding. It suffices to refold this figure in order to produce another. Origami is an exemplary "othering machine," to purloin a beautiful phrase from Pile (1994a, p. 505). Or rather, since the whole One *can* be refolded, and insofar as it is *nothing but* the relative stabilization of its own refolding, its apparent integrity and self-sufficiency is illusory. Indeed, the folds of space are never merely *around* the figure, they are *in* the figure. Everything comes from the middle. This is why I see only shape-changers now. For mine is a universe of alchemists, sorcerers, and lycanthropes, of cyborgs, schizos, and becomings.

As a point of departure, then, I offer you the non-reflective foil of origami: "Folding, leaping in place, and thus distorting or displacing the ground (the foundation, or its unfounding)" (Nancy, 1996, p. 109). I offer you the prospect of a perverse, motionless (s)trip. To take flight without ever leaving the ground, to voyage without ever moving from the spot, and to become the dissimulative other of the same. Such is the geographer's art, when it is radical, when it is perverted enough. Everything is in the interminable process of becoming what it will have been: *post modo*. Coherence is a retroactive effect, and only takes hold from the vantage point of a certain perspective. This is what I have distilled from my disparate encounters with those writers who have been burdened with the label 'Poststructuralist': Baudrillard, Cixous, Deleuze, Derrida, Foucault, Guattari, Irigaray, and Lyotard, to finger just a few. Some will find my inclination perverse indeed and not at all to their tastes. Others will no doubt moan that this is not 'Geography' or that it bastardizes its sources. Others will probably be looking for good sense and evidence of a truly critical appreciation of what I have lifted from others. As for myself, these worries are not my own. I simply want this book to go with the flow of what comes within its orbit, and, if possible, to get carried away by the s(ed)uctive force of spacing degree zero. So I will pick up where I will have been: in a holding formation.

Holding formation

> Language seems to be seized by a delirium, which forces it out of its usual furrows. (Deleuze, 1997a, p. 229)

> Crazy talk is not enough. (Deleuze and Guattari, 1988, p. 138)

In the twentieth century, theories have proliferated at an unprecedented rate, leading to innumerable and seemingly incompatible views on life, the universe, and everything. For some it is a matter of successive paradigm shifts, with the hegemonic perspective at any moment in time being a result of majoritarian consensus (cf. Johnston, 1991; Stoddart, 1981). For others, such as Peet (1998), distinct 'schools of thought' periodically separate out from the pack; yet lamentably Peet allows them minimal opportunity for confluence or braiding (although much sparring is in the offing). This belies his recognition of a continual 'dynamic shifting complexity,' since it implies an accumulation of complexity over time, as the 'schools' comprising the geographical enterprise are presented in terms of a movement from the few to the many. For example, his summary diagram of post-Enlightenment human-geographical thought since 1850 graphs the branching out of twelve streams across a given 'disciplinary space' (Peet, 1998, p. 10, figure 1.2). Oddly, at the diagram's terminal date of the year 2000, of the nine remaining schools, seven are presented in contraction – Berkeley-school cultural geography, humanistic geography, regional geography, regional science, quantitative–spatial geography, radical–Marxist geography (incorporating structuralism), and realism–structuration–locality – ; and only two are in dilation – feminist geography and postmodern geography. Even odder, at the year 2000 these schools cover less than half of the available disciplinary space diagrammed in Peet's two-dimensional pictogram. In fact, the majority of the figure is cast in grey-tones, and the resulting grey areas stand in stark contrast to the historicized white streaks of post-Enlightenment geography. One wonders what is lurking in the dark, uncharted, and unattributed portions of geographical praxis. I am reminded of Lyotard's (1997, p. 5) realization that "the true streams are subterranean," which tap into "an underground cavity full of black, cold, and still water."

Now, before we get swept up by these dark currents, it is worth noting that the plethora of perspectives available to us need not only be characterized in terms of succession and branching. One could think of our disciplinary space as a woven or fulled fabric that can be frayed and thereby reworked in all kinds of ways. Alternatively, Livingstone (1992a) usefully characterizes the geographical tradition in terms of a parallelism of discrete strands that fade in and out of focus over time. The image of thought specific to this – although Livingstone fails to develop it – is one of accords: a harmonics of resonance and dissonance that is ceaselessly in play across time and space (cf. Lefebvre's notion of 'rhythmanalysis'). The discreteness of integral positions, perspectives, and schools gets swept up by an untimely orchestration. Similarly, one could figure the multiplicity of theoretical-practices as a virtual matrix of incalculable possibilities that subtend any actual instantiation of geographical praxis (à la origami). Or again: the geographical tradition could be rendered as a swirling cloud within which discernible events crystallize out.

Despite the preponderance of dark bodies, harmonics, and vapoury, there has been a tendency to present the disciplinary space of geography in terms of the 'many' (one+) rather than as a 'multiplicity' (a singularity in the mathematical sense). Even Livingstone (1992a, 1992b) resorts to enumerating the constituent strands of the geographical tradition, just as Peet (1998) enumerates the post-Enlightenment schools: it is always a matter of *positive* differences – one and one and one ... (pointillism). Much like the crass depiction of the West at the 'end of history' as a utopian kingdom of Happy Shoppers, the range of neatly packaged theoretical perspectives available today seems to lend itself to the ambivalence of such a consumer society, where choice is increasingly a matter of signifying one's (in)difference and (in)distinction, rather than a reflex of either desire, need, or want. Consequently, one is invariably called upon to suspend one's disbelief in order to buy into a particular image of thought-and-action. One must first of all learn to let go in order to be seduced into the efficacy of *this* particular frame of reference over and against all of the others. And for all of the agonizing over the respective merits, coherence, and side effects of the various theoretical endeavours, we seem to be as far away as ever from either a hegemonic consensus or a peaceful coexistence, let alone a final (re)solution, to the problem of fabricating an adequate understanding and explanation of whatever it is that we want to understand and explain. To be sure, this situation has engendered much self-examination and voluminous debate, which has had the effect of both empowering some and freezing out others. Yet given the expansionist and totalizing pretensions of almost all theoretical enterprises, this incommensurability has also been accompanied by violence. Such violence has ranged from the dissimulation of contradictions and paralogisms, the obscuring of lacunae and aporias, and the suppression of dissenting voices and opposing forces, to the local skirmishes between competing theories, the all-out conflict of opposing war machines, and the terror tactics of hostage-taking, sabotage, and mutually assured destruction.

Disintegration

Since ideas and concepts never travel alone but always come in packs, any particular idea or concept can help support a theoretical edifice; but it can just as easily be employed as an explosive device for blowing the edifice apart. Sometimes these supports are manufactured in-house. At other times they are borrowed, begged, stolen or purchased from other discourses. Similarly, the explosive devices might be produced off-shore and launched towards the enemy's positions or else they might be components of the other's edifice, which are over-extended or given a strategic twist in order to destroy their load-bearing potential. Such a 'twisting to destruction' is at the core of a host of theoretical-practices – including immanent critique, negative dialectics, reflexivity, active nihilism, and deconstruction – , although for reasons that will become apparent in due course, I prefer the common-or-garden term *perversion* as an expedient way to convey what is at stake here.

Concepts, ideas, frames of reference, and theoretical-practices are never created *ex nihilo* or given as ready-mades, like a wondrous bequest from an anonymous benefactor residing in another dimension. They are fabricated and fashioned in particular contexts, from materials and practices that are already made available to us. As with energy, concepts and ideas can be neither conjured out of thin air nor destroyed without trace – "There are only transformations, redistributions of energy" (Lyotard, 1990b, p. 36). In this sense, all theoretical-practice is a perversion. *It has nothing whatsoever to do with representation.* Rather than the vertical ontotheology of obedient reproduction without remainder, poststructuralist geography follows the horizontal drift of interminable perversion with maximal modification. Perversion is not a difference that produces repetitions of the same (a distortion that nevertheless retains, negatively, the imprint of proper reduplication – hence perversion's duplicity: it affirms the normal through transgressing it). To the contrary, perversion is a difference-producing repetition: "it distorts without misrepresenting," remarks Macherey of Deleuze's 'expressionist reading' of Spinoza. Perversion "forces the text out of itself by introducing the minimal dislocations needed to get it moving ... not by introducing completely foreign elements, but by amplifying certain themes that are not fully developed, thereby modifying the internal economy of their relations" (Macherey, 1996, pp. 148–9). Likewise, in an exquisite turn of phrase, Sim (1992, p. 66) reminds us that Derrida once claimed that "Deconstruction interferes rather than analyses or critiques" (cf. Lyotard, 1993). Yet by misunderstanding the torque of deconstruction – its truly twisted nature – , he misconstrues the turning, gyration, and revolution of deconstruction as "leading us in circles" (Sim, 1992, p. 67). As with ploughing, it is the turning and the returning that opens the sedimented field up (Doel, 1994b). In other words, what Sim (1992, p. 55) characterizes as Derrida's "off-criticism" – in which "analysis is bracketed before it has been given a chance to begin", so that in skirting the text one effectively leaves it, and the power relations sustaining it, untouched (sous rature) – is in actuality an 'ex-orbitant' 'ex-centricity.' It revolves around that which is unhinged – and thereby borders on delirium and schizophrenia (Perez, 1990). This is no "extravagant metaphorical whimsy," "a kind of sophisticated doodling on the margins of serious, truth-seeking discourse," as Norris (1987, p. 79) says of the typical reception of Derrida's writing amongst philosophers. For the turning of deconstruction not only opens the constellation of forces (peeling, unwinding, exfoliation), but its amassing effects draw the event (or the text) out of itself. The proliferation of signs – through a "cancerization of theoretical discourse" (Lyotard, 1993, p. 96) – has gravitational and seductive effects (cf. Baudrillard, 1986, 1990a). I shall return to these motifs of poststructuralist geography in subsequent chapters.

Since something only ever exists through its differential relations, 'it' can always be reworked and refolded. Perversion does not so much overturn the *terms* of a particular context, as reconfigure its *spacings* and *p(l)acings*, through amplification, feedback, and superconductivity, for example. Hereinafter, "the interval takes all, the interval is substance" (Deleuze and Guattari, 1988, p. 478). "What is expressed everywhere intervenes as a third term that transforms dualities," writes Deleuze (1990b, p. 311). Everything comes down to (s)p(l)acing, origami, and rhythmanalysis. This requires a "philosophy of passage, and not of ground or of territory" for "traversing the chaos: not explaining or interpreting it, but traversing it, all the way across, in a traverse which orders the planes, landscapes, coordinates, but which leaves behind it the chaos, closing on itself like the sea on the wake of a ship" (Nancy, 1996, p. 112).

To that extent, it is futile to try to isolate discrete theoretical-practices – each with its own system of ideas, conceptual apparatus, phrase regime, frame of reference, proscribed territory, and logic of internal development – and to position each over and against the others. For each is endlessly other: it is not a whole being but a multiple becoming. Each theoretical-practice is a multiplicity without unity since it is always already open to difference, deferral, iteration, transformation, and perversion. Hereinafter, there are nothing but open systems that are always already everywhere shot through with vectors of disjointure, disadjustment, and dislocation. Differential spacing is not just around something; it is that something. This is why established positions and sedentary fixations are inseparable from voyages in place and motionless trips.

Since nothing is closed in on itself in this or any other universe, one could usefully approach a theoretical-practice, and the concepts through which it unfurls, as though it were a handful of sand. On certain occasions, one can lift a concretion of encrusted sand and maintain its fragile integrity, until, with an imperceptible twitch of one's fingertips, its holding formation disintegrates into a cascade of free particles. These free particles comprise "packets of singularities, packets that come undone in their turn," says Lyotard (1990b, p. 79). En route to a 'politics of incommensurability' that I will take up in the next chapter, Lyotard suggests that it "remains to establish between the grains of matter a 'regulation' whose function cannot be to unite them, but must leave them in regrets: each connection of grain to grain must be misrecognizable, alien not only to a different connection between other grains, but to a 'previous' one between the 'same' ones" (Lyotard, 1990b, p. 79). In accordance with such an image of thought, one could say that the "fundamental illusion of philosophy is the illusion of the autonomy and primacy of the concept" (Dews, 1987, p. 44); just as in geography, the fundamental illusion is the autonomy and primacy of the point. Concepts are fashioned through relatively stabilized practices of association and dissociation, coagulation and coalescence. Whenever one encounters something that appears to be unified, wholesome, and stable, one should perhaps recall the precariousness of coagula and the tensity of stiff little fingers. Thus, every concept, idea, act, event, frame of reference, and theoretical-practice is always already open to disadjustment, displacement, and reinscription. Little wonder, then, that so many should concur with Harvey's (1987, p. 368) conviction that "we should strive hard to eliminate 'the terrorism of isms.'" For thinking in terms of '-isms' invariably leads to the freezing of variation into a monolithic and seamless constancy. Yet there are no inalienable forms or invariant ideals in this or any other world. As a pervert and lycanthrope, I see only shape-changers now. Henceforth, to be perverted by language, and to pervert others in turn, is not to defile or debase; nor is it to denounce, critique or condemn. Perversion is an expression of love for the othering of the same. "Deconstruction, as I see it, can only take place if you love what you are deconstructing," says Spivak. "This is the 'love,' knowing from the inside, that you give to an enemy you respect, so that the clear-cut distinction between friend and enemy begins to shift and blur" (1989, pp. 213–14).

Strange attractor

For Bauman (1989, 1990, 1993), such a blurring between insiders and outsiders is exemplified in the ambivalent role that the 'stranger' came to play in the aesthetic, cognitive, and moral spaces of modernity. On the one hand, the figure of the stranger was essential for 'binding' together the increasingly distanciated and accelerated articulation of social relations. In this way, the stranger embodied both the traits of pure circulation – restlessness, homelessness, depersonalization, autonomy, etc. – and the disinterest required for successful market transactions. On the other hand, since the stranger necessarily disrupts the common-sensical distinctions between inside and outside, near and far, and friend and foe, as well as short-circuiting the homologous relation between distance in physical space and distance in social space, it should be clear why the stranger can all too easily be positioned as a threat to order and a focal point for the projection of fear, anxiety, and hatred (Bauman, 1989; Clarke, 1997; Clarke, Doel, and McDonough, 1996). Yet the stranger is not in actuality a threat to identity. Rather, the stranger acts as a fixative for the ambient fear that pervades the experience of modernity. Both identity and fragmentation are experienced retroactively: they are set off – and off set – in relation to a misrecognition and anticipation of a becoming whole. They are both shaped from the outside in. As a harbinger of things to come, it is worth underscoring with Bauman that:

> Identity as such is a modern invention. To say that modernity led to the 'disembedding' of identity, or that it rendered the identity 'unencumbered,' is to assert a pleonasm, since at no time did identity 'become' a problem; it was a 'problem' from its birth – was *born as a problem* (that is, as something one needs do something about – as a task), could exist only as a problem; it was a problem, and thus ready to be born, precisely because of that experience of under-determination and free-floatingness which came to be articulated *ex post facto* as 'disembeddedment' [*sic*]. Identity would not have congealed into a visible and graspable entity in any other but the 'disembedded' or 'unencumbered' form. (Bauman, 1996, pp. 18–19).

A strange and perverted theoretical-practice, then – such as poststructuralism – would not constitute a unique and self-contained position. Rather, it would take the form of a Möbius (s)trip, through which the apparently secure threshold between what is inside and what is outside gives way to an undecidable and open multiplicity in continuous variation (cf. Llewelyn, 1986). Thus, when one says that a theoretical-practice is always already other than itself, one is problematizing the historicist inclination for allowing the past to remain settled with itself. This is the curious, spooky, and funny disjointure whereby the 'othering' of the tradition is always already and everywhere *in* the tradition, and not merely *around* it or *after* it. Such a perverse theoretical-practice is (s)played out in Deleuze's 'screwing process,' Derrida's 'reversal and reinscription,' Lyotard's 'cancerization,' Irigaray's 'touching lips,' and Baudrillard's 'light manipulation.' So, let me begin by stringing together a few of these perversions in order to glean a sense of what a poststructuralist geography might be capable of. In this chapter I draw on Deleuze and Derrida to elucidate the perverse duplicity of spacing. Then, in the next chapter, I consider Lyotard's ethico-political practice of 'dissimilating the givens.' Finally, I turn to Irigaray and Baudrillard for a taste of the s(ed)uctive force of (s)pacing degree zero.

The schizoid quilting machine – a Deleuzean screw-up

I don't believe in things. (Deleuze, 1995, p. 160)

As a tactical response to the repressive and Oedipalizing function of the history of philosophy – through which "'you won't dare speak your own name as long as you have not read this and that, and that on this, and this on that'" – Deleuze (1977a, pp. 112–13) reports a disturbing ruse through which he viewed

> the history of philosophy as a screwing process (*enculage*) or, what amounts to the same thing, an immaculate conception. I would imagine myself approaching an author from behind, and making him a child, who would indeed be his and would, nonetheless, be monstrous. That the child would be his was very important because the author had to say, in effect, everything I made him say. But that the child should be monstrous was also a requisite because it was necessary to go through all kinds of decentrings, slidings, splittings, secret discharges which have given me much pleasure.

Deleuze forced his blind dates to give birth to monstrosities, a trait which he shares with Derrida and Baudrillard. This declaration seems utterly offensive as it appears to endorse sexual violence as a source of creation and pleasure, and our abhorrence should not be lessened by its homoerotic inscription as an unequal exchange amongst men within a tradition dominated by the Phallus and the Name-of-the-Father, nor by the fact that Deleuze derived such pleasure on the back of those whom he considered 'enemies' (e.g. Kant and Hegel) as well as from those whom he 'loved' (e.g. Hume and Spinoza). Unbelievably, this stratagem appears to advocate systematic rape as an effective weapon of war, to the extent that it might bring about a defilement of the enemy's blood-line through external contamination: not through (artificial) insemination; but through cloning a corruptible genetic code in order to frustrate the endless reproduction of the same. Worse still, perhaps, is Deleuze's repeated insistence that despite all of this, he has "nothing to 'admit'" – "Attorney-general, I admit nothing" (Deleuze, 1977a, pp. 115 and 112). He seems to be without guilt, remorse or shame. But then again, he does not even admit that a wrong has been committed. So, rather than confess and seek to atone for his 'crimes,' he informs us that he simply *stopped* screwing with the history of philosophy. Why did he stop? It was because he finally encountered someone who would not be screwed with: Nietzsche (in much the same way that Baudrillard (1996a) tells us that he encountered a place which was unmoved by his own musings on the aporetic spiralling of simulations and simulacra: Japan). "For it is impossible to submit [Nietzsche] to such a treatment," says Deleuze (1977a, p. 113). "He's the one who screws you behind your back. He gives you a perverse taste that neither Marx nor Freud have ever given you: the desire for everyone to say simple things in his own name, to speak through affects, intensities, experiences, experiments." After getting screwed by Nietzsche when he was not ready for it, he stops screwing with others. Yet he does not stop in order to practise celibacy. Rather, he stops in order to start screwing with himself, in order to produce immaculate conceptions out of himself. For Deleuze, this signalled the passage from the paranoia of a State philosopher – who is obligated to honour, cherish, and obey essential forms, universal values, and inalienable concepts, whilst nevertheless despairing about the apparent lawlessness of the world – towards the schizophrenia of 'nomad thought' – whereupon thinking dissolves into the disseminating flows of the world. Yet if philosophy loses its privileged position it nevertheless gains the ability to work productively alongside a host of other discourses through a reciprocal deterritorialization onto a no-man's land of affective experimentation or a blind zone of indiscernibility. Thus, theoretical-practice, like reading and writing, "is a flow among others; it enjoys no special privilege and enters into relationships of current and counter-current, of back-wash with other flows – the flows of shit, sperm, speech, action, eroticism, money, politics, etc." (Deleuze, 1977a, p. 114).

Now, before returning to this scene of perverse sexual violence, which

Deleuze assures us he eventually grew out of, I want to make three points. First, by coming out of his period of screwing with the history of philosophy, Deleuze tells us that he was free at last to speak simply and in his own name. Deleuze dubs this 'pop philosophy,' which runs counter to "philosophy's golden rule: a philosophy may be 'idealistic' or 'realistic,' dialectical or illuminative, but it cannot allow itself the luxury of not being *difficult*" (Descombes, 1993, p. 7).

Weird pop

A useful way into pop philosophy is to follow Deleuze (1977a, p. 114) in distinguishing between

> two ways of reading a book: either we consider it a box which refers us to an inside, and in that case we look for the signified; if we are still more perverse or corrupted, we search for the signifier. And then we consider the following book as a box contained in the first one or containing it in turn. And we can comment, and interpret, and ask for explanations, we can write about the book and so on endlessly. Or the other way: we consider a book as a small a-signifying machine; the only problem is 'Does it work and how does it work? How does it work for you?' If it doesn't function, if nothing happens, take another book. This way of reading is based on intensities: something happens or doesn't happen. There is nothing to explain, nothing to understand, nothing to interpret. It can be compared to an electrical connection.

So, we can *either* treat a work as a box, and we can endlessly interpret its content, attempting to maintain a fidelity towards the presumed unity and constancy of the author's intentions, formal structure, libidinal investments, historical context, etc., *or* we can consider it to be a machine coupled to other machines, and we can endlessly play with its workings, flows, and interruptions, experimenting with what a particular machinic arrangement can do. In the conventional approach, one is liable to be driven to distraction because one will never know whether or not one has hit bottom in the interminable and labyrinthine process of interpretation (Schrift, 1990a). The treasure trove of hermeneutics all too easily becomes the Pandora's box of anti-hermeneutics (cf. Gould, 1994a; Laplanche, 1996). For "if nature signifies, it can be a certain acme of culture to make it designify" (Barthes, 1972a, p. 203). In pop philosophy, by contrast, one is only concerned with exploring what is possible at a particular juncture. Similarly, whilst philosophy is traditionally thought of as working *on* its subject matter, pop philosophy works *alongside* it (cf. Carroll, 1987). For example, Deleuze (1986, 1989) does not reduce the cinema to philosophy; he does not turn the cinema into a ventriloquist's dummy for the Voice of Reason. Instead, Deleuze attempts to allow the images of thought specific to philosophy to reverberate with the images of thought particular to the cinema – such as the movement-image and the time-image. "This way of reading intensively, in relation to the outside – flow against flow, machine with machines, experimentations, events for everyone (which have nothing to do with a book, but with its shreds and are a new mode of operating with other things, no matter what ... etc.) – is a manifestation of love" (Deleuze, 1977a, p. 115).

All in all, then, pop philosophy approaches something as if it were a machinic arrangement of 'flows and interruptions,' where the only appropriate question is: 'How does it work (for you)?' If it fails to function, if it fails to *go off*, then the pop philosopher will pass on in silence and take up another event. This is why Deleuze encourages us to treat a book, theory or concept "as you would treat a record you listen to, a film or TV programme you watch ... There's no question of difficulty or understanding: concepts are exactly like sounds, colours or images, they are intensities which suit you or not, which are acceptable or aren't acceptable. Pop philosophy" (Deleuze and Parnet, 1987, p. 4). Likewise, Foucault (1989, p. 196) adds that "It's crazy, that people like to judge. It's everywhere, all the time. I can't help thinking of the critic who would not try to judge, but bring into existence a work, a book, a phrase, an idea ... He would bear the lightning flashes of possible storms."

Accordingly, Foucault (1984, p. xiv) has noted that the games, traps, and snares scattered throughout the work of Deleuze and Guattari are not those of rhetoric, but "those of humor: so many invitations to let oneself be put out, to take one's leave of the text and slam the door shut." Indeed, rarely has a theoretical-practice been so attuned to the fickleness of pop philosophy. Like Lyotard's *Libidinal Economy* (1993), "You take it or leave it, but if you leave it, it means that it has produced no effects" (Lyotard and Thébaud, 1985, p. 3). It is in this sense that a theoretical-practice is just like a bag of tools, filled with so many prostheses for enhancing, extending, and intensifying thought and action. "We have done with all globalising concepts. Even concepts are haecceities, events. What is interesting about concepts like desire or machine or assemblage is that they only have value in their variables, and in the maximum of variables which they allow. We are not for concepts as big as hollow teeth, THE law, THE master, THE rebel" (Deleuze, 1993a, p. 254). Concepts must therefore become events in the universe to which they give an immanent consistency, and a philosopher is therefore someone "who creates an event in thought" (Lechte, 1994, p. 102; cf. Baudrillard, 1987a). Thus, "The world of Deleuze is not a world of classifiable things, but of events" (Lecercle, 1985, p. 97). Something happens.

For Deleuze, "a philosopher is someone who creates in the domain of concepts, someone who invents new concepts" (in Bogue, 1989, p. 155). Little wonder, then, that Deleuze is not at all inspired by accumulating knowledge and still less by discerning the truth (as either a 'correspondence' between thought and reality, the 'coherence' of a system, or the 'integrity' of a position). Instead, he is inspired by immanent and contingent criteria, such as 'interesting,' 'remarkable,' and 'important.' On these criteria, Deleuze and Guattari (1994, p. 83) denounce both "flimsy concepts" and "concepts that are too regular, petrified, and reduced to a framework. In this respect, the most universal concepts, those presented as eternal forms or values, are the most skeletal and least interesting." There is therefore little point in collecting concepts. "Hitherto one has generally trusted one's concepts as if they were a wonderful dowry from some sort of wonderland" (Nietzsche, 1968, p. 409), but "trust must be replaced with mistrust, and philosophers must distrust most those concepts they did not create themselves" (Deleuze and Guattari, 1994, p. 83). So too with the conjuration of space.

Accordingly, "There is no heaven for concepts," insist Deleuze and Guattari (1994, p. 5). "They must be invented, fabricated, or rather created and would be nothing without their creator's signature." But what are concepts created for? On Deleuze's account, they are created to elucidate what the situation at hand is capable of: not representation, but experimentation. And perhaps this is why Deleuze and Guattari prefer the notion of a contextualized and transient 'mapping' of a given terrain to that of a 'tracing' or 'copying' of inalienable and transcendent forms. It is no small wonder, then, that Deleuze should put so much emphasis on "Godard's formula: not a correct image, just an image. It is the same in philosophy as in a film or a song: no correct ideas, just ideas" (Deleuze and Parnet, 1987, p. 9). Hence also Deleuze's claim that "The point of critique is not justification but a different way of feeling: another sensibility" (quoted in Bové, 1988, p. vii).

The task of creating concepts is, however, no mean feat. The creator of concepts is always in danger of succumbing, on the one hand, to "the miseries of personal language – my *idea* is no more than a *saying* for someone who does not find it striking, and likewise my *saying* might be nothing more than a *cliché* – and on the other hand, the reassuring stability of commonplaces, proverbs, and tried-and-true expression" (Descombes, 1993, p. 12). This double jeopardy is all the more pressing for anyone who eschews 'difficulty' and the pleasure of neologism, technonarcissism, and bibliophilia, opting instead for the expression of simplicity penned in one's own name. "One could say that the intellectual uses the axiom as a *proverb*," suggests Descombes (1993, p. 12), "whereas the philosopher uses it as a *maxim*." When a philosophical maxim is posited, it is the result of a thought process, and is adopted after serious reflection and consideration. The force of an intellectual proverb, by contrast, is not the force of reflection, but rather that of convenience.

Second, it might be tempting to use this transition from an entanglement within the strictures of the history of philosophy to the freedom of pop philosophy as a device for dividing between, on the one hand, the 'hermeneuts of suspicion' and the 'philosophers of hesitation,' such as Derrida, who paralyse themselves by endlessly fretting over the meaning and significance of this or that morsel which they happen upon, and, on the other hand, those happy-go-lucky souls, like Baudrillard and Deleuze, who opt out of all that scholastic agonizing in order to create and inhabit "imaginary worlds or alternative universes" (Bogue, 1989, p. 159). So, Deleuze and Guattari become-woman, -animal, and -imperceptible, literally, and not metaphorically (cf. Massumi, 1992a; Miller, 1993). Likewise, after playing 'the whole game,' as Baudrillard occasionally puts it, he now engages in pataphysics, the parodic science of the accidental and the particular, superinduced upon metaphysics, in an endeavour to account for the universe supplementary to our own. Pataphysics, "the invention of the pre-dadaist, protosurrealist Jarry, occupies the place of a comic intermezzo in the mise-en-scène of modern, primarily modernist, French thought," says Pefanis (1991, p. 121). "As a minor and absurd movement of infinitesimal brevity, pataphysics ... represents an obverse and parodic mirror to the philosophically and scientifically serious." Similarly, one might say that beyond the strictures of the philosophical and sociological traditions, both Deleuze and Baudrillard conjure theory-fiction à la science-fiction, just as Foucault and Lyotard construct anamorphic and dissimilatory projections of eclipsed events on the incommensurable screens of words and things, discourses and figures. Integrity, coherence, and commensurability are not givens. They are special effects created by approaching things from a certain point of view.

Deleuze "invents paradoxical concepts," says Bogue (1989, p. 159), "but rather than reinscribe these concepts within traditional texts," as Derrida does, "he uses them as the building blocks of an alternative world." On that score, Deleuze would be closer to Baudrillard's brand of pataphysics than Derrida's enigmatic deconstruction. Thus, "The basic strategy ... is to invent such paradoxical elements and develop their unsettling consequences across various disciplines" (Bogue, 1989, p. 155). Such is the dynamism of a deterritorializing theoretical-practice, which seeks resources to overcome blockages in innumerable, relatively stabilized contexts.

Be that as it may, I think it is problematic to contrast Deleuze and Derrida in this way, not least because Derrida's reinscriptions are not

only placed within a slackened and extended notion of the text that in
its 'generality' – or distension – spreads out to take in the 'entire-
real-history-of-the-world' (Derrida, 1988a), but also because these
reinscriptions displace and refashion what has hitherto been held in
place as inalienable. Deconstructive reinscription is a repetition, to be
sure, but it is a repetition with a difference. Through deconstruction,
repetition never returns to the same. So, Massumi's (1996a, p. 406)
distillation of Deleuze's theoretical-practice down to the formula "Repeat
to differ" would be an apt catchphrase for deconstruction as well (cf.
Derrida, 1994b; Derrida, 1981b). Consequently, it is simply spurious
to attempt to set aside the (other) 'worldly' Deleuze, Guattari, and
Foucault from the 'textualist' Derrida, Lyotard, and Lacan, not least
because all of them work against the reduction of the world to meaning.
Likewise, I think that it is a mistake to claim that whilst Deleuze is the
rebel who seems to break with the strictures of State philosophy, Derrida
ensconces himself and beds down in its plush texture.

A more pertinent distinction between Deleuze and Derrida might be
drawn on the basis of Deleuze's liking for empiricism and Derrida's
ambivalence towards it. "Why ... does Derrida eschew empiricism?"
asks Descombes (1980, p. 150). "It is because he never appeals to a
particular experience that might weaken a *general* proposition ... Derrida
places himself as it were in the hands of a *general* experience." Take
the reasonableness of Reason. One will never weaken the general proposition by highlighting a particular case of unreasonableness. Such a
revelation would presuppose and work in the interest of a more complete,
inclusive, and total form of Reason. Yet as Bennington (1989b, p. 38)
remarks, "deconstruction is ... eminently describable (with Gasché) as
a 'radical empiricism' which exposes to contingency and historicity (this
is why deconstruction is less a theory than a series of events)." Derrida
commits – 'intentionally' and 'impeccably' says Descombes! – the 'fault'
of empiricism. This fault amounts to displacing the logocentric dream
of pure identity at the source (such as the self-sufficiency of the Concept),
since identity is necessarily negatory and differential (Gasché, 1986).
Similarly, Deleuze's 'transcendental empiricism' is not a naive reduction
of *truths of reason* to *truths of fact*, a reduction of reason to experience.
Transcendental empiricism does not arrest itself upon encountering
so-called 'brutal' or 'primitive' facts, which are simply there like so
many stubborn and irremovable 'stains of the real' (Žižek, 1992). Like
Derrida, Deleuze's events open onto a *general* experience – of becoming,
indiscernibility, and the impersonal Life, for example. This is why it
is necessary to speak of Deleuze's *transcendental* empiricism.

> The 'transcendental,' as opposed to the transcendent, refers to the *limit*,
> the transformation zone where actual faculties, such as conscious

thought ... and individual sensibility, are taken to their highest power, and are blocked. The limit is *of* thought and *of* feeling, but it is not *in* them. It is their plane of mutual immanence, where they are *in each other*. This plane is not beyond, in the sense of being outside. For if it were outside, it would be relative to an inside. The limit is absolute ... because it beyonds all things. It de-forms them ... by *infolding* them. The limit is a deforming *force* no thing can withstand, powerful enough to make a thing what it is not, to turn it inside out and outside in, to the point that it transcends itself at the extremity of its immanence. This process cannot but be felt. (Massumi, 1996a, p. 406)

This characterization of Deleuze's transcendental empiricism is very close to my own understanding of the deconstruction of the metaphysics of presence (Doel, 1992, 1994a, 1994b). In harmony with Derrida, "Philosophy, for Deleuze, is either dialectical or empiricist, according to whether the difference between concept and intuition (in the Kantian sense of a relation to the particular entity) is taken to be a conceptual or a non-conceptual difference" (Descombes, 1980, p. 155). Such a distinction is also helpful in distinguishing between idealism and materialism. This is important not least because countless geographers writing on poststructuralism, deconstruction, and postmodernism have erroneously attributed to these latter what Peet (1998, p. 302) refers to as a *"discursive idealist"* position. "Idealism, in its sense of opposition to materialism and not realism, is the affirmation not that there do not *exist* objects external to the mind, but rather that the innermost nature of these objects is identical to that of mind – that is to say, that it is ultimately *thought*" (Laclau and Mouffe, 1987, p. 87). This is why Althusser (1979), like Adorno (1973), was so insistent that the work of materialism could never be finalized. For there is no final solution to the task of expressing the non-identity of thought and reality, even though each is composed of the same grain. Hence the fact that I take Deleuze and Guattari (1988) at their word when they speak of 'voyaging in place' and 'stationary trips.' Moreover, one of the key consequences of empiricism for Deleuze is a recognition of the externality of relations, so that inquiry does not so much *dwell* on the relata, as *take flight* upon the relation. "The basic thing is how to get taken up in the movement of a big wave, a column of rising air, to 'come between' rather than to be the origin of an effort" (Deleuze, 1992a, p. 281). Or again: "What counts has never been to go along with some related movement, but to make one's own movement" (Deleuze, 1992a, p. 285).

Contrary to the totalizing depictions of empiricism in geography, empiricism need not be naively pointillistic (a dispersion of atomistic events). Through the affirmation of the externality of relations, transcendental empiricism inaugurates a general relativity. One need not fret over the bisection of internal and external relations, the separation of those relations necessary for a thing's existence from those contingent relations that are not, since that is to remain within a *restricted* economy of relations. In a state of *general* relativity, by contrast, *all* relations take on a life of their own.

In the first place, then, Deleuze's desistance from screwing with the Oedipalizing history of philosophy allowed him to experiment with the free-form styles of pop philosophy: transcendental empiricism, schizoanalysis, rhizomatics, pragmatics, etc. In the second place, this shift does not suffice to divide the (other) worldly character of Deleuze's work from the textualism erroneously attributed to other poststructuralist theoretical practices. Finally, and on the basis of both of these points, it should be clear that speaking in one's own name is not as simple as it might appear. For it is not an individual person who speaks (I speak), but an impersonal multiplicity (a schizoid 'it' speaks): "Something happens to [the characters] that they can only recapture by relinquishing their power to say 'I'" (Blanchot, 1993, pp. 384–5). Or else one still says 'I,' but it no longer expresses a 'me' – it is no longer my 'I'; the 'I' that belongs to me alone. "To reach, not the point where one no longer says I, but the point where it is no longer of any importance whether one says I. We are no longer ourselves" (Deleuze and Guattari, 1988, p. 3). One never screws alone, but always in relation to others, even if those others are first and foremost the ones who populate ourselves. One becomes by way of another. This is why the minimal unit of be(com)ing is neither the 'one' of identity, nor the 'one plus one' of addition, but the 'twofold' of supplementarity. "There's no longer any secret," says Deleuze (1983a, p. 75). "We have become just like everyone else, or more exactly, we have made of everyone else a *becoming*. We have become clandestine, imperceptible. We have made a strange, stationary trip."

Retake

Having laboured these three points more than I had initially intended, let me return to the scene of sexual violence with which I began. For there is something amiss in the account that I have given. Recall the fact that whilst Deleuze imagined himself approaching an author from behind and giving him a screwed-up child, this monstrous offspring is in actuality the result of an immaculate conception. The monstrosity that Deleuze gets pleasure from (pro)creating is not derived from him; it does not come from him, but only by way of him. Rather than give the other a screwed-up child, Deleuze merely handles its (after)birth, in much the same way that a 'fence' handles purloined goods. He does not so much engage in sexual violence against an other, hoping to defile the purity of the blood-line, as bear witness to the fact that the perverse monstrosity does indeed come from the other. He countersigns the othering of the same (cf. Derrida, 1984a, 1995a). And this is no less true when Deleuze stops screwing others and starts screwing with himself. In short, Deleuze acts like a double agent, employing a double stratagem. He works both 'for' and 'against,' which is to say, his work is effectively undecidable.

The Deleuzean screw-up is not a deep-seated crisis that comes crashing in from the outside, like a tidal wave or tsunami. To the contrary, it participates in the re-release of difference by affirming the fact that the one is always already other. Moreover, the multiplicity as a 'whole' is forever open to the outside – to other flows and interruptions, to other recontextualizations – such that it never ceases changing its composition and arrangement. Accordingly, what Descombes (1980, pp. 150–1) says about Derrida's double agency is, I think, of a piece with Deleuze's screwing with the history of philosophy (amongst others):

> Every text is a double text, there are always two texts in one ... Only the first of these 'two texts in one' is preserved by classical interpretation; it is written under the aegis of presence, favouring meaning, reason, truth. Here all negation is a superior affirmation. If I denounce this or that unreason within reason, I am denying only the negative of reason, a defect of reason within reason. The second text – other and yet the same – is that which the classical reading never deciphers. The first text, however, the one which it is prepared to read, contains fissures or traces which give indications of the second. Now comes the vital point: between the two texts no synthesis is possible, no fusing into one, for the second is not the *opposite* of the first (which might be reconciled with it by a 'surmounting' of their 'differences'), but rather its *counterpart, slightly phased*. A reading of the general text therefore requires a *double science*, rendering apparent the duplicity of any text.

When Boundas and Olkowski (1994, p. 3) call Deleuze a "*Stutterer, thinker of the outside*," this image of thought would be equally apt for Derrida. Both seek to elicit from any particular configuration those halved-together points that re-release variation, those points which, when activated, will begin to slide and make the entire constellation of apparently stable and sedimented forces slide. And if Deleuze's stuttering becomes increasingly screwed-up, then Derrida's becomes increasingly unhinged. The destabilizing movements of differential (s)pacing know no bounds.

Thinking (in)difference – Derrida's double dealing

A barely perceptible displacement disjoints all the articulations and penetrates all the points welded together ... A trembling spreads out which
then makes the entire old shell crack. (Derrida, 1978, p. 260)

"Boiled down to its essentials," says Olsson (1991, p. 167), "telling the
truth is to claim that something is something else and be believed when
you do it. Others trust me, when I say that this is thus or that $a = b$."
Take any proper name and one of 'its' definite description: Venus = the
morning star; Venus = the evening star; so the morning star = the
evening star. "How small must the unavoidable difference between a
and b be to be blessed as a truth? How big shall it be to be condemned
as a lie?" (Olsson, 1994, pp. 215–16). Hence Olsson's whirligig spiralling
around the irreducible disadjustment between the senselessness of
tautologies ($a = a$) and the meaningfulness of falsehoods ($a = b$).
Although as Olsson knows only too well, the bars of identity are not so
much rigid designators that pin things down, as lines of flight into the
driftworks of dialectics, semiotics, semiurgy, and beyond. This is partly
why the so-called 'prison-house of language' – in which all kinds of
'semiotic animals,' that is to say, language users in the broadest sense,
are trapped in the aporetic binds of identity thinking, of the necessary
lies that secure (im)proper names to (in)definite descriptions – leaks in
all directions.

Through (re)duplication, then, nothing appears to change (it is the
same one) – and yet everything has changed (it is always already other
than itself). This paralogy is perverse, and surely the special effect of
a 'crazy logic.' How can two that are the same be different? How can
one be other than itself? Olsson (1991, p. 190), for example, considers
a stone: "we can easily agree that the stone that now sits on my writing
table is the same as the one I picked up fifteen years ago," he says; "It
is more difficult to determine whether it also contains the same hopes
and fears." Such a disjuncture between tangible materiality on the one
hand, and dematerialized symbolism on the other hand, is a common
enough one to invoke in geography. For example, Gottdiener (1995)
makes much of various physical 'vehicles of expression' for all kinds of
communicative effects in his attempt to recover 'authentic' material
cultures from 'inauthentic' ones. However, this disjointure between
revisable meaning and enduring matter is not disadjusted enough (cf.
Farinelli, Olsson, and Reichert, 1994; Gren, 1994). Consider Duchamp,
whose 'mechanics' – or 'machinations' – are in Lyotard's estimation
radically dissimilating. Through a 'mirrorish' practice, Duchamp endows
his objects with a dissimilating extra dimension. How can this be squared

with Euclid's perspectival space within which "reflected space is homogeneous to the space that it reflects? Isn't the specular operation *essentially* one that replicates and makes identical?" (Lyotard, 1990b, p. 91). For both Duchamp and Lyotard, there is a 'double game of the mirror:'

> A duplicating machine, the mirror can be taken as a duplex/duplicitous machine; you can have confidence in the first – it gives back what you give it; the second one is cunning. The cunning is not only the infidelity of the mirror, but also it stems from the fact that its fidelity and its infidelity are produced together, the latter dissimulated in the former. The cunning is itself included in a dissimilation without finality: the straight shelters the crooked and is worked over by it. (Lyotard, 1990b, p. 91)

Hereinafter, the "trick is to use the specular and the reproductive, those mechanisms of assimilatory terror, to engender something dissimilar, to invent singularities" (Lyotard, 1990b, p. 62: cf. Gasché, 1986). This is an ethico-political manoeuvre that I will take up more forcefully in the following chapter.

No doubt many geographers will be familiar with the 'double agency' found at play within Bhaskar's (1989) 'critical realism' and Giddens' (1984) 'theory of structuration,' both of which have attempted to overcome the ineffectual separation of structure and agency, one through a 'transformative model of social action' and the other through a notion of 'the duality of structure' (Bryant and Jary, 1991; Outhwaite, 1987). In fact, poststructuralism, deconstruction, and postmodernism have by and large been filtered through into the mainstream of human geography by way of these two takes on double agency: either structuralism unhinged or humanism gone berserk. However, the double agency of Deleuze and Derrida is very different. The need for a double strategy arises because of the closure of metaphysics and the absolute nature of reason (cf. Boyne, 1990; Critchley, 1992; Habermas, 1987b). Reason is absolute because "there is no Trojan horse unconquerable by Reason (in general) ... one cannot speak out against it except by being for it, that one can protest it only from within it; and within its domain, Reason leaves us only the recourse to stratagems and strategies" (Derrida, 1978, p. 36). Which is to say: "Since the revolution against reason ... can operate only *within* reason, it always has the limited scope of what is called, precisely in the language of a department of *internal* affairs, a disturbance" (Derrida, 1978, p. 36). So:

> To speak in order to say nothing (whether we approve reason, which can forego our approval, or whether we address our criticism to it in a highly reasonable manner) – this dilemma is Derrida's point of departure ...
> Derrida opts to play a *double game* (in the sense that a double agent serves

two sides), feigning obedience to the tyrannical system of rules while simultaneously laying traps for it in the form of problems which it is at a loss to settle. The strategy of *deconstruction* is the ruse that makes it possible to speak at the very moment when there is, 'when all is said and done,' nothing more to say since the absolute discourse has been achieved. (Descombes, 1980, pp. 138–9)

This double agency has been characterized by Critchley (1992) as a 'philosophy of hesitation,' to the extent that it is forever suspending its ethico-political obligations within the realm of the undecidable, and by Lyotard (1989a, p. 361) as "so many objections, or rather disjections, made to unobjectionable thought. The Latin word, *disjectio*, more or less covers the meanings of *dissemination* and *deconstruction*." Now, one might be excused for thinking that lessons in 'How to avoid speaking' when faced by an absolutely reasonable Inquisition (Derrida, 1989e), and instruction in the finer points of double dealing, are not only delaying tactics, pure and simple, but the nostalgic machinations of a Cold War mentality that has long since chilled out. For the stand-off is over: the eternal, the universal, and the transcendent have been returned from whence they came: the fleeting, the particular, and the immanent. Indeed, in truly enlightened currents of contemporary human geography, anti-essentialism, contextualism, and 'non-representational' performances reign. The recent interest of many geographers in actor-network theory is exemplary, as is the embodied and emplaced 'thought-in-action' of Thrift (1996b). However, the continuing failure to consider the specificity of difference belies the enormous potential of these currents. Difference has been taken as given – by context, for example – when in fact difference is what *takes place* (Doel, 1994c). If difference is *in* place, it is not in place in the same way that something could be said to be *in* a box. Difference is in place only to the extent that it puts place *out of joint*. Difference is what splays out. It is the harsh law of space. Only once positive difference has been shown to be unbecoming will the singularity of space and spacing come to the fore. Only then will poststructuralist geography have a chance of taking on consistency. So, it is to difference that I now turn.

Definitely maybe – On in/difference

It seems to me that the double strategies of both Deleuze and Derrida are important for at least two reasons: there would seem to be nothing beyond the tyrannical Inquisition of reason, which can always enumerate the difference (that is to say, give it a place, an identity, and a concept), and, therefore, what eludes reason is *difference as such*, "since difference is by definition that which has no name" (Baudrillard, 1998, p. 88). For difference, conventionally (mis)conceived, always comes back to identity and the same. Why is this so? It is because even if difference 'opposes,' 'contradicts,' or merely 'differs from' identity, it is nevertheless a different *identity*, and therefore dialectically identical with identity. Everywhere one looks, geographers are identifying what has hitherto been different, other, marginal, hidden, repressed, disavowed, etc. The many different identities swarm. Identity thinking – with its threefold laws of: *identity* (whatever is, is), *contradiction* (nothing can both be and not be), and the *excluded middle* (everything must either be or not be) – never encounters difference *as such*, but only different identities, identities that are reflected, represented, and returned through difference to the same. Fixated on presence, stability, and sameness – Being and beings – identity thinking never encounters becomings. "The 'meditation on non-presence' with which metaphysics debates is not, for the latter, another thinking than itself, as a foreign tradition, oriental wisdom or a return to myth etc. would be. It *is* itself as other" (Descombes, 1980, p. 151). Thus, movement, change, and becoming are not 'otherwise than being,' they are misconceived as the serialized phasing of the metaphysics of presence. Identity is phased; it is installed in instalments. Yet by the same token, identity stalls; it differs and defers in and of itself (Doel, 1992). Hence the possibility of a double reading, a double agency, a double strategy, and a double dealing. Iteration alters: something other takes place.

A positive difference *is* the same. It has its own self-sufficient identity, and this appears no less true for relational identities (A:B – e.g. capital–labour) and negatory identities (A/not-A – e.g. self–other), as it is for indifferent identities (A,B – e.g. dog–moon). This is why a difference without positive terms, a difference without identity (the pleonasm indicating my difficulty here), will have to avoid yielding "to circulation in a 'libidinal economy' of substitutions and significations [and become] utterly resistant to the demands of the Cartesian ego, which ... wants nothing more than a decentred digital field of interchangeable 'differences' into which it can project itself omnipotently, changing identities, positions and genders at will" (Levin, 1996, p. 181). Since 'difference' has become one of *the* key terms and stakes of many 'different' theoretical-practices and discourses, this inability to conceive of difference as such, to think the difference *of* difference, is calamitous. What will become of all of those efforts to take into account 'other' voices and practices, and the 'difference' that place, space, and context make? And what about 'sexual difference' and the "*Liberation of subjugated knowledge*" (Moss, 1993, p. 49), the emancipation of all of those other ways of be(com)ing-in-the-world that have been hitherto quashed by that most reasonable of Inquisitions, not to mention the more sensitive and humane reconsideration of the 'mad,' the 'bad,' and the 'ugly,' the 'childlike,' the 'beastly,' and the 'non-human'? Then again, what will become of the attempt to identify this and that, if the difference comes back to the same? Attempting to think difference as such, or rather, endeavouring to *make space* for the difference of difference: I cannot think of a more appropriate task for a geographer.

How can the geographer's ethico-political art of making space for difference be squared with the commonly held view that poststructuralism in general, and deconstruction in particular, revel in a self-indulgent and nihilistic linguistic turn: for example, Derrida's reduction of the world to a special effect of textuality, Lacan's return of the subject to the letter of the Law, and Baudrillard's insistence on the resolution (equals extermination and dissolution) of the real through ob-scene and hyperreal simulations and simulacra? Fortunately, the centrality given to the alleged linguistic turn in poststructuralism is fundamentally misplaced. It misses the essential point, which is that the turn towards language is not at all a retreat from the world, but an effective way to make space for difference *as* difference. So, whenever one is tempted to separate and oppose the world and language, or matter and meaning, or life and textuality, and so on, one would do well to recall both the texture of language and the rhythmic (s)pacing of the world: "Language is a skin I rub against the other," says Barthes (1978, p. 73). One of the sides is no less real than the other, nor is one of them any more substantial. As a rule of thumb: Don't side – slide. And slide all the way across (cf. Deleuze, 1990a). Take the inslide out and the outslide in. Such is the undecidable and reversible ins(l)ide-outs(l)ide of the Möbius strip/motionless trip. To deconstruct, then, is not to turn over the smooth side in order to reveal the rough side, as Eagleton (1986) would have us believe. The smooth s(l)ide gives way to the rough s(l)ide and vice versa – they are the same movement slightly phased.

Eschewing the typical (mis)conception of language as a naming process where there is supposed to be an essential connection between language and the world, such that the former is motivated by the latter, the (post)structuralist view of language begins with the fact that language functions as a *system*, rather than as a gathering of (*in*)*discrete* signs. Much has been made of the so-called 'arbitrary nature of the sign;' that the connection between sound-image (expressive signifier), concept-meaning (expressed signified), and worldly-thing (motivated referent) is a social construct and a matter of convention. For whilst the homology of word–meaning–thing is invariably naturalized, and thereby rendered both transparent and commonsensical, if not in fact, then at least in principle, this seemingly unproblematic connection is no less contrived, slipshod, and forced for all that. On the basis of revealing the arbitrary nature of the sign, one can then explore the innumerable ways in which human beings have carved out sets of signifiers on a *plane of expression* (why these sounds?), signifieds on a *plane of content* (why these meanings?), and referents on a *plane of substance* (why these things?), and then one can proceed to consider how this three-fold inscription has been variously stitched together in order to *give the impression* of an homogeneous, univocal, and seamless world, where a signifier miraculously expresses 'its' signified and conveys 'its' referent, without loss or remainder. One might also emphasize that whilst no (necessary) homology exists between the various planes, each is a shifting floe in continuous variation (Deleuze, 1988a). Moreover, it is worth recalling, with Baudrillard (1981), that this view of language finds an homologous counterpart in the Marxian critique of political economy, wherein exchange-value (*à la* signifier), use-value (*à la* signified), and value (*à la* referent) transpear retroactively across three shifting and incommensurate planes of expression, content, and substance (respectively: price on the market, usefulness in consumption, and labour expended in production) (cf. Derrida, 1992d, 1994b).

Likewise, one could also explain why it is not the subject who masters language, but rather it is language that articulates the subject. But again, all of this is to miss the point. For the much more significant feature of language's systematicity is that in language, as elsewhere, "there are only differences *without positive terms*," as Saussure (1974, p. 120) famously phrased it (although see Ellis, 1989; Tallis, 1988). The recognition that the system, structure, or code is irreducibly *open* is what launches one into poststructuralism proper.

Take colour, or rather, take two systems of colouration: traditional and functional. "In the traditional system colours have psychological and moral overtones ... Colour may be dictated by an event, a ceremony, or a social role; alternatively, it may be the characteristic of a particular material ... Above all it remains circumscribed by form; it does not seek contact with other colours, and it is not a free value" (Baudrillard, 1996c, pp. 30–1). Traditional colouration reunites the differentiation of discreteness and discreetness, from the Latin *discretus*. Colours are not only individually distinct and discontinuous, they are also unobtrusive and circumspect. Accordingly, shading does not imply a permeability and continuity of colours, but rather a negation of colour as such. In this way, "the 'chic' invariably implies the elimination of appearances in favour of being: black, white, grey – whatever registers zero on the colour scale" (Baudrillard 1996c, p. 31). So, traditional colours shade into the positivities that they themselves lack as colours. They refer and defer to external constraints. To this morality of colours, Baudrillard contrasts the atmosphere of functional colouration, which absorbs both the simulacra of 'natural' colours, such as pastels, and the violence of 'affected' colours, such as plasticky primary colours. Composed of *positive* differences, traditional colours appear discrete, with each deferring to its 'natural' law of value (for example: red for passion, white for purity, black for mourning, etc.). Composed from a spectrum of *negative* differences, functional colours appear wholly relative, with each deferring to the 'structural' law of value. A colour's value is determined not on the basis of discreteness, but by a calculus of difference. Indeed, the 'natural' law of value is itself absorbed by the spectral play of structural differentiation, becoming one component in the generalized play and indeterminacy of signs (Baudrillard, 1993c, 1996c, 1998).

> In the fully fledged system of atmosphere ... colours obey no principle but that of their own interaction ... The combination, matching and contrast of tones are the real issues when it comes to the relationship between colour and atmosphere. Blue can go with green – all colours are capable of combination – but only certain blues with certain greens ... colours are now contrasting ranges of shades, their value has less and less to do with their sensory qualities, they are often dissociated from their form, and it is their tonal differences that give a room its 'rhythm' ... colours lose their unique value, and become relative to each other and to the whole. This is what is meant by describing them as functional. (Baudrillard, 1996c, pp. 34–5)

Ins(l)ide-outs(l)ide

Now, without going through all of the ins and outs of semiotics, semiology, and the political economy of the sign, suffice it to say that a sign is what it is only because it differs from and defers other signs, in a disseminating chain which can be extended and proliferated ad infinitum. This is obvious for words which express differences of degree ('hotter,' 'deeper,' 'greener,' 'faster,' etc.), but it is no less true for those which express differences in kind ('me,' 'you,' 'today,' 'this,' etc.). Signification, like the exchange-value of a commodity, is the fleeting and retroverted effect of networks of signs; meaning and value only exist to the extent that they are meaning and value *in motion*. Moreover, it is not just that meaning, like value, is established retroactively through the relation of one term to another in a system of (differential) signs, but that the terms *themselves* are the effect of differential (s)pacings, of relations of speed and slowness, and therefore do not exist beyond the event-horizon of the system of differential relations within which they are inscribed. Strictly speaking, then, there is nothing outside of the system, not because the system is closed in on itself (bubble logic), but because it is always already everywhere open to the outside (logic of suppletion). And in passing, it is worth noting that, as a system, language is either a totality or nothing, although it is a strange totality, not least because it 'lacks' a positive term, a centre. Since this totality has no positive terms, it could be said to have its centre elsewhere, which sets in train an undecidable and disseminating inslide-outslide (cf. Derrida, 1988d). In short, the system of language, as a structured totality, requires a *given* identity *against which* difference/deviation/deviancy can be *calibrated* and *exchanged*, but this is precisely what it does not possess. Descombes (1980, p. 145) puts it like this:

> It must be said that the first is not the first if there is not a second to follow it. Consequently, the second is not merely that which arrives, like a latecomer, *after* the first, but that which permits the first to be first. The first cannot be the first unaided, by its own properties alone: the second, with all the force of its delay, must come to the assistance of the first. It is through the second that the first is the first.

Difference, then, is the condition of (im)possibility of identity. Identity thinking knows nothing whatsoever about difference *as* difference. Thus, in a discussion of Deleuze, Descombes (1980, p. 154) makes the following point:

> The more perfect the repetition (as in the case of twins or mass-produced objects), the less a rationalist philosopher is able to tell where the difference lies ... Repetition should therefore cease to be defined as the return of the same through the reiteration of the identical; on the contrary, it is the *production* (in both sense of the word: to bring into existence, to show) of difference.

If all of this is a little too abstract, consider a pile of near-perfect tomatoes: red, round, moist, and firm. Here, enumerable identities give way to a general relativity. The more exact the equivalence, the more unstable the identity of 'each' in the stack: "the greatest exactitude and the most extreme dissolution" (Deleuze, 1997c, p. 154). The instability *in* each, and not just *around* each, is what makes the flesh of the world vibrate. (Chapter 6 will pick up on this vibration through the notion of solicitation: from the Latin, *sollus*, 'entire,' and *citus*, 'set in motion.') Peppers, potatoes, and carrots are still too obviously differentiated. Only mushrooms come close to the dissimilative exactitude of virtually blemish-free tomatoes. Amidst *the* tomatoes *a* tomato rises as an incorporeal event from the depths of the tomatoey flesh like a haze. Unlike *the* tomatoes, which are merely one or more of a kind (the tedious repetition of the same through the actualization of a generic form, much like canned goods), *a* tomato is indefinite (disembodied) yet singular (fully determined). Beckett (1986, p. 82) expressed it wonderfully in *Waiting for Godot*: "Have you not done tormenting me with your accursed time? It's abominable. When! When!" says Pozzo to Vladimir [*suddenly furious*]. "One day, is that not enough for you, one day like any other, one day he went dumb, one day I went blind, one day we'll go deaf, one day we were born, one day we'll die, the same day, the same second, is that not enough for you? [*Calmer.*] They give birth astride of a grave, the light gleams an instant, then it's night once more."

If difference is spectral, incorporeal, and indefinite, then it should be clear why the taking on of identity is like a forced shutdown. Folding difference back on itself in an attempt to stabilize and arrest the difference-producing vibration is unbecoming and violent. Take the brutality of plucking *the* tomato from the singular variability that is *a* tomato. The indefinite article is what takes flight from the strictures of the universal and the particular, of identity and positive difference. It is a singularity freed of all personal traits: *a* tomato, not *the* tomato – nor an any-tomato-whatsoever. The indefinite article throws the logic of identity and equivalence into crisis, since all property and proprietorship has been shed. While *the* tomato may be an any-tomato-whatsoever, *a* tomato has only itself. Such is the violence of foreclosing on vibration, of forcing an identity on multiplicity, of imposing constancy on consistency. Perhaps this is why the greengrocery invariably comes first in supermarkets: not in order to get consumers into the joyful habit of handling and selecting produce, but to make the violence beyond a little more bearable. If one can be brought to do *that* to soft fruit and vegetables, then what one does to other produce should be a breeze. Take meat. With its variation of cut, weight, fattiness, texture, and bloodiness, one can almost have a social relationship with it. Laid out, it seems naturally inclined towards positive differences and integral identities. One can delude oneself that some meat is hailing you: 'Take me!' But there can be no such delusion with the stack of near-perfect tomatoes that know nothing but negative difference.

To sum up, then, "Difference without positive terms implies that this dimension in language must always remain unperceived, for strictly speaking, it is unconceptualizable," says Lechte (1994, p. 107). Whence the insistence that there is no (proper) name for 'it,' and that the marks called upon in order to allude to its 'trans-apparition' – such as *différance* or trace – are neither words, nor concepts, nor signs, etc. Such marks, whilst 'mantically indicating' the ineffable (Merquior, 1986), leak in all directions. "With Derrida," continues Lechte, "difference becomes the proto-type of what remains outside the scope of Western metaphysical thought because it is the latter's very condition of possibility." And this irreducible *openness* to the incommensurable – the differential spacing of alterity, singularity, otherness – problematizes the assumption that Derrida is trapped in a 'prison-house of language,' for it leads who knows where, ceaselessly distending space for the creativeness, inventiveness, and experimentation of thought-and-action. Moreover, owing to the fact that a difference without positive terms uproots the anchorage points of presence and identity – against which difference is typically calibrated as a (standard) deviation and deviancy from the Norm – it should be clear why both Derrida and Deleuze are incredulous towards depth and verticality. Instead, they linger and slide over the surface of events. Hence Deleuze and Guattari's affirmation of 'nomad thought' as an overturning and overrunning of 'sedentary thought,' and Derrida's affirmation of 'dissemination' as an overturning and overrunning of 'formalizable polysemy.'

'The interval takes all.' This is what the poststructuralists and many geographers tell us. It is certainly what comes out most strongly in my reading of Deleuze, Derrida, and Olsson, for example. Now, be that as it may, it is all too easy to revert to sedentary ways of thinking, and to let general relativity granulate into pointillism: what is between positions is collapsed into position. It is very difficult to keep pace with the differential spacing and thereby avoid falling back into the illusory stability of positive terms. So, here's the rub:

> Of course, in everyday life people readily speak about difference and differences. We say, for instance, that 'x' (having a specific quality) is different from 'y' (which has another specific quality), and we usually mean that it is possible to enumerate the qualities which make up this difference. This, however, is to give difference *positive* terms – implying that it can have a phenomenal form – so it cannot be the difference Saussure announced, one that is effectively unconceptualizable ... [Derrida] wants to distinguish the conceptualizable difference of common sense from a difference that is not brought back into the order of the same and, through a concept, given an identity. Difference is not an identity; nor is it the difference between two identities. (Lechte, 1994, p. 107)

It is the same with space and spacing – with what *takes place*. Here we find a precedent not only for being suspicious about the integrity of place and space but also an echo of our earlier discussion of empiricism and dialectics. Shifting our emphasis from 'identity' to 'integrity' has a number of important consequences. Focusing on *identity* tends to take for granted the presence of what is identified – such as a person, a concept or a place – and invariably restricts one's attention to judging between those identifications that have been attributed to it. In the case of *integrity*, however, one cannot avoid considering the extent to which identity itself holds together. Hereinafter, "nothing and no one can avoid *trial be space*" (Lefebvre, 1991, p. 416).

Coagulum unbound

So, having said a few words about difference, let me turn to the other slide of this motionless (s)trip: *concepts*. I have already insisted that concepts are never created *ex nihilo* or given to us as ready-mades. To the contrary, concepts are *acretive* because they are continually refashioned according to the materials, techniques, and forces made available within particular and only ever relatively stabilized contexts, and they are *acephalous* because the balance of forces within these acretions are contingent upon the open context through which they are eternally reinscribed. This is why Massumi (1988, p. xiii) insists that "The concept has no subject or object other than itself. It is an *act* ... It synthesizes a multiplicity of elements without effacing their heterogeneity or hindering their potential for future rearranging." By the same token, concepts never exist alone since "the undetermined cannot be established" (Lyotard, 1988a, p. 9). They always travel in packs, and are most frequently seen bound up in *twos* – dualisms, oppositions, polarities, complementarities, etc. – or huddled together in *threes* – trifids, triforms, trichotomies, triptyches, dialectics, etc. But it is not simply the case that a concept is always accompanied by others, to which it is more or less inextricably bound, since each *individual* concept is always already multiple; it is irreducibly *fractional*.

In order to flesh out this image of thought it may be appropriate to enumerate how the homogeneity and inalienability of concepts is compromised by the very process of their fabrication.

> First, since a concept is not a simple point but a structure of predicates clustered around one central predicate, the determining predicate is itself conditioned by the backdrop of the others. Second, each concept is part of a conceptual binary opposition in which each term is believed to be simply exterior to the other. Yet the interval that separates each from its opposite and from what it is not also makes each concept what it is ... Third, concepts are always ... inscribed within systems or conceptual chains in which they constantly relate to a plurality of other concepts and conceptual oppositions from which they receive their meaning by virtue of the differential play of sense constitution, and which thus affect them in their very core. And fourth, one single concept may be subject to different functions within a text or corpus of texts. (Gasché, 1986, pp. 128–9)

This fourfold disadjustment and disjointure within the very identity of the concept clearly echoes the notion of difference without positive terms. Now, given that concepts tend to come to us not only in twos and threes, but also in *hierarchical formations*, where privilege, prestige, and priority has been accorded to only one of the terms, it is necessary to dislodge this *forced stabilization* in order to release the variability at play within theoretical-practices. Hence the strategic importance of what Derrida refers to as the 'double movement' of deconstruction: reversal and reinscription, occasionally relayed as the trimerous work of extracting the re-pressed term, grafting it onto the formerly privileged position, and extending its disarranging effects into other contexts and conceptual formations. (The hyphenation of re-pressed alludes not only to an asymmetrical relation of force between the two terms, but also to a substantive transformation. For here as elsewhere, an 'and' is not simply a convenient space-filler, nor an expedient way to get from one position to another. It is the mark of grafting and suppletion *par excellence*. 'And' is the minimal transformer.)

Whilst *reversal* affirms the constitutive significance of the hitherto repressed term and provides a sort of interim compensation – such as when the apparently plenitudinous (e.g. identity, place, being, presence) turns out to be shot through with its others (e.g. difference, spacing, becoming, absence) – the *reinscription* of the opposition onto other registers frustrates the re-establishment of an inverted hierarchy. However, this act of reversal and reinscription should not be understood as two distinct phases. Deconstruction, like the postmodern, is neither just in time (the latest latest) nor out of time; it is counter-time. This is why deconstruction is neither negative nor nihilistic. It affirms becoming through the re-release of difference, otherness, and alterity. And these untimely effects chime with the deconstructive and psychoanalytic recognition that integrity in contradiction expresses the force of a desire. In short, an image of thought based on stable, self-present, and self-enclosed identities, which integrate themselves into twos and threes, is always already flawed and collapsing Thus, deconstruction, like schizoanalysis, assists that which wants to fall and helps that which wants to stall. However, it is not that something falls into nothingness, as may be inferred from the motifs of implosion, disappearance, the void, and the abyss. It is more like when tension is released or when an erection deflates. That which is held in defiance of gravity falls back onto the surface of things. "Since it is a certain *sliding* that is in question ... what must be found, no less than the word, is the point, the *place in the pattern* at which a word drawn from the old language will start ... to slide and make the entire discourse slide" (Derrida, 1978, pp. 263–4). And with this image of thought I have arrived at the postmodern predicament *par excellence*: not the multiplication of codes, but the decoding of flows: not the integration of the disparate, but the dissimilation of the given. Hereinafter, everything goes. It is to the differential (s)pacing of such a driftwork that I now turn.

CHAPTER 2

Lyotard's cancerous geography

To lose the *possibility* of recognizing (of identifying)
2 *similar things.*
2 colors, 2 laces,
2 hats, 2 forms of any kind
to arrive at the Impossibility of a *visual* memory
sufficient for transporting from one similar thing to the other.
(Duchamp, in Lyotard, 1990b, p. 75)

A vacillation of space between two incongruent positions or two
dimensionalities, dystopia. (Lyotard, 1990b, p. 106)

For me at least, things are beginning to break up nicely, and I hope that
the perverse romp through some of the Deleuzean and Derridean motifs
of differential (s)pacing in the last chapter has given you a taste for
poststructuralist geography. In this chapter I want to develop one motif
in particular – the cancerization of thought and action. Yet rather than
agonize over the loss of this or that organizing tissue of moral, ethical,
epistemological, and political codes, I want to follow Lyotard – and in
the next chapter, Baudrillard – in affirming the ethico-political implica-
tions of a certain experience of cancer. I could have pursued this by way
of Deleuze and Guattari. (This is taken up in Chapter 7.) Their two-
volume *Capitalism and Schizophrenia* (1984, 1988) teases out the
consequences of radicalizing the decoding of flows: firstly, through a
schizoanalytic philosophy of desire that overruns the various attempts
at a Freudo-Marxian synthesis; and secondly, through a nomadological
philosophy of becoming that overturns the sedentary fixation of what
they call 'State philosophy' and the regulated decoding associated with
contemporary mutations of capitalism. "What the paranoiacs cannot cope
with is, precisely, libido: the uncontrolled, the uncontrollable, the *excess*
of energy, drives and production," contends Sim (1996, p. 23). "And
excess ... is exactly what capitalism specializes in." Similarly, the motif
of cancerization could have been pursued via deconstruction. Derrida
(1994c, p. 12) once characterized his work as being "dominated by the
thought of a virus, which could be called a parasitology, a virology."
Like a carcinogen, a virus "introduces disorder into communication;" it

"derails a mechanism of the communicational type, its coding and decoding." Such a difference-producing repetition makes a return of the same infeasible (cf. Ansell-Pearson, 1997). Like the influenza virus, which has caught the imagination of many quantitatively-inclined medical geographers and spatial diffusionists, repetition, iteration, and cell division are all open to unexpected mutation. And through a bizarre twist of fate that is fortuitous given the consideration of an ontology of sexual difference in the following chapter, one should note that Deleuze's screwing process and Derrida's virology aptly resonate with Pefanis' (1991, p. 87) characterization of Lyotard as "an opportunist, in a way a *promiscuous* thinker."

Rather than focus on the viral and cancerous nature of either deconstruction or schizoanalysis, I have chosen to follow Lyotard. This is partly because his incorporation into human geography has been myopic and often ill-conceived (although see Barth, 1996). There is little in the literature beyond vague and opportunistic allusions to his timely quips in *The Postmodern Condition* of our need for "incredulity toward meta-narratives" and to "wage a war on totality" (Lyotard, 1984a, pp. xxiv and 82, respectively). Sadly, few geographers can resist the crass immobilization of difference to isolated fragments floundering in the ruins of some lost or shattered totality, which Mouffe (1992, p. 11) aptly refers to as "an essentialism of the 'elements.'" (This is perhaps a residue of critical human geography's long-standing distaste for atomistic forms of empiricism and positivism, which manifests itself in an aversion against anything that smacks of either unstructured spontaneity – i.e. events that are not overdetermined by the penetrative forces of capitalism and patriarchy, for example – or 'spatial fetishism' – contentless and contextless laws of space, such as the 'friction of distance.') Once drained of their speed and splay, such pacified fragments lend themselves to reassembly and totalization, usually via some dialectical machination. What appear as discrete – such as "fetishisms of locality," as Harvey once put it (1987, p. 375) – are revealed to be disingenuous effects of a wider field of folded forces. What appear as fragmentary – such as places, localities, and commodities – are "dominated, penetrated, and then recuperated" by an exorbitant agency, such as capital, Logos, or Phallus. Consequently, in a discussion of "Marxist geography of the Harvey type," Peet (1998, p. 188) sees it as self-evident that claims such as "totalities cannot be thought ... are contradicted by reams of studies of how localities are caught up in universal processes." This supports his conviction that the assertion that "Marxism, with its talk of 'totalities,' can never enter a 'never-never land of non-totalizing discourses" is a myth (Peet, 1998, p. 188). As we will gradually unfold in the chapters that follow, there is much in these lines that is deeply troubling, not least for a spatial scientist.

Whilst I agree with the penetrative thrust of the above statements, they fail to recognize that what penetrates and is penetrated are neither static nor isolatable, but vibratory. What resists both structuration and totalization – of fixing into place – is not difference, alterity, and otherness *per se*, but their irreducible disjointure, disadjustment, and displacement. Each is open. All of which is not to deny that certain forces are in play that nevertheless attempt to violently embed them. Just as places and events are processive, fragments drift and difference vibrates (Doel, 1994a, forthcoming). This is why poststructuralist geography does not shy away from totalities and structures in order to merely celebrate atomistic events and 'little narratives.' It declines totalities and structures not simply because they are too large or too rigid, but because they are unbecoming. Even capital, the Logos, and the Phallus vibrate. They not only throb according to the rhythms and flows that surge through them, but it is by way of such a throbbing that rigidity and identity are both erected and sustained. Conclusion: it is not just the fragments, but the whole, that is *set* in perpetual motion. This is what is meant by the impossibility of both totalization and commensurability – and it is this motility and mutability that is lost in so many of the geographical renditions of difference, alterity, and otherness: although Natter and Jones (1997) and Strohmayer (1997a) have an inkling of what is at stake here. A similar draining of differential-repetition and vibration from the reception of 'difference' and 'fragments' has bedevilled many geographical encounters with Derrida, and Deleuze and Guattari. For example, Cresswell (1997b, p. 362) lambastes authors such as Deleuze and Guattari who make the nomad "the subject of vast generalizations and misguided metaphorical play." "Just as the postmodern theorists enjoy the disruption of boundaries that the nomad necessitates," he says, "the modernists feel nausea at such a threat" (Cresswell, 1997b, p. 376). Like Miller (1993), Cresswell is dismayed by the fact that metaphorical nomads romanticize and violate real nomads. Suffice to say that nomadology, like schizoanalysis, does not designate a being but a way of being, a style, manner, and symptomatology. Similarly, nomadology is neither literal nor metaphorical; it is metamorphotic and processive. Finally, like becoming-woman, becoming-animal, and becoming-imperceptible – which have in their turn troubled many feminist geographers – becoming-nomad does not entail the sequestration of a marginal identity (howls in the face of appropriation). Rather, it is to affirm the vibration and solicitation in each and every identity, and not merely in some *other* identities. This openness within the 'cracked I' reconnects with Harvey's (1996) misunderstanding of monadology and the 'windowless world' briefly considered in the introduction.

Now, all of this occultation of vibration, solicitation, and metamorphosy is deeply ironic, since Lyotard's work, like Derrida's and

Deleuze's, is profoundly concerned with spacing and rhythm, especially with what is occluded in the folding out of the figure One. What leads me into a consideration of Lyotard, then, is not his infamous 'incredulity toward metanarratives,' 'war against totality,' and affirmation of 'little narratives,' but his emphasis on re-releasing vibration, solicitation, and dissimilation. What I love is his splaying out of "a hinge-logic, a hinge-style" (Lyotard, 1990b, p. 123). And this splay brings me back to virology and cancerization. Perhaps surprisingly, instead of 'anything goes,' the dreaded consequence of sliding into unrestrained relativism (Sayer, 1993), cancerization opens onto an 'ethic of the event' (cf. Bennington, 1988; Readings, 1991).

Lyotard's driftwork

The time of writing does not pass. (Lyotard, 1990a, p. 34)

There is an urgency to thought ... One is urged or pressed to think because something, an event, happens before one has the time to think it ... In claiming that thought is unprepared for the affair I am eager to maintain its urgency and its pressure, to leave it open to the most patient questioning. (Lyotard, 1990a, pp. 51–2)

So far I have relayed how a duplicitous, slightly phased, and screwed-up theoretical-practice might be able to take flight from a sliding and trembling penetration that makes the relatively stabilized discourses of identity, Being, and sameness crack open. Such a theoretical-practice of differential (s)pacing releases the uncontrollable play of difference, iteration, variability, and dissemination. Nevertheless, it is worth under-scoring the fact that one is not simply looking for a particularly charged word within a specific context. One is also searching for the space, the place, and the point of effective disjointure: that which *sets* the context in motion. Thus, not only should one be wary about attempting to 'maintain together the disparate,' like a shattered windscreen or crazy paving, but one should recognize that the emphasis on an irreducible disjointure renders the minimal unit of space a fold, and not a point. This is not simply because a "point – a *true* point, as a mathematical ideal – neither exists nor does not exist, since it locates a point (the pleonasm highlighting our difficulty) in space whilst not occupying any space" (Simms, 1996, p. 195). Rather, it is because a point can only ever transpear by way of an originary relay. A point orients. It is therefore always already applied, "if the word is taken across to its Latin roots in *applicare*, 'to be attached to,' 'to fold'" (Malik, 1996, p. 200). A point is literally duplicitous – twofold. It is in this sense that Deleuze's passion for origami and Derrida's love of difference *as* difference can be folded one into the other in an endeavour "to put oneself there where the disparate itself holds together, without wounding the dis-jointure, the dispersion or the difference, without effacing the heterogeneity of the other" (Derrida, 1994b, p. 29). Yet how *can* the disparate (itself) hold together? Addressing this question will form the basis of the third portion of this book. It is the geographical problem *par excellence*. For the time being, though, it is perhaps worth considering the carcinogenic effects of the poststructuralists' 'return to the surface,' since these tend to be the greatest cause for concern.

Cancer

> Matter is that element in the datum which has no destiny. (Lyotard, 1989a, p. 214)

> a process of cancerization of theoretical discourse (Lyotard, 1993, p. 96)

The allusion to a cancerous proliferation has come up on several occasions already: decoding, dissemination, overrun and overextension, difference without positive terms, nomadology, schizoanalysis, reversal and reinscription, etc. The difference that poststructuralist geography makes to the extant geographical tradition is cancerous in at least four senses: (1) it gives rise to a malignant growth that displaces 'normal' tissue through an uncontrolled and unmotivated division; (2) it gives rise to an evil or corrupting influence that spreads wildly (cf. Baudrillard, 1990d, 1993b); (3) it slides across a relatively stabilized constellation of forces in the manner of a crab, whose 'pincer movement' recalls the double agencies by which schizoanalysis and deconstruction plough up identity and constancy (Doel, 1994b); and (4) it is the fourth sign of the zodiac, alluding to an unruly fourth element – or accursed share – in the otherwise self-composed and trimerous dialectic of position, negation, and negation of the negation: such an unsublatable excess is what motivates the 'general economy' of deconstruction (Doel, 1992; Megill, 1985; Plotnitsky, 1994; Žižek, 1991). So, when Lyotard refers to a certain 'cancerization' of theoretical-practice, this is much more than a mere figure of speech. And since this "'Revolutionary' pathology of organic abandonment," as Baudrillard (1994, p. 102) puts it, opens onto an *ethic* of the event, it will not be possible to simply dismiss it as yet another instance of "terminological vagueness and outrageous theoretical excess" (Peet, 1998, p. 246).

Two forms of cancer immediately spring to mind: the serial and the parallel. Serial cancerization emerges from the prolongation of series. Parallel cancerization emerges from the potential divergence within series. Whether serial or parallel, extensive or intensive, actual or virtual, cancerization turns on the hinge-points, fold-points, and bifurcation-points of the series. Each element of the series can be dissimilated along these splayed vectors of disadjustment and disjointure. This is why no series ever truly adds up, except through an occlusion and occultation of the accursed share. Take serial cancerization.

> In a way the term 'series' does not have to be accounted for, because it is already defined in the dictionary: an ordered set of elements, governed by a principle of distinction (one and one and one) and a principle of total-ization, or synthesis ... But, at the same time, series may well proliferate in length or in number. Here lies the contradiction: proliferation is always a threat to order. Deleuze answers with two opposed metaphors: the tree of order (as a structured network of roots, trunk and branches), and the rhizome – a subterranean root-like stem – for anarchic and proliferating growth. (Lecercle, 1985, pp. 94–6)

Cancer is an excessive reduplication that scrambles and escapes the established constellation of cells, series, and forces. Any cell can become cancerous. Every cell seethes with virtual cancers that put it out of joint from the off: "In the beginning there will have been speed," comments Derrida (1984b, p. 20). In so doing, cancer strikes at the very core of modernity's controlling investment in the criterion of optimal perfor-mance: maximum output for minimum input (Lyotard, 1984a). For all of these reasons I am suspicious of Baudrillard's (1994) conflation of cloning and cancer in his 'Clone Story,' which he reworked with a different ending (*sic*) as 'Hell of the Same' (Baudrillard, 1993b). The "Cellular dream of scissiparity" that underwrites cloning "finally allows one to do without the other, to go from the same to the same" without need of mediation, transcendence, or departure (Baudrillard, 1994, p. 96). As distinct from twinning – a twosome that was never a lonesome – he offers the pithy formula "$1 + 1 + 1 + 1$, etc." as an illustration of "the reiteration of the same" (Baudrillard, 1994, p. 97). However, this progression is less additive than processive: the Hell of the Same goes nowhere and knows nothing of evolution. Freed from the dissimi-latory effects of context and contingency, cloning engenders always-already-still-more-of-the-same. Accordingly, a more apt formula for cloning would be: '1 into 1 into 1 into 1, etc.' Irrespective of the prolongation of the series, such a division/cutting always amounts to the same: '$1 \div 1 \div 1 \div 1$, etc. $= 1$.' It is on the basis of this "exacerbated redundancy" – an affine redundancy that Baudrillard (1994, p. 101) aligns with mechanical reproduction (of objects, commodities, signs, etc.) and "the virulence of the code," and which will recur in Chapter 7 in the guise of fractals – that he makes the link between cloning and cancer: "The individual is no longer anything but a cancerous metastasis of its base formula ... Cancer designates a proliferation ad infinitum of a base cell without taking into consideration the organic laws of the whole. It is the same thing with cloning: nothing opposes itself any longer to the renewal of the Same, to the unchecked proliferation of a single matrix" (Baudrillard, 1994, pp. 100–1).

Were Baudrillard's hellish characterization of cancer and cloning correct, this would make a mockery of any notion of an ethic or politics of cancer. My yearning for a difference-producing repetition (a processive and open dissimilation) would be little more than a difference producing repetition (a perpetual return of the same). Fortunately, neither cancer nor cloning return the same. The ontotheological *dream* of second comings is always declined by events. Strohmayer (1997a, p. 166) writes of a "cracked circle" where "Ends don't meet directly." Even Baudrillard belatedly acknowledges this, in a note suitably appended beyond the end of his 'Clone Story,' and purged from his 'Hell of the Same.' "One must take into account that cancerous proliferation is also a silent disobedience of the injunctions of the genetic code," says Baudrillard (1994, p. 102). Likewise, cloning "is at once the triumph of a controlling hypothesis, that of the code …, and an eccentric distortion that destroys its coherence. Besides, it is probable (but this is left for a future story) that even the 'clonic twin' will never be identical to its progenitor … Millions of interferences will make of it, despite everything, a different being."

Cancer begets a decoding and deterritorialization of the organizational fabric of a body that comes from the bifurcation-points that are held in tension on the frame of the text or tissue. "Open the so-called body and spread out all its surfaces," declares Lyotard (1993, p. 1) in the opening scene of *Libidinal Economy*: "perform the dissection of polymorphous perversion, spread out the immense membrane of the libidinal 'body.'" I am reminded of that exquisite moment in *The Western Lands* where Burrough's (1988, pp. 60–1) distils Joe-the-Dead's take on cancer:

> A cancer cell, a virus has no destiny, no human purpose beyond endless replication. It has no work to finish and no reason to die. Give it a reason to die and it will. The ultimate purpose of cancer and all virus, is to replace the host. So instead of trying to kill the cancer cells, help them to replicate and to replace host cells. Produce the first all-virus rat, it's more efficient – instead of all these elaborate organs we have just cells, an undifferentiated structure.

Cancers disturb. They unsettle bodies and agitate minds. They "cause language to flee, they make it run along a witch's course, they place it endlessly in a state of disequilibrium, they cause it to bifurcate and to vary in each one of its terms, according to a ceaseless modulation" (Deleuze, 1994a, p. 25). Now, one would be hard pressed to find a poststructuralist term that did not embody such a disturbed portion: writing, fold, supplement, seduction, rhizome, (s)play, etc. For example, schizoanalysis and *délire* take these 'disturbed elements' as their model. "It is a question of a model that is perpetually in construction or collapsing, and of a process that is perpetually prolonging itself, breaking off and starting up again," say Deleuze and Guattari (1988, p. 20). Similarly, Bennington (1988, p. 32) characterizes the cancerization of theoretical-practice as "a perpetual running out of control of what was to have been a rational theoretical enterprise." Referring to Genet's (1989) *Prisoner of Love*, Critchley gives a succinct glimpse of this at work. It "is like the growth of a cancer, where a cell departs from its usual metabolism, connecting with and infecting other cells, interconnecting to form the sentences of a page ... The book is bitty and flows awkwardly, employing or rather being employed by a language that at times appears to be out of control" (Critchley, 1990, pp. 26–7).

What splices together serial and parallel cancers, those of actual extension and those of virtual intension, are the hinge-, fold-, and bifurcation-points that compose a corpus: "A sheet of articulations connects pieces of white skin to other pieces," suggests Lyotard (1990c, p. 40). "Its arthrography, leading me to unhinge this ankle, will unhinge every other ankle too." I have drawn upon some extraordinary words to convey these points of scission, yet their cancerous tissue is exemplified in the simplest of terms: AND. For it is precisely when one is in the midst of things that a cancerous proliferation takes off:

> The middle is not at all an average – far from it – but the area where things take on speed. *Between* things does not designate a localizable relation going from the one to the other and reciprocally, but a perpendicular direction, a transversal movement carrying away the one *and* the other, a stream without beginning or end, gnawing away at its two banks and picking up speed in the middle. (Deleuze and Guattari, 1983, p. 58)

This bilateral movement takes on speed as it is no longer held in place by the strictures of dualistic or dialectic coding, and it is transversal since it decodes and disseminates the libidinal investments stored in its enfolded corpora. Yet insofar as the motion is twisted, the figure that emerges from between the folds is not so much helicoid as Möbian.

To have a taste for cancer may appear evil. To the contrary. "History, like politics," notes Lyotard, "seems to have need of a unique point of perspective, a place of synthesis, a head or eye enveloping the diversity of movements in the unification of a single volume: a synthesizing eye, but also an evil eye which strikes dead everything which does not enter its field of visibility" (Lyotard, 1977, p. 164: quoted and translated in Dews, 1987, p. 212). Cancer, however, permits no such synthesis or totalization. "It's the paradox of saturation, inversion," writes Baudrillard (1993a, p. 91). "There is a kind of reversible fatality for systems, because the more they go towards universality, towards their total limits, there is a kind of reversal that they themselves produce, and that destroys their own objective. It is what I call 'hypertelia,' a way of surpassing a function, past its own objective. One goes past finality. Things go too far."

For example, in *The System of Objects*, Baudrillard (1996c, p. 35) argues that "Just as modular furniture loses its specific functions so much so that at the logical extreme its value resides solely in the positioning of each movable element, so likewise colours lose their unique value, and become relative to each other and to the whole." The fully relativized spectra of sign-values modulated around the attributes of form, function, and colour do not so much overcode the specific use-values and exchange-values of objects, as short-circuit them. One need only think of food, gadgets, appliances, home furnishings, and clothing to comprehend the move from an ontology of substantial beings to a hauntology of immaterial spectra: "objects have lost the substantiality which was their basis," says Baudrillard (1996c, p. 21); "it is now space which plays freely between them, and becomes the universal function of their relationships and their 'values.'" Contra Gottdiener (1995), the distinction between 'dress' and 'fashion,' for example, does not allow one to distinguish between a deeply authentic response to environmentally stimulated needs, which demands really useful objects such as umbrellas, coats, and shoes, and all of those superficial games of emulation and differentiation based on sign-values: designer labels, branding, lifestyles, neo-tribalism, etc. The purportedly 'really useful' objects are themselves relative to the system of objects: function is merely one element to be composed and decomposed amongst others. "What such objects embody is no longer the secret of a unique relationship but, rather, differences and moves in a game" (Baudrillard, 1996c, p. 21). Paradoxically, then, within a functional system of objects, a system without positive terms, "space is the object's true freedom, whereas its function is merely its formal freedom" (Baudrillard, 1996c, p. 21). Such is the virtual and viral illusion: the yearning for a fatal perfection (Baudrillard, 1995, 1996b).

The ethic of cancer

> The adversary and accomplice of writing ... is language ... One writes against language but necessarily with it. To say what it already knows how to say is not writing. One wants to say what it does not know how to say but what one imagines it should be able to say. One violates it, one seduces it, one introduces into it an idiom unknown to it. (Lyotard, 1992, p. 105)

By overrunning established limits, cancer begets experimentation – and "to experiment means, in a way, to be alone, to be celibate;" it inaugurates "a situation in which one judges without criteria" (Lyotard and Thébaud, 1985, pp. 10 and 16, respectively). Since modernity endlessly dreams of itself being left alone with itself, it should be evident why it gives rise to autism, delirium, and cancer. What is striking about Lyotard is the extent to which he affirms these 'pagan' traits whilst denouncing instrumentalization, rationalization, and totalitarianism (cf. Beck, 1992; Beck, Giddens, and Lash, 1994; Giddens, 1990). For Lyotard, like Bauman (1989, 1990), modernity is ambivalent: its regimes of ordering and disordering are of a piece. Order is not given; it must be made. To that extent, the fabrication of order is simultaneously the fabrication of disorder. Symptomatology is creative. "The instability of criteria," argues Lyotard, "comes from this experimental situation" (Lyotard and Thébaud, 1985, p. 9). He carries such disturbed elements into his notions of postmodernism, paganism, the *différend*, and just gaming. However, rather than merely affirm the disordering portion, Lyotard (1984a, p. 81) adopts the experimental criterion of "working without rules in order to formulate the rules of what *will have been done*." To that extent, "*Post modern* would have to be understood according to the paradox of the future (*post*) anterior (*modo*)." Hence its anamorphic, untimely, and retroflex structuration.

> Postmodern (or pagan) would be the condition of the literatures and arts that have no assigned addressee and no regulating ideal, yet in which value is regularly measured on the stick of experimentation. Or, to put it dramatically, in which it is measured by the distortion that is inflicted upon the materials, the forms and structures of sensibility and thought. (Lyotard and Thébaud, 1985, p. 16)

Take the history of philosophy again: "It's rather like portraiture in painting," remarks Deleuze (1995, p. 135). "Producing mental, conceptual portraits. As in painting, you have to create a likeness, but in a different material: the likeness is something you have to produce, rather than a way of reproducing anything." It is always a matter of deforming materials and events. "You have to blind the eye that thinks it sees something; you have to make a painting of blindness that plunges the sufficiency of the eye into rout; you have to 'make a sick picture' (Duchamp)" (Lyotard, 1990b, p. 77). Paganism, deconstruction, rhizomatics, postmodernism, schizoanalysis, poststructuralism: "In every instance, one must evaluate relations: of force, of values, of quantities, and of qualities; but to evaluate them there are no criteria, nothing but opinions ... There is no metalanguage ... One works 'case by case' ... But in matters of opinion there is no adding up of accounts, no balance sheet" (Lyotard, in Lyotard and Thébaud, 1985, pp. 27–8). Hence the paganistic incredulity in respect of metanarratives. So, when differences proliferate wildly through "the racing of a discursive machinery" (Lyotard, 1993, p. 97), one should resist drawing up a balance sheet and judging them according to a common measure: such equilibration and equanimity are unbecoming traits, especially for a spatial scientist (cf. Dear, 1988; Dear and Wassmansdorf, 1993; Gregory, 1987, 1989a, 1989b). By affirming the cracked state, "the idea that emerges is that there is a multiplicity of small narratives. And from that, 'one ought to be pagan' means 'one must maximize as much as possible the multiplication of small narratives'" (Lyotard, in Lyotard and Thébaud, 1985, p. 59). Henceforth, the maxim of poststructuralist geography – whether inflected by deconstruction, paganism, or schizoanalysis – could be rendered thus: 'each according to its fractures.' Such is the motivation of an ethic of the event.

Totality = X

> We have paid dearly for our nostalgia for the all and the one ... Beneath the general demand for relaxation and appeasement, we hear murmurings of the desire to reinstitute terror and fulfil the fantasm of taking possession of reality. The answer is: war on totality. (Lyotard, 1992, pp. 24–25)

According to Lyotard (1992, 1994a), modernity legitimates itself through an appeal to a variety of metanarratives, such as the emancipation of a collective subject of history, the liberation of humanity from superstition through Enlightenment rationality, the world-historical mission of realizing universal democratization and transnational liberalism, and the onward march of instrumental reason and technoscience. Symptomatologically, a metanarrative has the function of accounting for all of the other narratives within its jurisdiction, proscribing their appropriate domains, and adjudicating between their competing claims. Like the commodity law of value, which is based on equivalence, substitution, and exchange, a metanarrative is a master code: a universal currency into which events can be translated without distortion or remainder. Above all, then, metanarratives claim to totalize the field of events so as to organize the succession of occurrences in terms of the revelation of an essential meaning. They are 'grand narratives' that seek to put an end to the work of narration by revealing the singular truth in the plurality of 'little' narratives. It is this that enables every event to be evaluated and discounted in terms of its contribution to and deviation from the 'totality = x.' (One thinks of the typical historiographies of disciplinary traditions and canons, for example.) Lyotard, by contrast, insists that these metanarratives devalue the specificity of events, inflicting numerous instances of violence and injustice upon them: "totalitarian bureaucracy likes to keep the event under its thumb," he suggests.

"When something happens, it goes into the dustbin (of history or the spirit). An event will only ever be retrieved if it ... is made into an example" (Lyotard, 1992, pp. 105–6). Moreover, the claim to a position beyond the play of narrative events is untenable: "We are always within opinion, and there is no possible discourse of truth on the situation ... because one is caught up in a story, and one cannot get out of this story to take up a metalinguistic position from which the whole could be dominated" (Lyotard, in Lyotard and Thébaud, 1985, p. 43). Furthermore, Lyotard argues that there are innumerable events – especially the Holocaust (Lyotard, 1990a) – that cannot be adequately set within a metanarrative and act as unsuturable rents in the 'incomplete' fabric of modernity (cf. Clarke, Doel and McDonough, 1996; Doel, and Clarke, 1998a).

So, whilst a 'grand' narrative strives to arrest narration by uncovering the timeless essence of the narratives over which it presides, a 'little' narrative is that which resists such an incorporation. A little narrative does not necessarily embody a small quantity or occupy a marginal position. A little narrative is a transformer and a vibrator. It suffices to find the frequency (repetition, recurrence) and the amplitude (deformation, differentiation) capable of setting the totality in motion. In other words, a little narrative is not a discrete *fragment* of a grand narrative, whose proliferation would multiply the injustice inflicted by metanarratives (one and one and one, etc.), but a deforming *figure* through which untimely events take place (one into one into one into one, etc.). "That is why it is important to increase displacement," maintains Lyotard (1984a, p. 16), "and even to disorient it, in such a way as to make an unexpected 'move.'" Grand narratives appear as discursive structures, where the rule of signification (meaning) organizes objects of knowledge into conceptual representations. Little narratives, by contrast, are figural, but that does not mean that the figurative opposes the discursive or that irrationality and desire are preferable to reason and understanding. The figural opens discursive structures to an experience of difference, heterogeneity, singularity, and multiplicity that cannot be integrated, subsumed or rationalized within the framework of representation (Lyotard, 1971). As with Duchamp's *Glass*, one halves together 'paralogies' and the like, "not to have a true effect, nor even several true effects, according to a mono- or polyvalent logic, but to have uncontrolled effects" (Lyotard, 1990b, p. 65). Such is the cancer of theoretical-practice. It brings together postmodern paganism and avant-garde agonistics: "the avant-gardes continually expose the artifices of presentation that allow thought to be enslaved by the gaze and diverted from the unpresentable," avers Lyotard (1992, p. 21).

Periodization and facialization

> Postmodern is not to be taken in a periodizing sense. (Lyotard and
> Thébaud, 1985, p. 16)

There are three broad ways by which people have sought to periodize
the modern and the postmodern. First, one can endeavour to periodize
them on the basis of an *absolute* break. Yet post-modern, in this sense,
is a contradiction in terms (McHale, 1989). If the modern means 'pertaining to the present' – *modus*: 'just now,' 'now' – , then post-modern
can only mean 'pertaining to the future.' Little wonder, then, that many
write off the postmodern as either idle speculation or as a "moderner
modern," "the continuation of the Modern and its transcendence"
(Brooke-Rose, 1981, p. 345, and Jencks, 1986, p. 7, respectively). Second,
a periodization could be established through a *relative* break. This move
is exemplified in all of those two–column, contrapuntal differentiations
of the modern and the postmodern, in which there is a shift of dominant
from, say, 'reason, unity, and order' to 'madness, fragmentation, and
disorder' (see, for example, Harvey, 1989). Yet such an epochalization
is easily unhinged through a dialectical image of thought that emphasizes
how the two apparently autonomous and self-sufficient sides of the
diachronic break are in actuality two mutually constitutive aspects of a
single synchronic structure. And since the negation of modernity always
already belongs to modernity, the post-modern negation is an impostor
bereft of either proper form or specific content. The final variation on
this epochalizing theme is when postmodernity is presented as the
reversal of the hierarchies and principles underpinning modernity, such
that power and significance now reside with those elements that were
devalued and re-pressed in modernity. But the lesson of deconstruction
is that the work of the minor is no less significant than the work of the
major in maintaining the structure's facade of unity, nor can the difference between the one and the other be rigorously maintained. Little
wonder, then, that McDonald (1988, p. 190) should note that "Reversal
only repeats the traditional scheme in which the hierarchy of duality is
reconstituted."

Periodization and epochalization invariably lead astray (cf. Latour,
1993; Strohmayer, 1997b). This is not just because such a "'breaking'
is, rather, a manner of forgetting or repressing the past. That's to say
of repeating it. Not overcoming it" (Lyotard, 1989b, p. 8), but also
because it is the presumed self-sufficiency and integrity of the 'now'
that has been put into question. Indeed, the postmodern is precisely a
figure through which the representable and recognizable 'now' may be
opened onto the disseminating affects of the untimely: "*in a certain
sense*, the postmodern might be said to *precede* the modern" (Bennington,

1989c, p. 86). Or again: "A work can become modern only if it is first postmodern. Postmodernism thus understood is not modernism at its end but in the nascent state, and this state is constant" (Lyotard, 1984a, p. 79). Likewise with little narratives. They do not signal the multiplication and proliferation of discourses and representations. Rather, they maintain our relation to the unpresentable: not on the basis of a given concept of justice, but through an indeterminate idea of justice towards which still other narratives are responding. As with the proceedings against K. in Kafka's *The Trial* (1992), no case is ever closed, no account is ever settled, and no event is ever finalized. Not only the whole, but also each element, is set in perpetual motion. Consequently, "the problem that faces us … is that it is no longer a matter … of reflecting upon what is just or unjust against the horizon of a social totality, but, on the contrary, against the horizon of a multiplicity or of a diversity" (Lyotard and Thébaud, 1985, p. 87). Such a horizon is always ahead of us, and it can never be represented. This is why "the term 'postmodern' implies contradiction of the modern without transcendence of it" (Kuspit, 1990, p. 60).

So, postmodernism, like paganism, is only ever a strategic term for opening up thought and action to deformation, experimentation, and transformation: "once the postmodern is formally recognizable, it is no longer opening up a hole in representation; rather than testifying to the unrepresentable, it will have presented it" (Readings, 1991, p. 56). Postmodernity is not an epoch, but the ceaseless refusal, from within modernity, to silence and forget what cannot be represented and remembered within modernity. The "postmodern would be that which, in the modern, puts forward the unrepresentable within representation itself" (Lyotard, 1984a, p. 81). Or again: "it is not up to us to *provide reality* but to invent allusions to what is conceivable but not presentable" (Lyotard, 1992, p. 24). "This being granted, the 'post-' of postmodernity does not mean a process of coming back or flashing back, feeding back, but of *ana*-lysing, *ana*-mnesing, of re-flecting" (Lyotard, 1989b, p. 10). The pagan sensitivity to that which is unpresentable opens a hole in representation. "One tries to listen and make heard the secret affection, the one that says nothing," writes Lyotard (1990a, p. 34): "one expends oneself, one exhausts oneself. Writing degree zero." This hole should not be confused with either the *vanishing point* traced by the infinitely receding horizon or the *point of view* from which projective geometry maps out its phallogocentric field of vision (thereby ensuring that the subject or actant who occupies such a position masters its space). For while vanishing points necessarily exceed and dissolve the boundaries, finitude, and fullness of hyperbolic spaces (i.e. those classical 'spaces of emplacement' that are closed in on themselves in the manner of a circle or hyperbola), points of view nevertheless ensure that unbounded,

infinite, and open spaces remain centred – on an observer – and distanciated – in terms of an abjected object that is cast 'outside' the
self-enclosed interiority of a subject. The third hole, then, is neither
the perspectival vanishing point that distends the hegemony of vision,
nor the point of view through which alterity, difference, and otherness
are condemned to return to the same. Instead, it is a 'point of flight'
that deconstructs the specular economy of representation. It short-
circuits the libidinal economy ensconced between two poles, two holes.
Sartre put it superbly: "It appears that the world has a sort of drain
hole in the middle of its being and that it is perpetually flowing through
this hole" (quoted in Burgin, 1996, p. 55).

Accordingly, perspectival space is "part of a surface-holes, holey
surface, system" (Deleuze and Guattari, 1988, p. 170). It is one facet
of the regime of facialization that has covered first the head, then the
body, then the socius, and finally the earth with a screen for identification,
subjectivation, and recognition. "A horror story, the face is a horror
story," warn Deleuze and Guattari (1988, p. 168). They suggest that
recovering what a body can do will require not merely an agonistics of
depersonalization and desubjectivation, but also a thoroughgoing
scarification of the facialized corpus and its disengagement from the
abstract machines that inscribe it with facial traits: "a whole scouring
of the unconscious, a complete curettage" (Deleuze and Guattari, 1984,
p. 311). As an apparatus of facialization, with its two symmetrical black
eyes (point of view and vanishing point) and white wall (striated field
of vision), perspective space is

> built not only upon a founding subject [at the apex of the cone of vision],
> the 'point of view,' but also upon the disappearance of all things in the
> 'vanishing point.' Previously, there was no *sign* of absence – the *horror
> vacui* was central to Aristotelianism. In classical cosmologies, space was a
> plenum. Similarly, in the medieval world, God's creation was a fullness
> without gap. In quattrocento perspective the subject first confronts an
> absence in the field of vision, but an absence disavowed: the vanishing
> point is not an integral part of the space of representation; situated on the
> horizon, it is perpetually pushed ahead as the subject expands its own
> boundary. The void remains abjected. In later, non-Euclidean geometry,
> we find the spherical plenum of classical cosmologies collapsed upon itself
> to enfold a central void ... In this changed space, this new geometry, the
> abject can no longer be banished beyond some charmed, perfectly Eucli-
> dean circle. (Burgin, 1996, pp. 55–6)

Inscribed on the surface of things, then, are at least three holes. The
first hole is the *peep hole* of representation, exemplified in the egocentric
apex of the cone of vision. The second hole, the *vanishing point*, structures
the field whilst withdrawing from it. The third hole, the *point of flight*,

deconstructs the orderly lineaments of Euclidean, non-Euclidean, and n-dimensional spaces. Whilst the complicity between the peep hole and vanishing point traps the unpresentable within the field of vision, the latter dislocates representation according to the incommensurability of the unpresentable. By way of this third hole, space resists unification and totalization and becomes dissimilatory – a conduit for difference, otherness, and heterogeneity. At the very least, then, this three-eyed installation suggests a disfigured and malformed face: a face that loses its abstract and representative traits in order to return to the singularity of a fleshy and meaty body (cf. Deleuze, 1983c). Parenthetically, it is worth noting that this dissimilation of perspectival space is distinct from the critiques developed by feminist geographers such as Blum and Nast (1996) and Rose (1993a, 1995a, 1995c), which typically dwell on the phallocentric distanciation of an active subject from pacified objects, others, and landscapes (cf. Pile, 1996). Nevertheless, the third eye is also a vibrator, which participates in the solicitation – setting in motion – of the ontology of sexual difference: the oscillation between fullness (presence, identity, stability) and lack (absence, difference, flow) proves to be unbecoming, so much so that 'polymorphous perversion' remains free to (s)play itself out once more. I will pick up on this in subsequent chapters.

Meanwhile, whenever facialization begins to come undone there is a strong temptation to suture the fraying seams, to apply skin grafts, or to engage in reconstructive surgery. One thinks not only of Franken-stein's piecemeal monster and cosmetic surgery, but more aptly of Pinhead and his minions in the *Hellraiser* trilogy of films (1987, 1989, 1992: Clive Barker, Randal Anthony, and Anthony Hickox, respectively), where heads are geometrically apportioned with tiny metal stakes set into the scalp and faces are pulled taut by hooks secured to surrounding frames. Yet in addition to violently composing the flesh, such 'appara-tuses of capture' can be made to work otherwise in order to explore what a body can do. Through a difference-producing repetition, such a Chamber of Horrors may become an Artaudean Theatre of Cruelty. Take the series of body-hangings undertaken by Stelarc, a performance artist who deforms his own body in order to experiment with what *a* body is capable of. A body is not given in advance. It is an articulation of forces and of the power to affect and to be affected by other bodies: a body is always indefinite and impersonal, even though it may traverse and subtend 'me' (cf. Ansell-Pearson, 1997; Lingis, 1994). Such a body changes with context. It has to be repeatedly composed, orchestrated, and performed (Doel, 1995). There is, therefore, no solution to the problem of what a body can do. To the contrary, the task for any and every body is to pose itself (as) a problem, to continuously reinvent itself (as) a problem. It is a matter of experimentation and not realism.

For example, in a consideration of Stelarc's bodily experimentations –
hanging his body from hooks, securing the limbs to electronic prostheses,
rendering audible the fluxion of his body, exposing the interior surfaces
and cavities through an invaginated visualization, etc. – Massumi (1996b,
no pagination) notes how: "The problem posed by a force cannot be
'solved' – only exhausted." It is not exhausted in the sense of realizing
a matrix of given possibilities, but exhausted in the sense of reworking
a problem until it mutates into a qualitatively different problem. Or
again: "The usual mode in which the body functions as a sensible
concept – possibility – is radically suspended. The body is placed at
the limits of its functionality. The answer to what is being suspended
is: embodied human possibility." Quite literally, the hooks upon which
the flesh hangs do not only render the force of gravity on the comportment of the body visible – on this "gravitational landscape" "ripples
and hills ... form on the hook-stretched skin" – they also serve to
enable the suspended body to engage in a transformative series of
irrational cuts. In other words, the hung body, counter-actualized to
the point of 'suspended animation,' knows only of immanence (what to
do?), and nothing of logical possibility (the body is/ought/should). It
no longer re(as)sembles a pre-given form that is posed for it in advance
of its (dis)connection and experimentation. Such is the paganistic 'incommensurability' and 'case by case,' and the postmodern 'sveltness'
and 'pointlessness,' which suspend the unseemly machinations of totalization and unification, engendering experimental dissimilation in their
wake (Lyotard, 1986/7). In shaking off a certain kind of organization,
the suspended body has opened onto what Deleuze and Guattari (1984,
1988) call, after Artaud, the 'Body without Organs.' Indeed, the problem
for a Body (without Organs) is that of counter-acting the forces that
constrict its capacity for action. In this regard, we know next to nothing
about what a body can do, even in the most banal of respects: eating,
loving, walking, fighting, falling, dreaming ...

Once the 'assimilatory terror' of organization is put under suspension
the swarming multiplicity of little narratives and degenerate traits of
faciality can no longer be fastened together into a whole. For there is
no unity of thread, no common medium nor measure. Hereinafter, each
thread, medium, or measure must be drawn out from the flesh that is
to hand. Such is an indefinite and impersonal life that is ceaselessly
strung out under suspension. Like a spiderish web-master, little narratives comprise "a patchwork of language pragmatics that vibrate at
all times," says Lyotard (Lyotard and Thébaud, 1985, p. 94). However,
it would be wrong to differentiate the spider from its web, or the event
from its context, insofar as vibrations are really all that ever take place.
Totalization, unification, finalization: all of these ways of imposing a
resolution of difference, heterogeneity, and otherness are for Lyotard

acts akin to terrorism and torture. They mark the snapping back of the extenuated flesh onto itself in order to dampen down its potential for vibration and experimentation. It is always a matter of regulating the flesh. This is why Lyotard insists that "Majority does not mean large number, it means great fear" (Lyotard and Thébaud, 1985, p. 93). But in staving off the regulation of flesh and the discounting of events, Lyotard also cautions against the 'bad side' of the pagan: indifferentism and adiaphorization.

Whilst I would insist that everything goes – not least through the point of flight traced by the migratory third eye – indifferentism means neither indistinction nor 'anything goes.' Rather, it is the rule of total commensurability, unlimited substitution, and universal exchange. It is the capitalist principle *par excellence*, exemplified in what Baudrillard (1981) calls the political economy of the sign. This latter consists of a homology of commodities and signs that is capitalized through a reciprocal conversion of economic-exchange value and sign-exchange value. The law of indifferent exchange does not respect difference, otherness, and alterity. It operates via a fully integrated code that carves up the identical into so many serialized equivalents. "Material in serialism is not valuable in itself, but in the relationship of one term to the next" (Pefanis, 1991, p. 93). And when the structural law of value reigns, the spacing of terms is no longer fixed, but enters into a condition of generalized motility and mutability. Such is the dream of general relativity: a pure circulation bereft of any terms (and Baudrillard, like Bataille, holds out for the return of the repressed, for that delirious excess that has been remaindered in modernity: symbolic exchange and the accursed share.)

In contrast to the ex-termination of quality and specificity, which would amount to a liquidation of all distinctions, the process of adiaphorization takes differentiation to a superlative degree: it exempts "a considerable part of human action from moral judgement and, indeed, moral significance" by hurling it outside of the subject's frame of reference (Bauman, 1996, p. 32). Adiaphorization seeks to sever the link between the one and the other, especially one's actions and their consequences. It has been inextricably bound up with "the tendency to substitute ethics, that is a law-like code of rules and conventions, for moral sentiments, intuitions, and urges of autonomous selves," suggests Bauman (1996, p. 32). Adiaphorization is exemplified in all of those bureaucratic practices that withdraw things, and especially social relations, from 'moral space' (where the justice and legitimacy of one's dealing with others are always at stake) into the 'cognitive space' of technical performance, instrumental rationality, and administrative competence. This process is at the heart of Bauman's (1989) investigation of the relationship between modernity and the Holocaust. It is also replayed in a different form in the relentless delegation and abandonment of social relations to networks of objects and immutable mobiles: "sociologists ... are constantly looking ... for social links sturdy enough to tie all of us together or for moral laws that would be inflexible enough to make us behave properly. When adding up social ties, all does not balance. Soft humans and weak moralities are all sociologists can get. The society they try to recompose with bodies and norms constantly crumbles. Something is missing," laments Latour (1992, p. 227). Yet "they will soon discover their missing mass. To balance our accounts of society, we simply have to turn our exclusive attention away from humans and look also at nonhumans. Here they are, the hidden and despised social masses who make up our morality." Like Lyotard, poststructuralist geography is obligated to resist the violence of attempting to force indifferentism and adiaphorization onto events. A sensitivity to the demands of difference, otherness, and alterity motivates the 'game of the just.'

Accordingly, the 'game of the just' – just gaming, just (s)playing – works against consensus and all of the apparatuses of assimilatory terror by heightening difference and deforming events. It works against indifferentism and adiaphorization, and in support of multiplicity and singularity, by demonstrating incommensurability and thereby affirming the irreducible agonistics of thought and action. In this way, the game of the just strives to do justice to all manner of *différends*. This is the name that Lyotard (1988a) lends to the silencing of others, such as through simplification, disavowal, translation, censure, expulsion, and extermination. A *différend* arises whenever something that should be put into phrases, actions, and events cannot be. It marks an unbecoming "point of difference where the sides speak radically different or heterogeneous languages," says Readings (1991, p. xxx). Or again: it "marks a point where existing representational frameworks are unable to deal with difference without repressing or reducing it." Theoretical-practices, then, are only games of the just if they seek to make space available for incommensurability to take place: and insofar as it takes place it *drains* the plenum of its integrity. While such incommensurability, incompossibility, and indiscernibility can neither be known nor seen, they may at least be felt. This does not mean setting aside or fossilizing *différends*, least of all through a timeless representation, but keeping them current and in play, and no amount of forgetting, repression or extermination will suffice to subdue their affects. 'We,' 'here' and 'now,' are riven with *différends*. To that extent, a *différend* has the character of the untimely: it haunts, disturbs, and disjoins. Hence Lyotard's interest in the sublime.

Sublimity

> We thought we knew how to see; works of art teach us that we were blind. (Lyotard, 1989a, p. 224)

> With the sublime we go a long way into heterogeneity. (Lyotard, 1989a, p. 406)

The sublime is "Not elsewhere, not up there or over there, not earlier or later, nor once upon a time. But as here, now, it happens that" (Lyotard, 1989a, p. 199). The sublime accompanies the taking place of an event, which Lyotard suspends under the phrase: *Is it happening?* For an event is "Not a thing, but at least a caesura in space-time" (Lyotard, 1987, p. 11, translated in Readings, 1991, p. xxxi). Or again: "An event is neither substance, nor accident, nor quality, nor process; events are not corporeal. And yet, an event is certainly not immaterial; it takes effect, becomes effect, always on the level of materiality" (Foucault, 1982, p. 231). The sublime is a sign of the failure of expression when confronted by the taking place of an event; it relays the introduction of undecidability, indeterminacy, and incommensurability into thought and action. As such, it is a sign of the *différend*, and a sign of history. Lyotard not only wishes to see justice done in relation to these signs of history, by frustrating any attempt to reduce them to an intelligible, denotative, and consensual discourse, he also wishes to exacerbate sublimity so that something other might have the chance of happening.

To do justice to the singularity of an event, to its specific *différend*, one must resist exchanging its affect (which disturbs) for a representation (which settles). This imperative is akin to the ethic of deconstruction, which "is a recognition that doing justice to texts is not a matter of fidelity to their content but of listening to the points at which they are torn apart by a difference that they cannot express, yet must express" (Readings, 1991, p. 128). Such an ethic is expressive, and not representative. "The gaps that deconstruction opens up in texts are not contradictions or failures; if they are lapses they are lapses in a Freudian sense, they arise at the site of radically heterogeneous libidinal investments, at points of incommensurability, at 'differends.'" As with Deleuze and Guattari, it is always a matter of *activating* the difference, of sending thought on an experimental line of flight. "Instead of critique we are offered ... the libidinization of all Enlightenment philosophy," comments Sim (1996, p. 23). Moreover, this desire to open up thought, action, and representation to an experience of the impossible and unpresentable is underscored by Lyotard's incredulity towards metanarratives, including the "great narrative of the decline of great narratives" (Lyotard, 1989a, p. 318).

This failure of expression gives rise to a pain, a kind of cleavage within the subject between what can be conceived and what can be imagined or presented. But this pain in turn engenders a ... double pleasure: the impotence of the imagination attests *a contrario* to an imagination striving to figure even that which cannot be figured, and that imagination thus aims to harmonize its object with that of reason – and that furthermore the inadequacy of the images is a negative sign of the immense power of ideas. This dislocation of the faculties among themselves gives rise to the extreme tension (Kant calls it agitation) that characterizes the pathos of the sublime, as opposed to the calm feeling of beauty ... Avant-gardism is thus present in germ in the Kantian aesthetic of the sublime. (Lyotard, 1989a, pp. 203–4)

It may be tempting to scoff at the power of the sublime, in much the same way as Smith has recently satirized the apparent "dismal failure of the various political programs of the New Left – a revivified Marxism, feminism, antiracism, and the new social movements" – by parodically chastising left-leaning scholars for their failure to explore the radical potential of "counterhegemonic sleep practices" (Smith, 1996, pp. 506 and 505, respectively). And in parenthesis, it is odd that Smith writes as though the destabilizing force of the (collective) unconscious and the dreamwork had never been felt (Halton, 1992), and even odder that the exchange that followed the publication of Smith's piece should veer into: "'uncritical social somnambulance'" (Hamnett, 1997), the encroachment of work-time into night-time and dream-time (Pile, 1997), and a parodic, ghostly death drive (Neil Smith, 1997). Be that as it may, Lyotard's characterization of the sublime chimes with Löwy's (1996) depiction of the 'Gothic Marxism' in the work of Walter Benjamin and some early surrealists, where the magical and enchanting aspects of the signs of history – especially the symbolically charged remains of cadaverous commodities – are drawn upon as aftershocks to awaken everyday life from its anaesthetized and amnesic slumber (cf. Buck-Morss, 1991, 1994; Frisby, 1985; Löwy, 1998). Like postmodernism, the point of Gothic Marxism and surrealism is not to hyperrealize the world as an aestheticized dreamworld. It is to re-release the enchantment that remains fossilized in even the most apparently disenchanted of objective systems. This is why the explosive aftershock of the dreamwork remains one of the best hopes for arousing the dreamer (Doel and Clarke, 1998b).

As well as being given over to experimentation and sublimity, deformation and abstraction, the game of the just seeks to maintain the difference that is set in play by a disturbed and disturbing element. I have pursued these motifs in terms of a cancerous ethic of the event. Lyotard, however, takes this ethic to mean defending the specificity of each from reduction to another. Hence much of the antagonism between Lyotard, the advocate of incommensurability and dissension, and Habermas, the champion of transparent communication and rational consensus (Habermas, 1984, 1987a, 1987b). Moreover, in order to ensure incommensurability, he claims that a 'great proscriber' is needed to enforce the identity of each party. (Little wonder that the dialogue between Lyotard and Thébaud on the game of the just should dissolve into laughter – a sure sign of the return of the repressed.) Thus, "the true function of the great prescriber is not so much to prescribe, but rather to *proscribe* ... while at the same time obscuring the necessity for proscription" (Weber, 1985, p. 104). Likewise, "To judge is to open an abyss between parts by analysing their *différend*" (Lyotard, 1989a, p. 326). No perfect translation, representation or communication is possible, nor are they desirable. There is always some remainder (Baudrillard, 1996b; Derrida, 1991b). Hereinafter, one should respect "the basic house-rule – NO TOUCHING" (Barnett, 1995, p. 417). As I shall develop in the next chapter, such an injunction remains enthralled by the Phallus. His defence of difference is in this instance aporetic since it reduces its deforming openness to a mere identity: "wanting to determine singularity as the other of the other can only end in the same, in the identical, in the 'pure' and the 'specific'" (Weber, 1985, p. 103). It would seem that Lyotard misconceives singularity as 'oneness' rather than as a 'break point.' However:

> a response to this criticism ... would be precisely to challenge the opposition 'singularity/totality,' 'incommensurable/equivalent,' etc., by pushing the notion of exchange, or of circulation, to the point that it is no longer conceivable within the horizon of the identical or the commensurable. It is at this point that the idea of a 'general agonistics' ... becomes indispensable. (Weber, 1985, p. 104)

In other words, we spatial scientists must decline proscription in the name of a cancerous and polymorphous perversity. Incommensurability is maintained not by refusing all intercourse between terms, but through the ex-termination of terms. Each is neither liquidated (zeroed) nor put into general circulation (rendered equivalent). Rather, each is 'without measure' to the extent that it puts itself out of joint. Such is the resonance of paganism, postmodernism, deconstruction, and schizoanalysis. Through experimentation and deformation, cancerization and dissimilation, theoretical-practice becomes (again) a driftwork (Lyotard, 1984b). Such a driftwork is exemplified in the dreamwork:

> We can never be in a position that is totally 'immanent' to the stories we tell because – here as elsewhere – the stories are not 'immanent' to themselves. They are always in the process of going elsewhere, in the sense

of *Entstellung*, and it is this movement – caught in the double requirement on the one hand to displace itself and on the other to arrest its movement [*s'arrêter*], to take a fixed position – that marks the unconscious agonistics as ambivalent. (Weber, 1985, pp. 110–11)

On the back of such a driftwork one could envisage a deconstruction of the widespread "archaeological outbidding by which psychoanalysis, in its archive fever, always attempts to return to the live origin of that which the archive loses while keeping it in a multiplicity of places" (Derrida, 1995c, p. 58). For this reason, Deleuze counterposes a carto-graphic conception of psychoanalysis to an archaeological one. "The latter establishes a profound link between the unconscious and memory: it is a memorial, commemorative, or monumental conception that per-tains to persons or objects, the milieus being nothing more than terrains capable of conserving, identifying, or authenticating them," says Deleuze (1997c, p. 63). "From such a point of view, the superposition of layers is necessarily traversed by a shaft that goes from top to bottom, and it is always a question of penetration." Such is the dominant charac-terization of databases, for example, the signs of which are routinely referred back to a human being as their proper measure. Whether in the domain of psychoanalysis, surveillance or credit scoring, this archaeological conception "has a mania for the possessive and the per-sonal, and interpretation consists in recovering persons and possessions" (Deleuze, 1997c, p. 65). But there are no returns of the same in this or any other universe – not even of the repressed. It is illusory to believe that all of these data trails and their derivatives belong to one subject: a subject that could or should be self-same.

So it is that Deleuze distinguishes the cartographic from the archaeo-logical conception of psychoanalysis:

> maps … are superimposed in such a way that each map finds itself modified in the following one, rather than finding its origin in the preceding one: from one map to the next, it is not a matter of searching for an origin, but of evaluating displacements. Every map is a redistribution of impasses and breakthroughs, of thresholds and enclosures, which necessarily go from bottom to top. (Deleuze, 1997c, p. 63)

Deleuze and Guattari (1984) dub the cartography of psychoanalysis 'schizoanalysis,' wherein "the unconscious no longer deals with persons and objects, but with trajectories and becomings; it is no longer an unconscious of commemoration but one of mobilization" (Deleuze, 1997c, p. 63). So one must insist that a subject is a multiplicity without unity. It can be folded, unfolded, and refolded in many ways. It can engender derivatives only because it is always already a difference-producing repetition caught up in, and splayed out according to, innumerable differential calculi. Each is manifold. Each is a variable pack. "How many of us are there altogether, finally? And who is holding forth at the moment? And to whom? And about what?" (Beckett, 1958, p. 70). "That is how we sorcerers operate. Not following a logical order, but following alogical consistencies or compatibilities. The reason is simple. It is because no one, not even God, can say in advance whether two borderlines will string together" (Deleuze and Guattari, 1988, p. 250), or what will happen to it. Case by case. Body by body. Intensity by intensity. Such is the prospect of "justice in a godless society" (Lyotard, 1989a, p. 123).

CHAPTER 3

The pornogeography of
Baudrillard and Irigaray

Obscenity is another world. (Baudrillard, 1993a, p. 62)

Erections, jetties, lips – Irigaray's twofold

There is something of One, but something escapes it, resists it, is always lacking; there is something of One, but it has holes, rifts, silences which speak, murmur to and among themselves, etc. (Irigaray, 1991, p. 97)

She is not infinite, but nor is she *one*. (Irigaray, 1991, p. 55)

As the foregoing discussion of differential (s)pacing, cancerization, paganism, and the driftwork begins to stiffen up, let me simply say that if I were pressed into distilling everything I have come to love in poststructuralism into one word, then it would not be one with an overtly architectonic resonance, such as destabilization, deconstruction or ruination. Nor would it be one with principally ethico-political overtones, such as difference, otherness, relativism, or nihilism. The word that I would choose would be: flaccid – a loose, limp, drooping, and relaxed word, but one whose allusion to fluidity and the skimpiness of partitions nevertheless serves to foreground the tensile and erectile desires of almost all theoretical-practices. After all, theoretical-practices are supposed to stand, and to stand firm against the "obscenity of the confusion of ideas, struggling against the promiscuity of concepts," as Baudrillard (1990d, p. 178) puts it. One has a concept, like an heirloom or talisman, and it is supposed to survive the ebb and flow of events. It is supposed to stand tall and erect above the fray, usually legislating from on high, and it is supposed to stand the test of time, context, and contingency. Whence the fact that the dominant forms of theoretical practice are arboreal, erectile, and turgid. However, poststructuralism does not *oppose* turgid theoretical-practices, least of all with flaccid ones. Instead, it discloses how the rigidity, stability, and standing of what is erected in the name of common sense or high theory is only achieved through a (forced = unbecoming) containment of flows, like the pressurized flood of spongy, penile tissue. Such an erection is nothing but a holding formation with an uncertain extension and duration. Furthermore, this emphasis on erection should sensitize us to the fact that solidity and constancy never cease to be worked over by fluidity and variation. This image of thought chimes with what Irigaray (1991, p. 73) refers to as the 'at least two' of a "perpetually *half-open* threshold, consisting of *lips* that are strangers to dichotomy." Such an 'at least two' distinguishes itself from the 'almost one' of the phallus, whose erectile tissue can detach itself from neither its surroundings, nor the fluidity that both ensures its turgidity and exceeds its holding formation. Identity arises on the basis of an ontology of sexual difference. One need not overthrow identity (which would be equally unbecoming). It suffices to pick up on the vibration that is set into place.

One and one does not make two

Always more than two, always 2 + *n*, always a mix or an open space – an ecstasy – within any given element or participant. (Krell, 1997, p. 34)

Unlike the 'at least two' of the lips, the 'almost one' of the phallus would wish to enforce the impermeable partition between inside and outside, the one and its disavowed (m)other, such that the fluidentity and viscous-mucosity of "woman, or more strictly, the maternal-feminine, [would be] said to be the sacrificial object, 'forgotten, repressed, denied, confused'" (Irigaray, 1991, p. 73; see also Canning, 1994a). "The debt owed to her is never acknowledged." The erect one needs his fluid other(s), such that this other "is always described in terms of deficiency or atrophy, as the other side of the sex that alone holds a monopoly on value: the male sex" (Irigaray, 1985, p. 69). Like the commonsensical notion of space-time as an empty *n*-dimensional region into which 'things' and 'events' are placed, Irigaray suggests that:

The dominant fantasy of the mother ... is as a *volume*, a "receptacle for the (re)production of sameness" and "the support of (re)production – particularly discourse – in all its forms." But man needs to represent her as a *closed* volume, a container; his desire is to immobilize her, keep her under his control, in his possession, even in his house. The fear is of the "open container," the "incontournable volume," that is to say, the volume without contours (*sans contours*), the volume which he cannot "get round" (*contourner*) or enclose, possess and capture in his nets, or master and appropriate. Or his fear is of the *fluid*, that which flows, is mobile, which is not a solid ground/earth or mirror for the subject ... To the male representations of woman, Irigaray opposes "an other woman," a woman "without common measure" who cannot be reduced to the quantifying measurements by which she is domesticated in male systems, who exceeds attempts to pin her down and confine her within a theoretical system, whose volume is "incontournable," whose lips touch without distinction of one and two ... Against the Lacanian image of woman as *hole*, Irigaray opposes the image of *contiguity*, of the two lips touching. (Whitford, 1991, p. 28)

The phallic misrecognition of the other as simply another one, as more of the same – as a slightly phased and in(tro)verted one – will not suffice to return the other to the same. Irigaray is right to draw attention to the numerous ways through which the one – ego, self, subject, identity, etc. – ceaselessly 'cannibalizes' the other, but one should add that "since *one must* eat," the imperative is "*how* for goodness sake should one *eat well*?" (Derrida, 1991c, p. 115). How indeed should one consum(mat)e an other, and in turn be consum(mat)ed by an other? The one and the other are mutually constituted: not as a one plus one $(1 + 1)$, but as a twofold $(1 \div 1)$. Libidinal economy finds itself supplemented by a 'placental economy' (Irigaray, 1993). The spatialization of the 'at least two' – lips, folds, schizzes – affirms a plethora of "Metamorphoses where no whole [*ensemble*] ever consists, where the systematicity of the One never insists" (Irigaray, 1991, p. 59). Or rather, since the one is only ever a transitory, superficial, and above all retroflex effect of the (s)play of folding, these metamorphoses are also anamorphoses. Like a spectral or special effect, an integrated one can only be glimpsed *from a certain angle* – exactly like looking back on eclipsed epistemes (Foucault, 1970). Paradoxically, then, ideal coincidence has its conditions of (im)possibility in parallax: the point, the subject, the one, the other, and the same are all split together. They are not so much reflected as defracted. As Caygill (1998, p. 119) perceptively remarks of Walter Benjamin's city writings: they "exemplify his speculative method: the city in question, whether Naples, Moscow, Berlin or Paris can only become an object of knowledge indirectly, obliquely refracted through the experience of other cities, each of which is its own infinite surface." Identity is always already *dis*-placed and *ex*-posed (such as the imaginary unity of the self as projected from the vantage point of an other).

> Everything, then, should be rethought in terms of volute(s), helix(es), diagonal(s), spiral(s), curl(s), turn(s), revolution(s), pirouette(s) ... An increasingly dizzying speculation which pierces, drills, bores a volume still assumed to be *solid*. And therefore violated in its shell, fractured, trepanned, burst, sounded even unto its most intimate centre. Or belly [*ventre*]. Caught up in faster and faster whirlings, swirlings, until matter shatters and falls into (its) dust. (Irigaray, 1991, pp. 64–5)

Lipos(ed)uction

> the necessity of the leap to the outside in both space and time ... the
> suction and seduction of radical exteriority. (Krell, 1997, p. 57)

On the disseminating scene of sexual difference, the granularity of this image of thought can all too easily lead astray, into what Thwaites (1995, para. 13) refers to as the "elementary error" of "a total and absolute granulation of time into an endless series of independent and monadic presents, and the equally total and absolute determinism of a single eternal present – to be collapsed into absolute equivalents." It is not for nothing, then, that in Irigaray's previous quotation, she repeatedly remarks this danger through the parenthetical addition of the disseminating letter *par excellence* – 's.' Now, concern over what Livingstone (1995, p. 420) refers to as "postmodern pluralization" is invariably couched in terms of a multiplication of granulated positions. It is as if the many were simply an amalgam. The challenge for spatial scientists, however, is put succinctly in Irigaray's (1991, p. 63) insistence that: "For the/a woman, two does not divide into one. Relations preclude being cut up into units." Hereinafter, then, the disseminating s's do not amount to add-ons, but to fold-ins. S + pace takes place on a line of flight. "And so woman will not yet have taken (a) place," continues Irigaray (1991, p. 53). "Never here and now because she is that everywhere elsewhere from whence the 'subject' continues to draw his reserves, his re-sources, yet unable to recognize them/her." The other woman subsists and transpears through a fluid identity, bereft of (a) place, or rather disseminated throughout the entirety of space-time, like a ghost in the phallogocentric machine. She solicits. She sets the whole in motion. She plays a duplicitous and ambivalent game, in the manner of a double agent who works both for and against the powers that be. This is why Baudrillard (1990a) is so wrong to restrict Irigaray's *parole de femme* to the 'anatomical speech' of the female body (cf. Grosz, 1994b). Her solicitation is of a piece with his seduction – on the twisted Möbian band, she vibrates and he withdraws. In general libidinal economy, solicitation and seduction form a complementarity.

So: "*Fluid* must remain that secret, sacred, *remainder* of the one" (Irigaray, 1991, p. 64). It is the 'dangerous supplement' and 'accursed share' without which and beyond which phallomorphism no longer holds firm. As a surplus value it participates without belonging, but since the system depends upon this surplus for its processive reproduction, leans upon it and bends towards it, such an excess perpetually puts the system out of joint. The system has its pivot elsewhere.

> She is not infinite, but nor is she *one* unit: a letter, a figure, a number in
> a series, a proper name, single object (of a) sensible world, the simple

ideality of an intelligible whole, the entity of a foundation, etc. This incompleteness of her form, her morphology, allows her to become something else at any moment ... Never completed in any metaphor ... But becoming the expansion that she is not, never will be at any moment, as a definable universe ... If she closes up around the unit(y) of [a] conception, enfolds herself around that one, her desire will harden. *Will become phallic because of this relation to the one?* ... Whereas what comes to pass in the *jouissance* of woman is in excess of it. An indefinite overflowing in which many a becoming could be inscribed. (Irigaray, 1991, p. 55)

Going with the drift of this dangerous supplement is how I understand Deleuze and Guattari's (1988) much misunderstood and maligned imperative to become-woman, become-animal, and become-imperceptible. Drawing on similar foldings of the 'almost one' and the 'twofold other' in fluidentity, Derrida (1990) speaks of stabilizing and destabilizing 'jetties,' some of which stiffen up, while others supple up (cf. Dixon and Jones, 1996). Deconstruction takes its place in the ebb and flow of such theoretical 'jetties,' but this place is not the 'almost one' of a secured position. It takes place – i.e. slides – amidst the unsutural 'at least twofold' (s+) disjointure of spacing.

For convenience I'll use again the word 'jetty,' in which I distinguish, on the one hand, the force of the movement which throws something or throws itself (*jette* or *se jette*) forward and backwards at the same time, prior to any subject, object, or project, prior to any rejection or abjection, from, on the other hand, its institutional and protective consolidation, which can be compared to the jetty, the pier in a harbor meant to break the waves and maintain low tide for boats at anchor or for swimmers ... I will call the first jetty the *destabilizing* jetty or even more artificially the *devastating* jetty, and the other one the stabilizing, establishing, or simply *stating* jetty ...

You may have had the impression that I was making a distinction between the destabilizing jetty ... and the stabilizing jetty ... as a distinction between the movement which gives momentum, on the one hand, and, on the other hand, the inert fallout which ... would take momentum and life back down, towards inert solidity. It would be a ... very serious misunderstanding. The destabilizing jetty doesn't go up. On the contrary, it is the stabilizing jetty that goes upward. It stands; it is a standing, a station, or a stanza; it erects, institutes, and edifies ... The destabilizing jetty goes neither up nor down; it may not go anywhere. (Derrida, 1990, pp. 84 and 93, respectively)

The undecidable double agency of stabilizing and destabilizing jetties is an exemplary motif of poststructuralist geography. Take *chora* (*khôra*), which participates in "the very foundations of the concept of spatiality and placing: it signifies, at its most literal level, notions of 'place,' 'location,' 'site,' 'region,' locale,' 'country': but it also contains an irreducible ... connection with the function of femininity, being associated with a series of gender-related terms – 'mother,' 'nurse,' 'receptacle' and 'imprint-bearer'" (Grosz, 1995b, p. 48). Binary oppositions saturate Western thought and act as the foundation of the metaphysics of presence. In the previous chapters I have maintained that poststructuralism in general, and deconstruction in particular, work through the perversion and cancerization of purportedly integral positions, opening forced and unseemly stabilizations onto the jetstreams of differential (s)pacing. *Chora* has played a pivotal role in the establishment and maintenance of binary oppositions, but it is also a disturbing portion that always already puts the articulation out of joint.

In Plato's account, *chora* was introduced by Timaeus in order to explain the *passage* from the pure and perfect realm of unchanging forms, paradigms, and ideas (the intelligible) to the impure and imperfect world of actuality, change, and becoming (the sensible). For example, the paradigmatic circle as distinct from worldly circles, or the Idea of justice as distinct from the actual practice of justice. Without *chora* – or some such apparatus and rite of passage, a "tropological texture," as Derrida (1995b, p. 93) refers to it – there would be no passage between the one and the other. The world of becoming would be bereft of form, and perdurant being would be unrealizable. The details are less important than the fact that when one begins *in division* one must have recourse to something that will span it. But if *everything* is divided, then from whence does this excess come? And should it prove to belong to one side of the division, how can it operate on the other side without bringing into question the security of the division with which we began? "Timaeus says he needs a mixing bowl, a kind of container or receptacle in which the 'originals' can operate on and somehow influence what will become their 'copies.' The mixing bowl will turn out to be called $\chi\omega\rho\sigma$(*khôra*). Yet where will he find the mixing bowl – is it up there on the shelf with all the other paradigmatic forms and intelligible moulds of 'being,' or is it down here below, where all the other materials of 'becoming' are strewn"? (Krell, 1997, p. 19). Despite an instability in its nature, or rather owing to such an instability, *chora* enables passage, translation, and commensurability between everything that is given to us in division. (This is why it leans towards the dialectic from the off: it effects a proto-sublation.) It is the 'space' through which universal (i.e. atemporal and spaceless) forms become imparted onto temporalized and spatialized matter. *Chora* is a (s)pacing irreducible to 'space' and 'time;' it comes and takes place from an altogether 'other' dimension. One could call it a 'third space,' were it not for the fact that its place in the series is far from clear; and that its number is incalculable. *Chora* comes between the one side and the other, participating in each without being included in each.

> [*Chora*] is the mother of all qualities without it itself having any – except its capacity to take on, to nurture and to bring into existence any other kind of being. Being a kind of pure permeability ... infinitely transformable, inherently open to the specificities of whatever concrete it brings into existence ... [it is] an incubator to ensure the transmission or rather the copying of Forms to produce matter which resembles them ... *Chora* can only be designated by 'its,' by 'her,' function: to hold, nurture, bring into the world. Neither an 'it' nor a 'she,' *chora* has neither existence nor becoming. *Not* to procreate or produce – this is the function of the father, the creator, god, the Forms – but to nurse, to support, surround, protect, incubate, to sort, or engender – the worldly offspring of the Forms. Its function is a neutral, traceless production ... [which] allows the product to speak indirectly of its creator without need for acknowledging its incubator. (Grosz, 1995b, p. 50)

Yet for *chora* to perform in this way – or rather pro-ject and trans-form, as Lyotard (1990b) aptly puts it when considering Duchamp's TRANS/*formers* – it itself can neither be intelligible nor sensible, neither being nor becoming, neither material nor immaterial, neither subject nor support (*subjectile*), and so forth. Or else it is *both ... and ...* This is more than mere oscillation and vacillation. *Chora* is (s)played out on the frame of a certain quadruplicity (X): a double exclusion (neither, nor) criss-crossed by a double participation (both, and). So "how is one to think the necessity of that which, while *giving place* to that opposition as to so many others, seems sometimes to be itself no longer subject to the law of the very thing which it *situates*?" – except by way of a sort of "hybrid, bastard, or even corrupted reasoning" (Derrida, 1995b, p. 90). *Chora* participates without belonging, and as such its (im)propriety is twofold: that it possess nothing of its own (*anessence*), and that it be formless (*amorphon*). "*Khora* must not receive for *her own sake*, so she must not *receive*, merely let herself be lent the properties (of that) which she receives. She must not receive, she must receive not that which she receives" (Derrida, 1995b, p. 98). Moreover, so far as structure and not essence is drawn on/from the baselessness of *chora*, it should be obvious why "*khora* is anachronistic; it 'is' the anachrony within being, or better: the anachrony of being. It anachronizes being" (Derrida, 1995b, p. 94). And here one can catch a glimpse of the unpresentable and uncontrollable dissimilation that always already undercuts the yearning for similitude and resemblance: "there is only one, however divisible it be" (Derrida, 1995b, p. 97). Hence the strategic importance of *chora* for a solicitation and deconstruction of the ontology of sexual difference. "It dazzles the logic of non-contradiction," maintains Grosz (1995b, p. 49); "it insinuates itself between the oppositional terms, in the impossible no-man's land of the excluded middle." Rather than simply regularizing the realization of ideal forms in some substantial actuality, *chora* is "Just the reverse: the chora, as indeterminacy, is a harbinger of pure chance" (Lechte, 1995, p. 120).

The anachronized and plasticized, splaying, drawing, and quartering of *chora* exemplifies the structuration of all of those poststructuralist passage-works that exceed the phallogocentric calculi of differential (s)pacing: they are neither one thing nor another, nor both one thing and another, but an infinitely disadjusted becoming-other, which carries away the one and its other into a blind zone of singular, free-form, and immanent experimentation. Such a 'no-man's land' is the abjected, destabilizing otherness without which the institution, erection, and inflation of a phallogocentric position would not take place. This is why Kristeva insists that abjection – *ab-jectus*: thrown off, before, and away – is the "degree zero of spatialization," such that "abjection is to geometry what intonation is to speech" (quoted in Burgin, 1996, p. 285, note 39). Consequently, spatial scientists must affirm an other woman and femininity that are not just others *of/for* man and masculinity. Such an other would not be confined to the conventional familial, patriarchal, and phallogocentric reductions of 'woman' to a reflective medium (motifs of screen and foil), a negative double (motifs of lack and abjection), or a womb (motifs of gestation and propagation), for man. This has nothing to do with an anatomical essentialism. In attempting to foreclose on its debt to the unpresentable and unknowable virgin (m)other – (dis)figured here as *chora* – , the phallogocentric edifice yearns for coherence, correspondence, and integrity; yet the repressed will have always already returned to haunt and destabilize the fortified and petrified house of reason. No small wonder, then, that Irigaray (1984, p. 15) should insist that: "In order for [sexual] difference to be thought and lived, we have to reconsider the whole problematic of *space* and *time* ... A change of epoch requires a mutation in the perception and conception of *space-time*, the *inhabitation of place* and the *envelopes of identity*" (quoted and translated in Grosz, 1995b, p. 55). Quite simply, this requires other calculi of differential (s)pacing, other chor(e)ographies of how s + pace take place.

By picking up on the solicitation and vibration of sexual difference the poststructuralist predilection for folding and differentiating, rather than adding and integrating, sets thought-and-action on course for twisting free of naive polarity and opposition. Nothing is given, except, perhaps, for the shakes. Hereinafter, everything will have been (s)played out along the lines (of flight) of so-many disseminating foldings and unfoldings. And in order to lend a certain fragile consistency to this image of thought, one might usefully resituate it within the orbit of psychoanalysis, where the force of sexual difference is most explicitly felt in the flesh.

The s(ed)uction of psychoanalysis

Now, without wishing to go into the ins and outs of psychoanalysis, let me simply stick to a profound possibility put forward by Laplanche (1992, 1996): that contrary to prevailing opinion, psychoanalysis is an *anti*-hermeneutic. It is commonplace to align Freud with 'the hermeneutics of suspicion' – along with Marx and Heidegger – , for whom significance lies not so much with the intended and motivated outpouring of a conscious and rational subject, as with the escape of sense and affects from the machinations of so-many unconscious drives and structures, via slips of the tongue, jokes, and dreams, for example (Benvenuto and Kennedy, 1986; Shamdasani and Münchow, 1994). On that score, psychoanalysis is positioned as a 'regional hermeneutics,' which is devoted to dredging the murky depths of the (collective) unconscious for a spattering of signs, in the hope that it might then be able to decode those cyphers for the benefit of the analysand. Yet as with any hermeneutic enterprise, one will never know if the cypher is meaningful or meaningless. For a cypher is not only both a secret or disguised way of signifying and the key to decyphering it; a cypher is also the arithmetic symbol (o) for 'signifying nothing' in a vacant place (Rotman, 1987). Moreover, in its typical usage, cyphering–decyphering is "phallic logic, a binary logic of 'plus' and 'minus.' ... it is directly linked to the expansion of binarism, the foundation of the modern occidental world," says Laplanche (1996, p. 9). "But despite the irresistible conquest of the world by binarism, it is worth recalling that this expansion remains contingent, in relation to so many civilizations whose founding myths are not binary but plural – accepting ambivalence instead of staking everything on difference." If hermeneutics are part and parcel of the long-standing endeavour of the (hyperactive) subject to gain mastery over a universe of (pacified) objects, then the possibility of a semiotics of zero, in which the quest for meaning exhausts itself, is a truly 'fatal strategy.'

Both Freud and Lacan have been accused by some of wielding rigid, totalitarian, and ahistorical codes, whilst others have emphasized that these codes are always embedded by Freud and Lacan within particular contexts that lend consistency. For example, in considering Lacan's understanding of the Ego as an 'illusion of synthesis' established on the imaginary 'point of convergence,' it becomes clear why "Lacan argues that the ego is a specifically modern form of conceiving of self-identity," which crystallized out around the turn of the sixteenth and seventeenth centuries, and was only possible in the wake of "the establishment of geometrical laws of perspective formulated at the end of the fifteenth and beginning of the sixteenth centuries" (Lacan, quoted in Evans, 1996, p. 37). He also locates the onset of the Oedipus complex in the transition from matriarchal to patriarchal social formations. However, the contextual relativity of psychoanalytic concepts should not blind us to 'the lure of the already-there,' the lure of the ready-made. "When something comes to light, something which we are forced to consider as new ... it creates its own perspective within the past, and we say – *This can never not have been there, this has existed from the beginning ...* What appears to be new thus always seems to extend itself indefinitely into perpetuity, prior to itself" (Lacan, quoted in Evans, 1996, p. 38).

Be that as it may, suffice to note that whether or not these concepts establish codes that are eternal discourses or ones that are historically relative, one still needs a code in order to interpret. After all, asks Laplanche (1996, p. 9): "What is theory for? To master an *enigma*." Since the turn of the century, psychoanalytic codes have come to dominate through the interplay of the *symbolic*, which does more than fix the symbol to what it symbolizes since the symbol is also the murder of the thing, and the *typical*, which ensures the translation of the manifest (dream) content into a (quasi-)universal scenario. Codes not only enable interpretation and translation; they also ensure that the analyst trusts and invests in the manifest cyphers. But there is another psychoanalytic approach, which Laplanche claims pre-dates this *synthetic* interplay of cyphers, codes, symbols, typicalities, and complexes.

> This method is constantly defined as *analytic*, associative-dissociative; 'free association' (*freie Assoziation*) or 'freely occurring ideas' (*freie Einfälle*) are only the means employed for the dissociation of all proposed meaning ... It is a strictly individual method, favouring an individual's way of conceiving things, element by element, through 'associations,' to the detriment of all self-construction and self-theorization. The method is ana-lytic in the true sense of the term, associative-dissociative, unbinding. One might call it 'deconstructive' – and the term *Rückbildung* is certainly there in Freud. (Laplanche, 1996, pp. 7 and 10, respectively)

Little wonder, then, that Laplanche should refer to psychoanalytic anti-hermeneutics as a "general theory of seduction:" a symptomato-logical and asymptotic "'refusal of knowledge' (*Versagung des Wissens*) by the analyst" (Laplanche, 1996, pp. 7 and 12, respectively). All of this brings me to Baudrillard's fondness for s(ed)uction and the void: "Radical thought does not decipher. It anathematizes and 'anagramatizes' concepts and ideas," says Baudrillard (1996b, p. 104). Or again: "Cipher, do not decipher. Work over the illusion. Create illusion to create an event. Make enigmatic what is clear, render unintelligible what is only too intelligible, make the event itself unreadable." This affirmation of the s(ed)uction of the void engenders the fatal strategy of offering the system of regulated codes an unanswerable symbolic exchange. "The absolute rule is to give back more than you were given. Never less, always more. The absolute rule of thought is to give back the world as it was given to us – unintelligible. And, if possible, to render it a little more unintelligible" (Baudrillard, 1996b, p. 105; cf. Baudrillard, 1983a; Clarke and Doel, 1994a, 1994b).

Baudrillard's light manipulation

Why become stuck undermining foundations, when a *light* manipulation of appearances will do? (Baudrillard, 1990a, p. 10)

If the infrastructure is curved, that changes everything. (Baudrillard, 1990a, p. 68)

Gasché (1986, 1994) insists that the out-turn of Derrida's serious philosophical labour can be formalized as a cluster of interrelated 'infrastructures,' which spread out to take in even those texts that are often assumed to be more 'playful' and not, strictly speaking, 'philosophical.' For Gasché, Derrida's work "*always might* be seducing us, leading us astray, especially if we were 'literary' people, because the *apparently* literary feel of some of his work *always might* hide its *true* or *genuine* philosophical import" (Bennington, 1996b, p. 252). So, one should perhaps distinguish between style and substance, superstructural adornment and basal infrastructures, to avoid being diverted from the recognition that Derrida, like Deleuze, has written philosophy, nothing but philosophy. Deleuze created 'concepts.' Derrida creates 'infrastructures.' However, both work in relation to the non-philosophical, in the dual sense of that which philosophy projects and recognizes as *its* other, like an uncanny shadow or virtual double (a 'non-philosophy' that paradoxically belongs to it), and that which philosophy *misses* in misrecognizing 'its' other as *the* other (a 'non-philosophy' that escapes – absolutely – the hold of the philosophical idiom). Now, it goes without saying that it takes a lot of hard graft both to create concepts and infrastructures in a 'deterritorialized' relation to a duplicitous non-philosophy and to resist the "prospects of seduction and wandering, keeping [oneself] firmly away from temptation, on a rather puritanical straight and narrow that looked as though it would require constant vigilance, lots of honest hard work, and a good deal of self-denial" (Bennington, 1996b, p. 252).

Bennington, like Derrida, and to a certain extent like Gasché himself, is right to be nervous about the notion of 'infrastructure.' This is not least because the word cannot help but connote foundational, architectonic, and skeletal significations. Moreover, even when such an infrastructure is brought to the surface in order to emphasize its anti-foundational and ornamental roles – like the circulation systems and 'wall of services' encasing Renzo Piano and Richard Rogers' Pompidou Centre in Paris, or the make-shift 'scabs' that Woods (1993) proposed as a temporary shelter for the reconstruction of Sarajevo's war-torn urban fabric – it is still too rigid, secured, and programmatic for my liking. Endoskeleton or exoskeleton, an infrastructure cannot but lend support. This is why I have chosen to unfold my take on poststructuralism in terms of superficial, destabilized, and liquescent motifs. They have exfoliated all semblance of essential depth. Perversely, then, the apparent gap between Derrida's 'hard graft' and Baudrillard's 'light manipulation' is not metered out in terms of depth and solidity, but in terms of breadth and fluidity. So too with Lyotard's cancerous proliferation, Irigaray's touching lips, and Deleuze's immaculate conceptions. They are all profoundly 'horizontal' notions, to borrow an apt image of thought from Lechte: "This radical horizontality, perhaps paradoxically, does not lead to an order of sameness (everyone on the same level)," notes Lechte (1994, p. 102), which would amount to little more than the indifferentism of unlimited exchange so beloved by capitalism and crass renditions of relativism alike, "but to the instability of differences." As I sought to demonstrate in relation to cloning and cancer, poststructuralism works through horizontal driftworks: "the play of repetition and difference has supplanted that of the Same and representation" (Lechte, 1994, p. 102).

Poststructuralist geography articulates two movements across such a horizontal driftwork (a difference-producing repetition) and not across vertical reduplication (the eternal return of the Same): the s(ed)uction of superficial abysses – (s)pacing degree zero – and the unhinged play of foldings – differential (s)pacing. Deleuze, Derrida, and Lyotard excel in the latter, whereas Baudrillard offers the most intense experimentation with superficial abysses. However, one needs to approach Baudrillard's work with extreme caution. The aphoristic simplicity and the prevalence of everyday phrases can be deceptive. One needs to bear in mind that these distilled terms have been repeatedly experimented upon, deformed, and perverted in many other contexts. It is extremely problematic to seek to periodize Baudrillard's *œuvre*, such as the claim that the role of the sign undergoes a dramatic reversal in his work – from fetish to enigma – or that the tension between a critical-emancipatory impulse gives way to the fatal strategies of seduction, where these latter are exemplified in the 'enigmatic attack by fascination' that accompanies every cypher (and recall that in the West at least, the cypher not only signified nothing – as zero it stood in for absence – it also possessed the seemingly magical and potentially diabolical capacity for effortless multiplication: 1, 10, 100, 1000, etc. Only later did the ambivalent artifice of this phantasmagorical sveltness divide itself between something – a secret – and nothing – absence pure and simple). In a manifold space-time, one which is necessarily disadjusted and disjoined, the partitions upon which periodizations and other segmentations are built cannot hold. Through the play of folding, the distinction between what is inside and what is outside is rendered undecidable, as is the distinction between what is close to hand and what is far away. (Hence the difficulty of affirming 'co-presence' as somehow more authentic, wholesome, and intimate than so-called 'distanciated' interaction: the notion of 'mis-meetings' captures this difficulty perfectly.) Likewise, the folding that holds things together is reversible and revisable. At no point is anything strictly speaking fixed or sedimented into place. What matters is how a particular surface has been folded, unfolded, and refolded. This is no less true for concepts, functions, and sensory aggregates, than it is for sediments, organisms, and buildings. In every situation, the fold obliges one to 'play the whole game.' So, let's take up the Baudrillardian fold where I have happened upon it: in s(ed)uction. The parentheses are mine, but the propellant comes from Baudrillard.

S(ed)uction

At first glance, seduction seems opposed to production. Pefanis (1991) uses this to parodically set Lyotard's productivist analytic of desire against Baudrillard's anti-productivist symbolic exchange. However, not only is such binary thinking constitutive of the productivist schema itself – since polarity ensures the conservation of energy (nothing escapes the mutually-exclusive opposition), the circulation of terms (exchange, reciprocity, substitution, etc.), and the accumulation of value (meaning, sense, profit, etc.) – , but that which is put forward as 'oppositional' invariably functions as an accomplice and alibi – in both the erroneous sense of an 'excuse' and the root sense of an 'elsewhere' – for the perpetuation of the dominant term: "one of the two terms must die, and it is always the same since the other is already dead," says Baudrillard (1990a, p. 123). "Now suppose that wherever relations of opposition presently exist, relations of seduction are put into play," he continues. "Imagine a flash of seduction that causes the polar or differential, tran-sistorized circuits of meaning to melt" (Baudrillard, 1990a, p. 104). This 'flash of seduction' succinctly relays the overloading, short-circuiting, and fusing of binary op-positions, not into an amorphous and synthetic material (such as an end Result), but into a multiplicity of polymorphous undecidables (the 'op' of op-positions here alluding to the swirling and flashing moiré effects of op art, an "abstract equivalent of Pop" says Lucie-Smith (1996, p. 268), which fortuitously puts Baudrillard's 'light manipulation' in touch with Deleuze's 'pop philosophy'). Bereft of positive terms – centre, positions, partitions, boundaries, etc. – the 'flash of seduction' could be compared to a passage of light amidst a parallelogram of mirrors, each plane of which being always already *withdrawn* at absolute speed into the vanishing points (the lines of flight) excavated into the virtual space-times of all of the others. Such an overexposure of the mirrorish and specular is truly ob-scene. It is the ob-scene of the perspectival space-time of modernity. The 'flash of seduction' over-exposes the ob-scene of modernity's fixation on the rational and orderly grids of an abstract and striated space-time.

Now, such an easy-going image of thought sparks readily off the drier versions presented in the previous discussion of the perverse double agency of Deleuze and Derrida. Indeed, much of Baudrillard's effort has been directed at elucidating and discharging – rather than reversing and reinscribing – the duplicity of oppositional (i.e. dialectical) movements. Once again, it is a matter of cancerization, proliferation, and hypertelia, of moving to extremes: 'More X than X.' "For thought, the internal scandal produced by its simulated apotheosis is unbearable," says Baudrillard (1990b, p. 158). This scandal is bound up with his 'philosophy of disappearance.' "Even the most iconoclastic dissidents evaluate themselves primarily in the light of their productivity – their competition to create culture, to generate disturbance, and to 'produce difference,'" notes Levin (1996, p. 129). "Baudrillard is no exception in this regard: he 'produces' culture at a phenomenal rate." Yet Baudrillard invests neither in production, nor in accumulation. To the contrary, he divests – discharges – through a threefold disappearance: death, cloning, and transubstantiation (Baudrillard, 1987a, 1987b; Clarke and Doel, 1994b). Whereas instrumental, hermeneutic, and emancipatory theoretical-practices seek to be productive and progressive, Baudrillard's theoretical-practice is destructive, perverse or, more accurately, s(ed)uctive (Baudrillard, 1988b, 1990a). Having declined the myth of ideal forms, he affirms the 'procession of simulacra.' What I find most adorable in Baudrillard's work is not one of the usual motifs with which his name has become most associated, such as simulation, hyperreality, nihilism, and fatality, but that of s(ed)uction.

> You can't fight the aleatory by imposing finality, you can't fight against programmed and molecular dispersion with *prises de conscience* and dialectical sublation, you can't fight the code with political economy, nor with 'revolution.' All these outdated weapons (including those we find in first-order simulacra, in the ethics and metaphysics of man and nature, use value, and other liberatory systems of reference) are gradually neutralized by a higher-order general system. Everything that filters into the non-finality of the space-time of the code, or that attempts to intervene in it,

is disconnected from its own ends, disintegrated and absorbed. This is the well know effect of recuperation, manipulation, of circulating and recycling at every level. (Baudrillard, 1993c, pp. 3–4)

For example, one thinks of the absorption of anti-art by art, such as Duchamp's 'ready-mades' and Oldenburg's 'wrappings' (Leslie, 1996). "This is why the only strategy is *catastrophic*," continues Baudrillard (1993c, p. 4). "Things must be pushed to the limit." Hereinafter, "The only strategy against the hyperrealist system is some form of pataphysics, a 'science of imaginary solutions;' that is, a science fiction of the system's reversal against itself at the extreme limit of simulation, a reversible simulation in a hyperlogic of death and destruction" (Baudrillard, 1993c, pp. 4–5). Consequently, the pataphysical and fatal strategies of s(ed)uction should not be conflated with the *différantial* and spectral strategies of deconstruction, although they are virtually homologous.

Seduction affirms the void into which all polarity is cast in order to be annulled – whether or not that charge is held in the traditional form of 'binary opposition' (e.g. ritual antagonism) or in the newfangled form of 'digital coding' (e.g. cold simulation). The ethico-political task of s(ed)uction requires the creation of a vacuum around the more or less rigidly encoded system, so that a strategic puncture will cause the pressurized content of its bubble-logic and bubble-memory to be sucked out into the void. "The real joy of writing," confides Baudrillard (1990b, p. 29), "lies in the opportunity of being able to sacrifice a whole chapter for a single sentence, a complete sentence for a single word, to sacrifice everything for an artificial effect or an acceleration into the void." Thus, he readily admits that he does not "have any doctrines to defend. I have one strategy, that's all" (Baudrillard, 1993a, p. 82).

Curvature and declension

It's not so easy to create a void. (Baudrillard, 1987a, p. 129)

Now, the assumption that the void is 'out there,' where there is nothing, is to forget that "There is a curve we can't escape" (Baudrillard, 1987a, p. 127). Seduction is what is left once totalization, unification, and transcendence are declined. Hereinafter, events are perpetually turning away from integration. Such is the resonance between seduction, cancer, and the void. And in a certain way, all of these modes of disappearance affirm an ethic of the event; an ethic that affirms singularity by declining totalization. "Things aspire to be straight, like light in an orthogonal space, but they all have a secret curvature. Seduction is that which follows this curvature, subtly accentuating it until things, in following their own cycle, reach the superficial abyss whereupon they are dissolved" (Baudrillard, 1988c, p. 70). This is what is implied in his games of symbolic exchange – as distinct from the nostalgic lure for an illusory, pre-capitalist primitivism uncorrupted by the commodity law of value.

First and foremost, then, s(ed)uction calls for "an attempt to identify the curvature of things, the mode in which things try to disappear" (Baudrillard, 1993a, p. 38). This image of thought not only frames Baudrillard's interest in the aesthetics of disappearance – mortal (death and entropy), generic (cloning and obesity), and ritual (fashion and obscenity) – it also figures his desire to play the 'whole game' of production and seduction: "The original sense of 'production' is not that of manufacture," Baudrillard (1987a, p. 21) reminds us; "rather, it means to render visible, to cause to appear and to be made to appear: *pro-ducere*." Hence his (symbolic) response to all manner of restricted economies is to adopt a "strategy of displacement (*se-ducere*: to take aside, to divert from one's path)" (Baudrillard, 1990a, p. 22). In seeking to return the 'accursed share' from whence it came, it becomes a fatal strategy to be sure. Little wonder, then, that Levin (1996, p. 84) should suggest that "Symbolic exchange might be described as the 'trickster' version of *différance*, the demonic version of strategic essentialism."

Elsewhere, David Clarke and I have attempted to diagram this curvature of the s(ed)uction of the void in relation to both transpolitical geography and transpolitical urbanism (Clarke and Doel, 1994b; Doel and Clarke, 1997b). Such a diagram is composed of two parts: the first consists of three *superficial abysses* – the terminal velocity of ecstasy (disorientation through spinning), the metastasis of obesity (decomposition through massification), and the overexposure of obscenity (absolute proximity in the wake of implosion, transparition, and duplicity) – whilst the second traces three *modes of s(ed)uction* – the drift from passive nihilism into active nihilism (potentialization, intensification, and overextension), the scission of infinitesimals (schizoanalysis, rhizomatics, multiplicity), and the Möbius spiralling of a difference-producing repetition (undecidability, ghosting, transvestism). These superficial abysses and modes of s(ed)uction exemplify "the suction of the transparent void" (Baudrillard, 1987a, p. 22). One could call it a pornogeography.

As with David Cronenberg's *Videodrome* (1982), the clandestine, indiscernible, and overexposed universe of pornogeography is not only mutant, anomalous, and cancerous; it also folds seemingly secure partitions – such as those between the real and the illusory, between pleasure and pain, and between transgression and complicity – onto a single surface of undecidable spin, direction, and phasing. And as *Videodrome* so graphically illustrates, 'simulation' is not simply an additional layer of special effects that is overlaid upon the body of the earth, like a sediment or mask; it turns the inside out and the outside in. This invagination is neither inversion nor reversal, but Möbius spiralling:

through a simple twist of fate, the ins(l)ide gives way to the outs(l)ide – and vice versa. Hence the fact that a poststructuralist geography must seek to diagram the curvature *in* things, and not merely *around* them. Accordingly, the specificity of poststructuralism – especially in comparison to structuralism, which also foregrounds differential spacing, grids, and relations – should not be (s)played out in terms of its emphasis on 'difference,' 'discontinuity,' 'incommensurability,' 'alterity,' 'superficiality,' etc., but in terms of its sensitivity to folds and curves, volutes and helices. (Hence the link between poststructuralism and the Baroque: Deleuze, 1993b; van Reijen, 1992.) There is nothing particularly difficult or mysterious about this: it amounts to experimenting with the settings of various torque converters that currently serve to regulate and control the forces of destabilization within specific contexts of relative stabilization. For it is torque which transforms a structured space into a constricted space, structuralism into stricturalism. S(ed)uction, fatal strategies, and deconstruction are less to do with drawing out, wearing down, dismantling, and ruining established positions, as with giving them an unforeseen spin. As with the media and the masses, it is not a matter of ideology and propaganda, which supposedly manipulate or dissemble truth and clarity, but of spin-doctoring. And one can only spin an event by learning how to release it.

Each of these modes of disappearance inaugurates a line of flight, a vector of absolute deterritorialization, or, more simply, a perverse and obsessive propensity to get carried away. Yet as both Baudrillard, and Kroker and Cook (1988) understand, getting carried away is not merely a movement from the apparent liberty of sense and determination to the terror of senselessness and undecidability; it is also a dash across the void. Getting carried away should be understood as the short-circuiting of Baudrillard's (1990c, p. 183) fateful gambit: "Seduction versus terror: such is the wager, since no other exists." There is little left except for the s(ed)uction of the void, but at least our encounter with it still gives rise to appearances, traces, and special effects. Following the declension of transcendence, s(ed)uction is what draws out events: this is what takes place.

To cap it all, I would argue that Baudrillard's 'whole game' is not so much a game of the just – *à la* Lyotard – as a game of the hole. It traces the first movement across the horizontal driftwork of a difference-producing repetition by carving out a powerfully s(ed)uctive black (w)hole in the Order of Things. But there is another movement across this superficial abyss that is just as forceful and enigmatic. It is what I want to call, after Deleuze and Derrida, the (s)play of folding. In the chapters that follow, it is this second movement that I will take up: first in the context of the geographical tradition, then in the work of deconstruction, and finally in the pleats of rhizomatics and schizoanalysis.

Meanwhile

something would finally have a chance of happening (Derrida, 1990, p. 81)

As I bring this peregrination to a close I would like to add a brief addendum to my opening comments concerning the flaccid condition of poststructuralist geography. It is something of a commonplace to differentiate between the 'hard' sciences and the 'soft' humanities. Social scientists have become accustomed to the misfortune of falling between the precision of quantity and the inexactitude of quality, between hard sums and fluffy meaning, and between rigorous formalism and hazy interpretation. Openshaw (1996, p. 761) has claimed that a "numerate scientific geographer can readily deride his or her nonnumerate colleagues as producing rubbish, unverifiable stories: the so-called 'Catherine Cookson' approach to reconstructing plausible and knowledgeable geographical fairy-tales that fit the scraps of evidence." Like a cruel fitness instructor, Openshaw's factitious 'numerate scientific geographer' wants the geographical community to toughen up: not necessarily to the core, but at least on the surface, so that others might no longer recognize human geography as a soft, woolly, and scatter-brained affair. Since it is a tough and hard world outside, geography would do well to rigidify its components. (And Openshaw's gambit is to propose a fuzzy resolution, whose combination of hardware and software will attempt to reconcile the hitherto incommensurate worlds of the numerate and the non-numerate, the quantified and the qualified, the objective and the subjective, the non-discursive and the discursive, and the hard and the soft.) Here, however, I would like to entice spatial scientists into softening up, loosening up, limbering up, and going with the flow (cf. Dixon and Jones, 1996, 1998). This image of thought is less that of a latter-day crusader encased in plate armour, and more of a rubberized surfer catching the crest of a wave. For our world is not as hard as it might first appear – it rolls, pulsates, and ebbs and flows. This is why both Deleuze and Lefebvre (1996) insist on the necessity of a 'rhythmanalysis.' Given this fluidity, one would do well to note Demeritt's repudiation of his earlier 'discounting' of the feminist insistence on the role of "subjective psychological factors" in the formation of so-called "hard facts of nature." He now realizes that he "was constructing a thoroughly social and intensely gendered hierarchy of knowledge to distinguish [his] own objective scientific knowledge from silly and subjective social theory," so that "rigorous and rational hard sciences are differentiated from soft and sentimental forms of feminine thought" (Demeritt, 1996, p. 489).

Accordingly, what I want to achieve in this book is neither a secure identity for poststructuralist geography, which one or two readers may attest to being the 'Real Thing,' nor a justification for reducing the geographical idiom in all of its heterogeneity to the theoretical-practices of figures such as Deleuze, Derrida, Lyotard, Irigaray, Baudrillard, and Olsson. I hope that my actual aim is much more modest. I want to participate in generating a different way of feeling about events, about the world, about others, and about theoretical-practice. Hence Deleuze's claim that "The point of critique is not justification but a different way of feeling: another sensibility" (quoted in Bové, 1988, p. vii). I have chosen these authors, then, not because of their 'authority' or 'currency' within the contemporary conjuncture – when all is said and done, such majoritarian considerations amount to nothing – but because they give me a *passion* for thinking the geography of the event. Others will no doubt find their inspiration elsewhere. So, "The question is not: is it true? But: does it work? What new thoughts does it make it possible to think? What new emotions does it make it possible to feel? What new sensations and perceptions does it open in the body? The answer for some ... will be 'none.' If that happens, it's not your tune. No problem" (Massumi, 1988, p. xv). As for the rest, "a lightning storm was produced ... new thought is possible; thought again is possible ... springing forth, dancing before us, in our midst" (Foucault, 1977, p. 196). More importantly, in the midst of this lightning storm responsibility comes to the fore. "Responsibility cannot responsibly be thought of as following a programme of ethical (or political) correctness: responsibility can be taken only when such programmes are exceeded or surprised by the event of the advent of the other," Bennington (1996b, p. 254) reminds us. "Responsibility occurs on the occasion of a singular event which escapes prior normative preparations." It is obligated to come by way of the 'undecidable,' under the auspices of a certain 'perhaps,' in the name of an anonymous and unrecognizable 'name X,' and through an (impossible) experience of incalculable alterity (e.g. aleatory and infinite estrangement). If a poststructuralist theoretical-practice were perverse through and through, it would be no less ethico-political for that. Indeed, the folding, unfolding, and refolding of an ethic of the event will have been our entire affair. For what I am after is just spacing.

Responsibility will perhaps not take place within the strictures of a holding context. It is to our good fortune that every context differs and defers in and of itself: that each is a vibrator and open to cancerization, solicitation, and s(ed)uction. Moreover, neither the past nor the future hold the present securely in place (cf. Baudrillard, 1986). For historicity is always already unhinged and disarranged. This is why one must employ a perverse historicity, which is exemplified in Deleuze's expressionist screwing process, Derrida's deconstructive double agency,

Lyotard's paganism and postmodernism, Irigaray's touching lips, and Baudrillard's light manipulation. For example, "Derrida's thinking of historicity and traditionality exceeded all historicist determination, making it very difficult to situate deconstruction 'in' history, for example as coming 'after' Heidegger. Take 'Plato's pharmacy:' it showed deconstruction happening in fifth-century BC Athens at least as much as in '70s Paris," notes Bennington (1996b, p. 255). Yet

> this means not that we are therefore forever condemned to re-working that tradition, but that Derrida's loving and meticulous readings of texts from the tradition partially *liberate* indebtedness to Heidegger (but also Plato, Hegel, Marx or Blanchot) [and] does not so much indebt us in our turn to those same texts, as in part (whence our gratitude and indebtedness to Derrida 'himself,' who is, however, just this liberatory reading machine) open us to other, always different debts and engagements.

Before unfolding my own take on poststructuralist geography, I want to turn this perverse historicity onto the geographical tradition itself, with delirious results. For I want to open up spatial science to a schizoanalysis, and whilst I do so, one will have been obligated to make space for what is still coming. "The past went that-a-way," wrote McLuhan (1967, pp. 74–5). "We look at the present through a rear-view mirror. We march backwards into the future."

Part II

Schizoanalysis of the
geographical tradition

The schizophrenic voyage is the only kind there is.
Gilles Deleuze and Félix Guattari, *A Thousand Plateaus*

Individual or group, we are traversed by lines, meridians, geodesics,
tropics, and zones marching to different beats and differing in nature ...
The lines are constantly crossing, intersecting for a moment, following
one another ... it should be born in mind that these lines mean nothing.
It is an affair of cartography. They compose us, as they compose our
map. They transform themselves and may even cross over into one
another. Rhizome.
Gilles Deleuze and Félix Guattari, *A Thousand Plateaus*

Should the history of geography be X-rated?
David Livingstone, *The Geographical Tradition*

CHAPTER 4

Geography unhinged – probe-heads, eraser-heads, and dead-heads

There is no more system of reference to tell us what happened to
the geography of things. We can only take a geoseismic view ...
Things no longer meet head-on; they slip past one another.
(Baudrillard, 1987a, p. 126)

Go slowly. Leave blank, leave ... space for transitions, passages.
(Strohmayer, 1997a, p. 177)

In this chapter I want to take up the struggle against commensurability
and totalization, not so much through a cancerization (difference-producing
repetition) and the diabolical art of s(ed)uction (declination, leading
astray, and withdrawal), although these will be in play, but through a
schizoanalysis and a polymorphous perversion of geography. Given that
geography is invariably depicted in terms of its lineage and lineaments,
I will be concerned with how these lines are spaced out and splayed out,
and to what extent they short-circuit. What I will be seeking to recover
is a scrumpled geography that is ceaselessly worked over by scission and
pullulation (cf. Doel, 1993, 1996). Now, to misquote an apt catchphrase
from Bennington (1989a), geography is not what you think. It is not
what you think if you think that geography is concerned with addressing
such questions as: What is ...? or Where is ...? Despite an all-too-
frequent misrecognition, geography does not locate, place or pinpoint,
even when it employs an encyclopaedia, a map or a Geographical
Information System. Still less does it localize, glocalize or earth the
so-called global flows or abstract spaces of late (post)modernity. To the
contrary: geography spaces. The trembling of space does not so much
reduce to points as open them up. Geography is cracked, fissured, and
fractal. Clearly, the field of geography will prove to be a poor ground
for sinking foundations and erecting structures. Even the name itself
relays an irreducible perturbation and solicitation: geography, from the
Greek 'geo-graphia,' means earth-writing or earth-drawing. Many would
have us believe that geo-graphy is merely representational, that it presents again (it copies and reproduces) in innumerable media what is

always already present to itself 'out there' in the so-called 'real world.' As good Platonists, geographers would then be consumed by the quest for accurate and truthful reproductions. By contrast, the more perverse amongst us might argue that if geography really were representational, then the status of its works would be undecidable since one could not be sure in the braiding of ... writing-earth-writing-earth-writing ... which came first: this earth or this writing, this map or this territory, this (social) space or this perspective. Geography would lose itself in the complication and explication of the simulacrum (cf. Baudrillard, 1983b, 1994). Worse still, the assumption that one can return to the same is predicated on an aporetic contextual hermetism. It assumes that something can survive intact its grafting onto another context. However, a reiteration entails a transformation, a redistribution of energy and effects, where "the terror of the True and the False has no place" (Lyotard, 1990b, p. 48). As a reinscription and reiteration, geography is an exemplary transformer. Its iterability – 'iter,' once again, from *itara*, the Sanskrit 'other' – provokes new moves through which geography will no longer recognize itself: "it is within a certain experience of spacing, of space, that resistance to ... authority can be produced" (Derrida, 1994c, p. 10). Or again: "To write means to graft. It's the same word ... The graft is not something that happens to the properness of the thing. There is no more anything than there is any original text" (Derrida, 1981b, p. 355).

To slacken the hold of Platonism in geography, of that dutiful reproduction that disavows its own participation in transforming the texture of things, one needs to carry through the thoroughgoing defamiliarization of space and spacing that I have been engaged in thus far. Specifically, I want to pick up on such a schizoanalysis by perverting two recent accounts of geography: Stoddart's (1986) *On Geography: and its History* and Livingstone's (1992a) *The Geographical Tradition*. Meanwhile, one should bear in mind Barnett's (1995, p. 418) warning about the tendency "to assume too easily that all geography in the past is the past of today's geography." Defamiliarization is also defamilialization.

Anxious curiosity

Arguing for a 'contextual history' of geography rather than a mere narrative emplotment of a 'chronology of events,' Stoddart (1986, p. 30) enumerates three "prerequisites for the development of modern geography:" a "recognition of the immensity of time, for on this depends our understanding of processes and rates;" an appreciation of the significance of "space and scale" (Stoddart 1986, p. 31); and an understanding of the importance "of man's capacity to interpret and to

modify his environment, and so to influence his position on the planet."
Time, space, and agency are the foundations upon which modern geography rests. Now, according to Stoddart (1986, p. 32), these 'contexts
of change' situate geographers before a twofold question: "When did
truth become our central criterion? When did geography become an
objective science?" In addressing himself to these concerns, Stoddart
highlights the difference in kind between the European reactions to the
so-called 'discovery' of America in the sixteenth century and of Australia
in the eighteenth, and turns this into the essence of all subsequent
endeavours in the geographical tradition. For whilst the former allegedly
stirred up theological and philosophical anxiety, since what was 'dis-
covered' could not be readily subsumed within the existing theodic
depictions of the world, the latter aroused largely scientific curiosity
(Wylie, 1996). On this account, the European passion for annihilating
the intrusion of Evil into the divine Order of Things gave way to a
thirst for knowledge about the infinite variety of the world. And between
the extermination of Evil and the collection of Truth there was, or so
Stoddart insists, a dramatic change of perspective: from the eternal
reduplication of Ideal forms to the direct observation of immanent
variety, from divine deduction to secular induction, and from the closure
of perfection to the openness of anomaly. Such a change in perspective
is exemplified in the shift from circular and helical images of thought
towards gridded and tabular ones. Whilst the former tend to be closed,
complete, and can only be extended through reduplication, the latter
are usually open, partial, and can be extended through accretion.

In the classical episteme, centred on God, "objects of science include
only those things which can in principle be extended to infinity, constructed in indefinite series out from *one* central 'creative' point," writes
Hallward (1997, p. 12). "The great effort of knowledge in the classical
age is thus the effort to represent or *locate* itself within the infinite, and
to explain is here to extend to infinity, to 'unfold' the Real without
losing this location" (cf. the humanistic ethic of place that strives to
resist the estrangement and alienation consequent upon the disembedding forces of globalization, universalization, etc.). In the wake of the
Enlightenment, the 'death of God,' and the 'birth of man,' "human
finitude becomes more 'positively' constituent (with Kant) than negative
or limiting. Rather than construct general series referring back to one
infinitely creative point, each element in a series takes on a self-consti-
tuent energy, and diverges in an ongoing 'evolution' of living beings,"
continues Hallward (1997, p. 12). "*Specific*, comparative histories replace
a general deductive order, histories in which the coordinating agent is
of course 'Man' himself." So, whilst circular and helical images of
thought entail variations on a theme, gridded and tabular ones tend to
consist of independent variables strung together along revisable axes.

Whilst Evil portends the destruction of complete worlds, truth merely proliferates. Hereinafter, a grid can be cast over the world in order to hold it in place; but it can also be amended, revised, and replaced. This is why latter-day soothsayers can at least allow themselves the luxury of laughter, which was formerly the Devil's share. "Things deprived suddenly of their supposed meaning, of the place assigned to them in the so-called order of things ..., make us laugh," writes Kundera (1996, p. 86).

> In origin, laughter is thus of the devil's domain. It has something malicious about it (things suddenly turning out different from what they pretended to be), but to some extent also a beneficent relief (things are less weighty than they appeared to be, letting us live more freely, no longer oppressing us with their austere seriousness). (Cf. Smart, 1993)

For Stoddart (1986, p. 39), then, "geography ... emerged as Europe encountered the rest of the world ... and all other geographical traditions are necessarily derivative and indeed imitative of it." Openness towards the truth, as exemplified in the empiricist passion for direct experience and observation, stands out as the indelible mark of geographical identity, to which all differences and deviations of practice are fated to return. As Olsson (1991, p. 17) reminds us, "the Greek word *aletheia* meant 'true,' whereas its opposite, *lethe*, meant 'forgotten.'" So it is that Stoddart (1986, p. 305) can close his ruminations *On Geography: and its History* by concluding that the geographical ideal of providing a "comprehensive view" on earthly 'distributions' "has in large degree been lost sight of in our increasingly technical and specialist concerns." It has been forgotten, but not falsified or nullified. It is our geographical unconscious, a repressed drive that will never cease returning. Little wonder, then, that Stoddart should express his dismay with those who "retreat into increasingly restrictive and esoteric specialities, where they protect themselves with secret languages and erudite techniques" (1986, p. ix). Geography remains open to an experience of the truth *in toto*, even if, in fact, it never ceases to depart from it and fall short of it in practice. "I read with astonishment ... of the 'vacuum' at the heart of the subject, that it is a 'formless discipline', 'unproductive and disillusioning', 'lacking any rigour'. There is a simple remedy: do some *real* geography" (Stoddart, 1986, p. 1986).

Unfortunately, the whole of this account is shot through with difficulties. First and foremost, not only do the 'prerequisites' required for the development of modern geography occlude many other salient features – not least its imbrication with sexism, racism, and violence -- they are also anything but 'modern.' Likewise, the difference in kind between the extermination of Evil and the collection of truth is not so clear cut, even in the 'pivotal' case of Cook's 1769 voyage to the Pacific (Carter,

1987). One could develop the hypothesis that each has always and everywhere been escorted by a diabolical version of the other. One should recall, for example, that there have been dark sides to both the Enlightenment and modernity (Bauman, 1989; Darnton, 1979; Habermas, 1987b; Horkheimer and Adorno, 1993; Hulme and Jordanova, 1990; Porter and Teich, 1979). Moreover, even if one were able to secure a workable partition between the principle of Evil and the will to truth, it would not be self-evident that either direct observation attested to the latter rather than the former, nor that all subsequent geographical efforts have subscribed to the yearning for truth, which is itself paradoxically modelled on the theodic principle of reduplication.

Lightning-conductor

Despite the disparate nature of the activities clustered together under the name of Geography, perhaps 'we' can at least agree on this: we geographers are all heirs of the Enlightenment tradition, and this legacy is not diminished by the obligation to highlight its contradictions, lacunae, pitfalls, duplicity, partiality, and heterogeneity. Geography aspires to be enlightening. For Gould, this ensures that the community of geographers will hold together: our yearning for a 'reasonable' and 'humane' geography is ineluctable. Hence his conviction that "the idea of fragmentation is absurd" since "The important thing is an ability to *illuminate* ... to bring something out of the darkness and into the light of human understanding" (Gould, 1994a, p. 195). Or again: "let us remind ourselves that the 'thea' of 'theatre' and *'theoria'* means a 'making public,' of bringing a representation of the world and its human affairs into the public gaze' (Gould, 1994a, p. 197). Thus "The Heideggerian emphasis upon *aletheia*, truth as unconcealment, with the *a* negating the darkness of *lethe*, need not be played out again, but what else could characterize Geographies *from* the Enlightenment?" (Gould, 1994a, p. 199). In the wake of a God-head who (de)posited ready-made forms into our world for our reverential reduplication, we are fated to become Probe-heads engaged in the illumination of our own acts of (de)positing. And "there are no privileged positions here, no ideological stances capable of sustaining exclusive claims, no *meta-hodos-logos*, no path-to-knowledge, no methodology, that constitutes an exclusive choice" (Gould, 1994a, p. 195). Hereinafter, there will have been only "A community of the question about the possibility of the question," as Derrida (1978, p. 80) once put it in a somewhat different context.

For Gould (1994a, p. 197), what agglutinates the multifarious geographical tradition together is simply this: "enlarging the horizon." The function of the horizon, like that of art, "is to incite its viewer to ask what is *beyond* ... it leads us not 'to see,' as Lacan would put it, but 'to look.' For the human animal is blind in this respect, that it *cannot simply see*, but is *compelled to look* behind the veil, *driven*, Freud would say, beyond the pleasure of seeing. This is where one finds the split between the eye and the gaze that Lacan takes from Merleau-Ponty" (Shepherdson, 1995, para. 5). However, there are difficulties with this attempt to hold the geographical community together. For example, one should note that such an image of thought rests upon the assumption of a 'detached' and 'distanciated' perspective. Indeed, one could underscore difficulties with both this type of visual mastery, which distanciates an active subject from a passive world of objects (Jay, 1993; Levin, 1993), and the dream of incorporeity implied by it (Butler, 1993; Grosz, 1994a; Haraway, 1991; Jung, 1996). Yet in this particular case I think that Gould is right to shrug off the angst of 'corporeity,' since his own version of distanciation is less to do with God-like omnipresence, and more to do with the at least minimal 'standing apart' in order to satisfy the requirements for (perspectival) representation. What is most problematic about Gould's image of thought of geography as an enlargement of the horizon is the strange reduplication at play within the questioning stance itself. It is one that unwinds in the figure of a double helix. On the one hand, and in spiralling towards the left, there is always the temptation for Reason to become involved with itself, to turn against itself, and to exhaust itself in a cancelling cycle of relativism and reflexivity (Kearney, 1988; Lawson, 1985). It is not for nothing that Smart (1993) foregrounds the masochistic drive of what he tellingly refers to as 'heretical reason,' which insists upon subjecting itself to the unrelenting force of the critical tribunal. "Reflexivity makes a general mockery of any pretensions to objective or certain knowledge," Demeritt (1996, p. 496) reminds us. Yet he is too quick to add that: "Evermore clever displays of reflexivity are narcissistic, accomplishing little more than calling attention to their own (usually masculine) presence" (cf. Marcus, 1992). For narcissistic infatuation is never a solitary affair: there is always the loving Echo of at least one other; even if s/he is the other within. "There is no *one* narcissism" runs the header to an interview with Derrida (1995a, pp. 196–215; cf. Pile, 1994a). On the other hand, and in spiralling towards the right, there is always the temptation for Reason to distend itself like a cancer, to turn against its 'others,' and to annihilate everything in a vicious concatenation of Inquisition and Terror (Kroker and Cook, 1988). The heretical nature of reason propagates waves of Inquisition and terror: *outwards* into other discourses, practices, and institutions; *inwards* into the foundation, coherence, legitimacy, and reasonableness of reason itself. These waves produce destructive rather than constructive interference. Little wonder, then, that Thrift (1993, p. 92) should suggest that paradoxically "our own theories have disenfranchised us, becoming a recalcitrant, even timid, kind of enterprise that has nothing left to say."

Now, neither the reigning in of the 'heretical' and 'Inquisitorial' impulse, nor the positing of a 'radical alterity' and 'irreducible otherness,' will suffice to ward-off the excesses of these temptations. The questioning stance is always already tempted by the short-circuit, by the path of least resistance, by the Earth. "And where does that leave freedom?" asks Baudrillard (1988a, no pagination). "In nowhere land. There is no choice, no final decision." Heretical reason is always already (over)-exposed to an "uncertainty that terminates our freedom," to an uncertainty that is paradoxically exacerbated through its critical and conceptual perfection: "SOPHISTICATING THE UNDECIDABLE." For there is no question that is not accompanied by what Pynchon (1975b) aptly dubs 'doubt paralysis' (cf. Doel, 1993). So:

> We must learn to live after truth ... In front of us is an abyss. We cannot 'know' what lies there because it is 'knowledge' that we leave behind ... We tell a tale of nihilism in two stages: relativism and reflexivity. When we consider the status of our theories and our truth, we are led to relativism. Relativism, in turn, turns back on itself and disappears into the vicious spiral of reflexivity. Nothing is certain, not even this ... This is no ordinary time. The modern age opened with the destruction of God and religion. It is ending with the threatened destruction of all coherent thought. The age was held on course by stories of progress and emancipation ... But these stories are now exhausted. There are no new stories to replace them ... The paradigm for constructing paradigms is now collapsing ... We are entering a period of 'abnormal' thought ... We are paralyzed by the performance and we cannot leave the theatre. All the exists are blocked. (Manifesto of the 2nd of January Group, 1986; quoted in Kearney, 1988, p. 360)

Given the fact that critical reflexion inscribes a black hole on the holey surface cast out by the questioning stance, I imagine the will to truth to be a superficial abyss traversed by a twofold movement of s(ed)uction. An apt motif for this interlacing of relativism and reflexivity is the X of deconstruction which I will take up more fully in Chapter 6. "X marks the spot ... X crosses through, does the *sous rature*, leaving legible what it simultaneously cancels," writes Bennington (1996a, p. 1). "I imagine X as a three-dimensional representation: of a pyramid seen from above, rising to its definite point, or of a rectangular shaft disappearing into the infinite depths, the central point a mere perspectival vanishing never arrived at, however long the fall." After God-heads and Probe-heads come the Eraser-heads. "From that point on, theory maintains absolutely no relation with anything at all," suggests Baudrillard (1987a, pp. 127–8): "it becomes an event in and of itself ...

Strictly speaking, nothing remains but a sense of dizziness with which you can't do anything." S(ed)uction is what takes place: something comes to pass.

What is at stake here, in this twofold short-circuiting of Reason, is the dissolution of the pact between "the questioning tradition of the Enlightenment" and the "opening of horizons" (Gould, 1994b, p. 210: cf. Gregory, 1994b). A question is an occasion for thought that takes place before an infinitely receding horizon that precludes finalization (cf. Wood, 1990). Like a space-filling fractal, the iterability of even the simplest of questions is interminable: "meaning is never given here and now, but 'at infinity'" (Descombes, 1980, p. 144). One is reminded of the 'invisible labyrinth of time' in Borges' (1985) 'The garden of forking paths,' whose infinite pullulation of divergent, parallel, and converging series of time engenders agitation, ontological flickering, and phanto-malization. The heresy of reason is therefore not to be found in its re-solutions, which could always be discounted by orthodoxy as mani-festations of Evil or Divine artifice. Consider, for example, the possibility that God secreted all of the 'evidence' of the earth's longevity – geological strata, indications of plate tectonics, traces of polar reversal, fossilized signs of evolution, and so on – in order to provide us with the perfect simulacrum of an extended past in order to cushion our 'Enlightened' existence from the shock of creation *ex nihilo* (Baudrillard, 1996b). Real heresy resides within the questioning stance itself: ask and one shall receive; question and be damned.

If the geographical tradition has a passion for interminable questioning by curious Probe-heads, then this is accompanied by Eraser-heads who withdraw into the darkness of cavities "full of black, cold, and still water," to pick up on Lyotard's (1997, p. 5) exquisite image of thought once again. Alongside the voyages that are assured in advance of returning home there are also voyages in place (cf. de Certeau, 1986; Deleuze and Guattari, 1988).

Death drive

In our 'world' the god has been displaced, and once the world is made, not given, the human possibility of curiosity is unleashed – for good or ill. Pandora's box, that compartmentalized closure, was prised ajar by the Greeks, and has been gaping wide open since the 18th century. We will question unto death. We know this, fear this, and still we do it. (Gould, 1994b, p. 212)

One assumes that Gould means that we will question as long as we live. That to live is to question, and that to stop questioning is to be as good as dead. In the wake of the Enlightenment, which reanimated human reason as the measure of the world only to find itself bifurcate into a humanizing impulse on the one hand and an instrumental rationalization on the other hand, to give up on questioning is not only to forsake the possibility of 'maturity,' it is also to become one of the undead. Probe-heads and Eraser-heads would give way to the Dead-heads that popuate most versions of the postmodern dead end. For Gould, posing questions is a sign of life: it is the pulse of reason. However, one could take his insistence in another way: questioning deadens; it murders the thing (cf. Baudrillard, 1996b). To question unto death is to sound the death knell of human reason. In its wake something monstrous begins to stir. "If there is a distinction between deconstruction and any other fashion, doctrine, method, whatever, it is that deconstruction began by dying," says Derrida (1996, p. 225). "What I see these days ... is the multipli-cation of necrologies." Hence the need to interrupt and defamiliarize the question. It is on this basis that Baudrillard (1988c, p. 100) claims that "The distance theory takes is not that of retreat, but that of exorcism." Likewise, "what ultimately drives Foucault is a desire, not to construct a more accurate history (the truth about the past – that of the historian), or to erect a great theoretical edifice (a universal truth – that of the philosopher)," notes Shepherdson (1995, para. 33), "but to dismantle the narratives that still organize *our present experience* (a truth that bears on the position of enunciation)." "I set out from a problem expressed in current terms today, and I try to work out *its* genealogy," says Foucault (1988, p. 262). "Genealogy means that I begin my analysis from a question posed in the present." This does not lead to a settled reading. It leads to an affirmation of an excess that cannot be integrated: "the stark impossibility of thinking *that*" (Foucault, 1970, p. xv). Yet this excess is not *beyond* knowledge – like a long-forgotten origin to which one could return or an infinitely receding horizon that one could venture towards. It is not an unknown that one day may come to be known. Such an excess haunts the Enlightenment's questioning unto death like a shadow and opens it to an experience of untimeliness, disadjustment, and indiscernibility. In the wake of the Enlightenment comes speleology (caving), sciagraphy (the art of shading), sciamachy (shadow fighting), and spectrography (spectral analysis). It is to the spectroscopy of the geographical tradition that I now turn *en route* from an ethic of cancerous spatialization and polymorphous perversion to-wards the unfolding of a deconstructive and schizoanalytic hauntology.

Spectrography

Spectrographic analysis investigates the position of emission and absorption lines and bands of a material in order to match it with spectra of known substances. Each substance has a unique signature. When one spectrographs the geographical tradition, however, one cannot find such a signature. For geography is itself spectral. To convey the difficulty that ensues from this phantomalization I will screen just a couple of diffraction patterns and their resulting spectra: one from Livingstone (1992a) and another from Agnew, Livingstone, and Rogers (1996).

Unlike Gould, Livingstone's (1992a) spectrographic take on the geographical tradition does not entail the presence of a break that ushers in a modern discipline derivative of the Enlightenment. His account is more of a parallelism, in the form of a base–superstructure model held together through a loosely-woven environmental determinism: "My argument is simply that geography changes as society changes, and that the best way to understand the tradition to which geographers belong is to get a handle on the different social and intellectual environments within which geography has been practised" (Livingstone, 1992a, p. 347). The text of geography changes in concert with changes of context, yet the causal – *choral* – link is left vague, and may even go by way of numerous third parties. Nevertheless, one is led to believe that the geographical tradition is continuous and incremental, processive if not entirely progressive. Livingstone's "aim is – in the words of Steven Shapin and Simon Schaffer [1985, pp. 16–17] – to avoid 'preferring idealizations and simplifications to messy contingencies'" (Livingstone, 1992a, p. 28). Despite the "postmodern pluralization imperative" – which he misconstrues as merely a '+s' phenomena (1 + 1 etc.) rather than as a 's+' solicitation (1 ÷ 1 etc.) – Livingstone (1995, p. 420) still wishes "to maintain the notion that we can coherently speak of the geographical tradition," "that geographers belong to a tradition of inquiry that, whatever its internal differences and debates, does have a narrative history." What makes geography a tradition, then, is its reflexivity as "'an historically extended, socially embodied argument' – an argument precisely about what constitutes the tradition" (cf. Shotter, 1993). It questions itself unto life. Indeed, a number of geographers have been engaged in a wonderfully creative engagement with the double jeopardy of reflexivity, even if, as Rose (1997, p. 305) suggests, this openness invariably comes "from a sense of failure" (see also Barnes, 1993, 1994; Bassett, 1994, 1995).

If, for Livingstone, reflexivity integrates, then spectral analysis differentiates. Just as a spectral diffraction pattern is produced via the passage of light through a diffraction grating that consists of equidistant parallel lines inscribed onto either a transparent medium (transmission grating) or a reflective surface (reflecting grating), so too with the spectral diffraction pattern of geography. Livingstone's spectroscopy uses different social and intellectual environments as the grating for producing the spectrum of the geographical tradition. On this basis Livingstone records a spectrum comprising ten 'conversations' that geographers have been engaged in since the age of reconnaissance. Exploration and cartography are two of the most well-known conversations in the Western tradition, and they have been inextricably bound up with imperialism and colonialism (Bell, Butlin, and Heffernan, 1995; Godlewska and Smith, 1994). To these, Livingstone adds not only the conversation that has been absorbed by the lure of unveiling a 'mechanistic world picture,' but also a cluster of long-standing conversations concerned with the magical, the mystical, and the theological (cf. Matless, 1990, 1992). In turn, all of these conversations resonate with the attempt to engage in regional recitation, and to integrate the human(e) and the physical, although this latter has been strained with the advent of orthodox spatial science, and all but extinguished in much of the post-positivist turn towards the ins and outs of social space. Disparate and frayed as these conversations are, the tenth one listed by Livingstone at least lays claim to a certain totalization of the geographical tradition. In the wake of the split between 'structural' and 'agental' accounts of socio-spatial transformation – exemplified, for example, in various Marxist and humanist strands of human geography (see, for example, Harvey, 1973, 1982; Harvey, et al., 1987; Ley and Samuels, 1978; Massey, 1995) – and its recent sublation through notions such as 'structuration,' the 'duality of structure,' and the 'transformational model of social activity' (Bhaskar, 1989; Giddens, 1984; Gregory, 1989c; Thrift, 1983), he suggests that "Where geography enters the picture is in the need to 'earth' this general model of historical change" (Livingstone, 1992a, p. 357). Indeed, earthing 'situated messiness' has rapidly become one of *the* key motifs in the present nexus of geographical conversations, especially in response to so-called 'globalization' and 'time–space compression.' Yet in this attempt to locate geography within a historical field of situated messiness, such that there can only be "a *situated* geography" (Livingstone, 1992a, p. 28), he cautions against "earthing ideas in the all-too-mundane world of social and economic interests, bodily needs, and psychological yearnings" (Livingstone, 1994, p. 368). By implication, and complementing my deconstruction of the ethic of emplacement and embedment sketched in the introduction, "it is as if the mind remains potentially clean, messed up by its placing in body and soul," says Matless (1995, p. 405). "One might suggest that a history proceeding through the cultures of geography would show, rather, an indissoluble mingling of intellectual debate, political power, bodies in landscapes, environmental and spatial dreams and desires, and that from this mingling is derived geography's historic fascination, its history at once both treasure chest and can of worms." It is as if Livingstone wanted an earthing without earthlings. By contrast, Rose has been at pains to demonstrate the relationship between forms of spatialization and regimes of sexual difference (see, for example, Rose, 1993a, 1993b, 1994, 1995a, 1995b; and the perceptive, homological reading of gendered spatialization in Lacan and Lefebvre by Blum and Nast, 1996).

Livingstone's decimalized diffraction pattern could be recast and multiplied indefinitely without taxonomic closure. He has chosen, however, to collapse the innumerable spectra in continuous variation and solicitation onto a line spectrum: only certain wavelengths are allowed to filter through. Perhaps it is only by fortuity that he arrives at 10, the motif *par excellence* of binary logic, digitality, and the metaphysics of presence. Nevertheless, it is symptomatic of his attempt to immobilize spectra in secure forms. However, he has enormous difficulty in doing so. The spectra transpear across different social and intellectual milieux, and eschew what Livingstone (1992b, p. 35) refers to as the "integrity of each of these diverse discourses in their own terms." Although he insists that "if we are to take history seriously we will have to learn to understand past geographies in *their own contexts* without subjecting them to twentieth-century judgements" (Livingstone, 1992b, p. 27), this is to ignore the fact that a context is never closed in on itself or settled into place. Like the unconscious, context is untimely. Finally, to earth something is not to settle it, but to short-circuit and discharge it. It is the same in geography as it is in electronics (cf. Driver et al., 1995). By taking for granted the insulation of contexts Barnett (1995, p. 417) is therefore mistaken in his conviction that:

> 'contextualization' runs aground when it comes to openly and critically addressing the only context that really matters: the contemporary one. It also indicates that contextualization works only on something which is not still changing its shape – on something which is dead – and which can therefore be made into a clearly defined and recognizable object of knowledge.

Everything remains current and potentialized, so to speak: not by being insulated within the endless circumnavigation of closed circuits – the eternal return of the same – but by ceaselessly passing through the earth – what Deleuze and Guattari (1988) call the Body without Organs – as a difference-producing repetition. That which is *current* is therefore always already *untimely*: it will have been spectral (*post modo*).

Operating on a somewhat different spectroscope, Agnew, Livingstone, and Rogers (1996, p. 5) separate out "five frequently expressed views about geography as a field of study – that it is 'empirical', 'practical', 'integrative' of the physical and human domains, the field uniquely concerned with 'the geographical', and intellectually 'isolationist.'" Unsurprisingly, they find this spectrum and diffraction pattern vague and ill-founded. Geography is neither more nor less 'empirical' and 'practical' than many other fields of study. In those limited contexts within which it held sway, the 'integrative' function of geography was invariably asymmetrical. One thinks of environmental determinism, natural theology, and regional surveying, for example. Presently, the dream of a truly integrative geography is not only deeply problematic but also little more than a promise of things to come. Integration has rarely been little more than rhetorical glue, and where efforts have been made to bring them together, these have not been developed on the basis of a *rapprochement* between the one side and the other. Rather, each side has invariably attempted to integrate with the mirror-image of itself. Each has projected itself onto the other side. The rhetorical force of integration also applies to the claim that geography has been effectively 'isolated' and insulated from the ebb and flow of other fields of inquiry. Such an isolation allegedly parallels the long-standing 'devaluation' of space and place in twentieth-century social thought. Whilst the latter is often said to have been impoverished by an unhealthy obsession with time and duration, space and place have thereby been effectively abandoned to professional geographers (cf. Smith, 1992; Soja, 1989a, 1989b, 1993). This is a rhetorical glue through which the geographer who secreted it is in danger of being the first to become unstuck. For not only is the so-called 'devaluation' of space and place in twentieth-century social thought overly inflated and far from convincing (see, for example, Carlstein, Parkes, and Thrift, 1978a, 1978b; Game, 1995; Giddens, 1984; Lefebvre, 1991), but the work of whole swathes of geographers has been dominated by unbecoming expressions of space and time, place and duration, and the global and the local.

In order to get a handle on the proliferation of conversations amongst geographers, Agnew, Livingstone, and Rogers eschew 'encyclopaedism,' 'biobibliographies' of key authorities, and the 'genealogy' of discrete entities, such as 'potted philosophies' and the interests of particular groups. Instead, they opt for a notion of a geographical tradition that, although bereft of an essential nature, is nevertheless strung together through contextually reinscribed 'clusters of concepts.' Geographers, they say, invent (constellations of) 'geographical' concepts. Such concepts fade in and out of usage for a variety of reasons: normative significance, explanatory adequacy, the dictates of fashion, etc. (Mohan, 1994). Moreover, since they crystallize the prevailing complex of power–knowledge interests, their semantic density and polysemy ensure that they can effectively resist reduction to a single meaning or function, even within the most stiflingly hegemonic and totalizing of contexts. Such an excess of signification means that geographical concepts are fated to undergo endless reiteration and remain subject to all manner of disputation. For the sake of convenience, Agnew, Livingstone, and Rogers 'impose' on this polysemic constellation a loosely-woven fabric knotted together through three sets of geographical concepts: nature, culture, landscape; region, place, locality; and space, time, space-time. Not only does each cluster relate "to one of the 'three traditions' of geography that conventional approaches to geographic thought have seen as competing with one another: the cultural, regional, and spatial traditions," but when summed up, they supposedly "define the main vocabulary of modern human geography," from which 'other concepts' are derived (Agnew, Livingstone, and Rogers, 1996, pp. 11 and 10, respectively). Human geography is stitched together through the criss-crossing and interlacing of these discursive filaments as they fade in and out of focus. It is almost as if geography were being cast on the loom, an apparatus for weaving (and also the first, vague appearance of land on the horizon whilst at sea). Geography is cast as a series of parallel lines forming a warp, around which the tradition will be woven into shape.

Now, in spinning out their yarn about modern human geography, Agnew, Livingstone, and Rogers tantalize us with, on the one hand, a tradition left in stitches, and, on the other hand, a tradition intimately woven together through a common idiom. Nevertheless, even when inverted to expose an "unglamorously dishevelled tangle of threads" (Eagleton, 1986, p. 80), such images of thought will not suffice to do justice to what they consider to be the actual texture of the geographical tradition: a "'situated messiness'" in relation to which one should endeavour to avoid "cleaning up intellectual history to make it smoother and more coherent than it really was" (Agnew, Livingstone, and Rogers, 1996, p. 11). To achieve that goal would require a texture akin to felt rather than fabric. For whilst a woven fabric is restricted by the rigid segmentation of warp and weft, felt is rolled and pressed, matted and fulled. To that extent, sewing, knitting, crochet, embroidery, and lace-making fall between weaving and felting. Although they are liberated from the taut strictures of the loom, they nevertheless remain subordinated to the supple strictures of needle, bobbin, and thread. In bobbin lace-making, for example, one can witness the increasing degrees of freedom as one moves from tape lace, through torchon lace, to plaited lace (Nottingham, 1983).

So much for these brief spectral analyses of the geographical tradition. Rather than culminating in one or more distinct signatures they have left us in stitches. Hereinafter, texts, textiles, and textures will all loom large, but only on condition that they are slackened, generalized, and overextended. When one approaches such texts, what one finds is that some hang loose whilst others are tightly bound. Some endlessly repeat the same motifs and techniques, even though others are free-form and polymerous. Some are closed off and hemmed in; others are splayed out and proliferate wildly. No matter. The crucial point is to realize that they are not woven from point to point, but from fold to fold. What I am groping towards here is Deleuze's insistence that the smallest portion is the fold, not the point. At this juncture on the schizoanalytic switchboard spectroscopy has opened onto origami.

One moves from fold to fold, rather than from point to point. "As a general rule the way the material is folded is what constitutes its texture," says Deleuze. "It is defined less by its heterogeneous and really distinct parts than by the style by which they become inseparable by virtue of particular folds ... In relation to the many folds that it is capable of becoming, matter becomes a matter of expression" (1993b, pp. 36–7). Geography is *expressive* (it is either becoming or unbecoming) rather than *expressed* (by a being, milieu, substance, etc.). Hence the futility of seeking to flush out one or more signatures and parephs from the spectra that express the variable and solicitous consistency of geography. Deleuze continues:

> the search for a model of the fold goes directly through the choice of a material ... But the point is that the composite materials of the fold (texture) must not conceal the formal element or form of expression ... This formal element appears only with infinity, in what is incommensurable and in excess, when the variable curve supersedes the circle ... Only then will ensue material Textures and, finally, Agglomerations or Conglomerations (felt made by fulling and not by weaving). (Deleuze, 1993b, pp. 37–8)

The schizoanalysis of the spectroscopy of the geographical tradition has returned me to the surface of things, a surface that is ripe for unfolding. The diffracted spectra and woven textiles no longer attest to secure forms and solid materials as the basis of the geographical tradition. However, before getting swept up by the fold I want to consider the diffraction gratings and looms themselves. Or rather, I want to consider the parallelism that invariably accompanies the pointillism in geography. Returning to the surface will not suffice as long as that surface remains riddled with points and holes, and striated by lines and partitions. Schizoanalysis can ready the surface for origami by demonstrating not only the unbecoming nature of points and lines, but also the fact that "folds replace holes" and points, and that "folds are always full" (Deleuze, 1993b, pp. 27 and 36, respectively). This is what is taken up in the next chapter.

CHAPTER 5

Plastic space – geography splayed out

More than a substance, plastic is the very idea of its infinite transformation;
as its everyday name indicates, it is ubiquity made visible ... Plastic
remains impregnated throughout with this wonder: it is less a thing than
the trace of a movement ... The hierarchy of substances is abolished: a
single one replaces them all: the whole world *can* be plasticized, and even
life itself. (Barthes, 1972b, pp. 97 and 99)

It is always a matter of experimenting with materials, of working with
the plasticity of the geographical tradition. Deform! Deform! Deform!
Yet deconstruction and schizoanalysis are not at all negative operations.
Such acts of deformation affirm the plasticity of the materials that are
worked over. What is most significant, then, is neither the perversion
nor the distortion of the material *per se*, but the fact that the material
puts *itself* out of shape. Perhaps there would be less scope for misunderstanding if I were simply to say that what interests me is the *contortion*
of materials, the manner in which they are twisted together – and
therefore apart. The material – in this case geography – is (s)played,
drawn, and quartered not only by folding, unfolding, and refolding, but
also by doing the twist: athleticism, dance movement, freak show.

In this chapter I want to be a plasticizer. I want to recover the
plasticity and metamorphosy of the geographical tradition. Plasticity
comes between forms. In the foregoing schizoanalysis we saw how the
geographical tradition has invariably been cast in terms of the bringing
together of distinct elements: points, lines, surfaces, volumes, etc. Insofar
as the twist of plasticization deforms the integrity of positions, and is
neither one form nor another, it could be called a 'thirdspace.' However,
this thirdspace of polymorphous perversion should not be confused
with the thirdspace of dialectical sublation that conserves and preserves
the difference between contrary positions whilst resolving and overcoming it. Indeed, it would be better to call the space of plasticization a
'fourthspace' in order to foreclose such a misunderstanding (this is taken
up in the following chapter).

Without realizing the dialectical mopping-up operation lurking in the
wings, Pile adopts a fluid and hybrid 'thirdspace' to prize apart the
closure of dualistic epistemologies in the hope of providing "another

place from which to criticize" (Pile, 1994b, p. 268). However, thirdspace is not merely a dumping ground for 'matter out of place.' It is not just another site for gathering together everything that does not fit into the established apportionment of identity, reality, gender, race, class, sexuality, ethnicity, etc. Falling on neither one side nor the other of the series of oppositions that have been arrayed in Western thought (self–other, male–female, pure–base, etc.), thirdspace vacillates between incommensurate positions. Unlike the dialectical third of sublation, through which the procession of unfolding oppositions is miraculously sutured together into a seamless whole, thirdspace forms a *hole* within periodic series: one, two, –, four, etc. This hole is not an absence or rent in the onto-theological Order of Things, but a collapsar, a black hole into which the entire work of serialization plunges. Since thirdspace is criss-crossed with hybridity everything participates in it without properly belonging to it. Nothing escapes the pull of the third. For this hole turns out to contain the *whole* world; it is the milieu (mid-place) into which, and from which, everything is drawn. For the boundary of a black hole is, precisely, the 'event horizon' itself. Nothing is missing, but everything is out of place. Such is a space of general relativity and disjointure. Yet in Pile's account thirdspace is nevertheless swept up by the Hegelian dialectic of *Aufhebung*, which conserves and maintains the integrity of the series while apparently dislocating it (cf. Strohmayer, 1997a). Here, the third relieves the tension that is transmitted throughout the series. It dampens the solicitation of the system. In this way thirdspace comes to act as a kind of shock-absorber for thought-and-action.

In the account given by Pile (1994b) there is a tendency to figure thirdspace as a milieu of synthetic resolution (a relieved whole), rather than as a milieu of s(ed)uction (a collapsar). It is presented as a reserve for everything that escapes the strictures of binary opposition. Thirdspace explodes the reduction of the field of possibility to a series of polarized choices (cf. Pile and Rose, 1992). So, he informs us that 'domesticity' is a disruptive thirdspace for prizing open the dualism of capital–labour; that 'sexuality' is an excessive thirdspace for rupturing the closure of bourgeois–worker, man–woman, and public–private; and that 'hybridity' dislocates the hermetism of centre–margin. However, since Pile yearns for a *place* from which to intervene, his thirdspace solidifies into an unbecoming form. It suspends its differential pullulation to take on a position. Similarly, Soja casts his own 'thirding-as-Othering' as a response to the reduction of thought-and-action to only two alternatives "by interjecting an-Other set of choices;" "critical thirding" takes place when the "original binary ... is subjected to a creative process of *restructuring* that draws selectively and strategically from the two opposing categories to open up alternatives" (Soja, 1996, pp. 5–6).

He tries to maintain the mutability of thirdspace by slipping it through Lefebvre's 'trialectics of space,' with particular emphasis on the lived spaces of representation as disruptive of the habitual realm of spatial practices and the disembodied realm of abstract representations of space. However, the addition of a third space does not disable dualism: it merely opens the metaphysics of binary opposition to a dialectical resolution of contradiction. Like Pile, Soja's thirdspace lends relief to the charge stored between polarized positions. It is not simply fortuitous that Soja's illustrations of the 'Trialectics of Being' and the 'Trialectics of Space' spiral inwards towards the integral positions of 'being' and the 'spatial' respectively (Soja, 1996, pp. 71 and 74). Likewise with Gregory's (1994a, p. 401) depiction of Lefebvre's take on the decorporealization of lived space as an 'eye of power.'

Without wishing to broach the relationship between deconstruction and dialectics, which is the theme of the next chapter, suffice to say that it is the spacing and not the spaces that declines and twists free of dualisms, oppositions, and contradictions. As I have repeatedly sought to demonstrate, space is always already a transformer and deformer of identity and positive difference. Nothing will come of a third space that has not already been relayed by spacing from the off. After thirdspace, the space which finally seeks to take control of the accursed share and disturbing portion, comes spacing (s + pace) in its generality. Whilst the thirdspace of dialectical relief inserts itself in the series in order to syphon off its charged content, that of spacing in its generality disjoins and deforms the integrity of the previously arrayed positions. Consequently, it is less a fourth space than a collapsar that subtends the entire series. Whilst it is undoubtedly true that the black hole is insinuated into the series (the fourth element), it should be recalled that *sinuare* is to curve. One can no longer rely on the straightness and periodicity of the series and matrices: 'one, two, three, –, five, etc.' Neither metaphysics nor dialectics can function flawlessly in a curved space.

Now, I would wager that virtually all of the possibilities for expressing the specificity of the geographical tradition – everything from the particularity of place and the generality of space to the polyphony of heterogeneous geographical conversations and the polysemy of clustered geographical concepts – are part and parcel of the conventional division of academic labour that typically assigns geographers three interrelated tasks: *enumerating* the properties, attributes, and adjuncts of various spatial entities (a comprehensive and encyclopaedic task of ascription and description, which lends itself immediately to empiricism and story telling); *mapping* the areal differentiation of manifold phenomena (a cartographic and diagrammatic task of relative localization, which thereby assumes a frame of reference and orientation); and *synthesizing* numerous aspatially conceived processes in geographical situations (an integrative and unifying task of contextualization, actualization, and localization that more often than not leads to their paralysis and decomposition). Furthermore, in the contemporary maelstrom it is worth emphasizing the remarkable pliability of these tasks in both form and content, to the point where this threefold detail division of labour can legitimate almost anything. Whilst other social sciences can claim a segment of the *real* – such as the economy, polity, media, culture or society – in order to set off their domain of legitimate intellectual jurisdiction, inquiry, and competence, geography would seem only to have *dimensions* and *scales* (point, line, surface, volume, region, etc.), a trait which it shares problematically with history. For if there seems to be a homology and complementarity between geography and space on the one hand, and history and time on the other hand, then clearly this cosy relationship does not hold for the irreducible space-time that is currently in vogue.

The trimerous division of labour and dimensional character gives geography a derivative, subsidiary, and ultimately redundant status. Like part of an archetypal 'hollow corporation,' which profits from holding together a network of subcontractors, its content would be given to it as ready-mades that would simply require assembly in place (localization, glocalization, earthing, embedment, etc.). Any defective materials would have to be returned to the appropriate manufacturer. Such is the conventional subordination of *contingent* spatial structures to *essential* social relations, of spatial form to social content (cf. Gregory and Urry, 1985). Geography and history act like a blank page or an empty box into which the essential features of reality can be set to work. They participate without belonging. The reality to which geography refers is not, therefore, the fundamental reality of universal, essential, and necessary forms, but rather the apparent reality of 'mere facticity,' the dispensable reality of possibility, actuality, and happenstance. Like history, geography concerns real-*ization*, and not reality itself. It is worldly without ever being fundamentally ontological. It concerns 'mere' becoming rather than the being of becoming, and whilst the former is the stuff of TV quiz shows, it is unbecoming in a scholar. As Fyfe (1996, p. 437) notes sardonically: "Would Haggett's [1979] *Geography: a modern synthesis* have been so successful and influential if it had had the title *Geography: a modern parasite?*" (cf. Urry, 1995).

Beneath the surface of 'realized' events – which are timed, periodized, and serialized by history, and enumerated, diagrammed, and synthesized by geography – there is another, invariant, and more basic reality, of which the surface phenomena are merely the superficial expression. Geography is not only superficial because it clings to the surface of what actually takes place, and is thereby exposed to the uncertain drift of events; it is superficial in a much more profound sense. What takes place can be accounted for as a mere actualization of the possible. For all of its hard graft and highly skilled labour, geography is idle repetition. Geography is a supplement that strictly speaking adds nothing of any significance: just like a demonstration or performance adds nothing to what is demonstrated or performed, or like a branch plant of a gargantuan corporation. It simply confirms that the eternal resides within the fleeting, that this or that essential social relation really is to be found in the ebb and flow of events.

Consider Descombes' (1993, p. 3) take on 'up-to-date philosophy,' through which "our gaze has turned away from the invisible beyond and toward daily events." Like the "spiritual attitude evident in the predilections of avid newspaper readers," we must reorient ourselves "in the light of what is." In such circumstances the status of geography should rise insofar as it is ideally placed to chronicle, (em)plot, and (re)count the passing of events. Other disciplines, such as philosophy, become "modern by renouncing the effort to ground the transitory in the eternal. It now turns toward the present, toward the 'now'" (Descombes, 1993, p. 3). Yet this state of affairs changes nothing about the 'unbecoming' character of geography. It will not enlighten us about the present *as* present since this latter is an ontological concern. For example:

> If someone does not exhibit the putative indices of the 'modern,' it will not be said that *he does not exist* ..., but rather that *he is different* ... However, if the [historical geography] of the present truly had an ontological significance, one would have to suppose that whatever does not seem to conform to the (ontological) index of the modern *does not exist*, cannot really be, or has only the appearance of presence ... If ontology pays particular attention to the 'present' to the 'now,' it is so that the decisive reduplication can be performed on present-being, the kind of being that is ours insofar as we exist *now* ... by which we therefore denote more than a date, more than a period, namely, a specific mode of being. (Descombes, 1993, p. 21)

Geography and history may chronicle, emplot, and recount events (their realization), but they can tell us nothing about these events *as* events (their mode of being). Little wonder, then, that in the current division of academic labour, so many geographers should find themselves lumbered with the turgid work of enumeration, mapping, and synthesis. However, even here the supplemental status of geography is not so clear cut. The work of enumeration, mapping, and synthesis is not simply an idle repetition since it is also remedial. It is charged with the task of accounting for, precisely, the contingency of realization. (Hence the enthusiasm for critical realism and structuration theory amongst many poststructural spatial scientists.) In dealing with the transiency of actual

states of affairs rather than the permanency of essential forms, geography, like history, is supposed to contain the return of the repressed:
chance, contingency, and uncertainty. For some spatial scientists, the
search was on for the ideal form of realization: to distil the power of
space *per se*. Yet for all of the grand talk of a spatial science uncovering
spatial laws that are independent of context or content, this would
always remain impostrous so long as the spatial is an expression of
contingency. As Aristotle insisted: there can by definition be no philosophy of the accidental. So, Massey (1992, p. 70) rightly notes how
the quest for "an autonomous sphere of the spatial in which 'spatial
relations' and 'spatial processes' produced spatial distributions" was
flawed from the start. Such was the aporia of the first structural revolution in geography, an aporia that serves as a timely signpost towards
poststructuralist geography. For were there to be a law of space and
spacing, it would have to be a law of context – and a non-saturable
context at that. This is why it is a *harsh* law of space. The breakthrough
in spatial science comes, then, when one realizes that a context remains
open to the differential play of iteration and solicitation.

Parallactic paralogism – Poststructuralist geography is not what you think

There was another geometry to come. (Derrida, 1981b, p. 366)

Situated as we are at one of the "signposts toward a poststructuralist
geography," as Natter and Jones (1993) aptly refer to them, it is worth
noting that in many accounts of the recent ins and outs of the geographical tradition one can locate the same decisive turn (that for many
has resulted in catastrophe). This is the so-called 'linguistic turn,' which
is taken when one acknowledges not only that our encounter with the
world is *mediated* by language, technics, and is irreducibly theory-laden,
but that signifying practices *constitute* our world no less than material
processes, that discourses, ideologies, and the whole linguistic caboodle
really do have substantive effects. Owing to the 'theory-laden' nature of
thought-and-action, any appeal to the 'facts' is naive. Reality "cannot
be used to explain why a statement becomes a fact, since it is only after
it has become a fact that the effect of reality is obtained," note Latour
and Woolgar (1986, p. 180). "It is *because* the controversy settles, that
a statement splits into an entity and a statement about that entity; such
a split never precedes the resolution of controversy." Everywhere one
looks, signs seem to be at work and at play. Interpretation takes centre
stage, steadily eclipsing both description and classification – and the
spectres of relativism, perspectivism, and nihilism lurk in the wings.

Thus, beyond the linguistic turn, the world is no longer *like* a text; it *is* a text. Everywhere one looks the world *makes sense*, which is not necessarily to say that it communicates meaning, carries authorial intention, or establishes reference.

Accordingly, the pressing task is no longer one of distinguishing the textual from the extra-textual, the immaterial from the material, the imaginary/symbolic from the real, the semiotic from the politico-economic, and so on and so forth. Having been set in motion such partitions no longer hold. Henceforth the important tasks would appear to be the development of a logic of interpretation (*à la* hermeneutics, semiology, and semiotics), a logic of analysis (*à la* psychoanalysis, schizoanalysis, and deconstruction), and a logic of sensation (*à la* Stoicism and rhythmanalysis). Such tasks easily merge with the so-called 'cultural turn' (Chaney, 1994). For if the linguistic turn effectively nullified the appeal of a universal and transcendental tribunal of the true, the just, and the beautiful, then at least contextualizing regimes of meaning within specific communities and milieux may help to shore up the traditional vocations of philosophers, intellectuals, and activists, and so block off the 'dangerous slide' into relativism, indifferentism, and nihilism.

To cut a long story short, the come-uppance of this linguistic-cum-cultural turn, which effectively extends the notion of the text to take in the texture of 'the-entire-real-history-of-the-world,' as Derrida (1988a) once put it, is that what geography deals with can be refigured as textual: not as a linguistic idealism, but as an affective texturing. Accordingly, the gambit that Natter and Jones (1993) make is the striking suggestion that there may have been a parallel trajectory followed by those disciplines that have been self-consciously engaging with 'texts,' narrowly conceived, and those that have been unconsciously engaging with 'texts,' broadly conceived. In short, they postulate that there may be a parallelism, and perhaps even a homology, between literary theory and geography.

For the moment I have little interest in the specifics of this parallelism and homology. So here is an accelerated run-down. The parallelism of the two disciplines resides in their sequential valorization of first authorial intention, then the object itself, and finally the interpreter. In the case of literary theory, this succession finds its expression in the serial privileging of first the author, then the text, and finally the literary critic, whilst in human geography, the same threefold transvaluation is expressed in the primacy of first the agent (some real-world process or actor), then space 'itself,' and finally the geographer. In both cases, then, one can posit a parallel and homologous movement: first, an original, founding *act* towards which analysis and interpretation are obliged to return (such as the intentions of an author or the irreversible determination of a causal process); second, a self-sufficient *medium* towards which analysis and interpretation are obliged to return (such as the formal structure of a text or the auto-referential play of the spatial); and third, an *interpretative community* that is empowered to have its way with the world and the text (such as when 'the' text becomes an effect of contested readings). Thus, Natter and Jones flag parallels between romanticism and behavioural geography (where each emphasizes the centrality of authorial intention); between Russian Formalism and the Chicago School, between New Criticism and regional geography, and between literary structuralism and spatial science (all advocating the primacy of a largely self-sufficient object: THE text, THE spatial); and between reader-response theories, phenomenology, Marxism, structuration theory, and poststructuralism (all of which entail a redistribution of agency from some original authority towards a more situated, overdetermined, decentred, and reflexive agent-cum-actor-network).

Lest one mistake this parallelism for a forced totalization and unification of two rather disparate and raggedy nexuses of theoretical-practices, it is worth noting Natter and Jones' (1993, p. 196) own disavowal of plotting a disciplinary "'trajectory' – that is, a discipline *soaring above* context and *directed*, even if nonlinearly, *toward* its target, the full and final presence of true knowledge." Indeed, they emphasize the contingent, immanent, and playful nature of their parallelism – it is a 'montage,' they say – whilst recognizing that both disciplines have been inscribed within overlapping and far from secure contexts. Their parallelism is not a given, a ready-made; it is not the unfolding of a teleological master narrative. It is a composition, a montage, a special effect. It would not take much to make their holding formation disintegrate. Clearly, both disciplines are far too heterogeneous to be squeezed into their two by three parallelogram, and the specificity of each of the six cells is far from evident. The whole thing could easily be blown apart. However, I want to stick with their parallelism, which strikes me as a smashing image of thought. I have no interest in the two by three box itself or with its cellular spaces. What draws my attention are the parallels through which their account is (s)played out. For it is here that one can sense the stirrings of a specifically poststructuralist geography.

So, let's agree not to touch this little two by three container, because it should go without saying that it is a pig in a poke (and Natter and Jones let the cat out of the bag themselves). But if one eyes it up in the manner that I have been suggesting, then it should be clear that something other than 'disciplinary trajectories' and 'intellectual affinities' is at stake here – the *contortion* of geography. How can one get from the inflexibility of parallelism to the plasticity of contortion? The obvious solution would be to project the parallels onto a curved surface so that they interlace with and affect one another. "Our argumentation suggests two propositions," they say, "that the author→text→critic model must be problematized in terms of space ... and that the agent→space→ geographer model must be problematized in terms of representation" (Natter and Jones, 1993, p. 190). Furthermore, this overlaying of parallels is why their montage is less a totalizing frame of reference for collapsing one disciplinary trajectory onto another, and more a parallelogram of forces or velocities. In short, the montage does not so much spotlight parallelism *per se* – a gesture that would be very close to the 'empty square' of formalism and structuralism – as open up the transversal move- ment of double invagination that carries the one into the other and reciprocally, of spatiality into representation and representation into spatiality. Hereinafter, the ... earth-writing-earth-writing-earth ... of geo-graphy is not merely strung out in series but is ramified in parallel. "Overcoming the rigid distinction between that which is thought of as 'representational' and that which is thought of as 'material' requires a recognition of their mutual determination," a transversal movement that "would be better conceived dialectically" (Natter and Jones, 1993, p. 190). Such is the disclosure not of a homology between geography and literary theory, but of a distortion or contortion that carries each through the postures of the other. Hereinafter, the parallels of identity thinking, whose *modus operandi* is naive negation (x = x = not y), gives way to the zigzagging parallels of dialectical thought, whose *modus operandi* is sublation (thesis→antithesis→synthesis). And whilst the par- allels of identity are irredeemably essentialist and static (as a reduplication of being and nothingness), the zigzagging dialectic unfolds dynamically and spectrally (as a differential becoming) (cf. Castree, 1996; Harvey, 1995; Ollman, 1993; Olsson, 1991). Either way, everything gets caught up in the twisted net of parallelism, in these lines of power. Everything becomes tangled up in either the warped lines of identity or the swerving lines of dialectics.

To pick up on Natter and Jones's (1993, p. 168) "prolegomena toward both a spatialized poststructuralist critique of representation and a post- structural geography," I want to focus on the twisting of parallelism itself, which threatens to unhinge and disarrange all of the partitions that have been called upon to separate geography from non-geography, the material from the immaterial, reality from representation, text from extra-text, and so on and so forth. For me, this is the nub of poststruc- turalist geography. Whereas the parallelogram depicted above on the basis of the montage of elements provided by Natter and Jones plotted a *historical trip* – whose itinerary included several landmark encounters between space and representation, and eventually culminated in an appeal for an urgent recognition of their co-determination – the trans- versal connection of the Möbius strip is a *motionless (s)trip*, whose modality is that of the always already, or more precisely, of the continuous future perfect: it will have been (*post modo*). Once again, everything changes. No longer will the image of thought be caught up in the strictures of textuality or the interminable attempt to twist free. No longer will thought gaze towards the horizon. Instead, it will have become a matter of folding. Hereinafter, the pictographic notation 'V' and 'X' will need to hesitate between a fixation on the *vanishing point* and a sliding across the variegated surface of the *fold*. (For more on the disarranging effects of 'V,' see especially McHale, 1989; Pynchon, 1975a.) Yet before I take this up in the final part of the book, I want to end my schizoanalysis and plasticization of geography with a consideration of the work of one of the most skilled geographical plasticizers – Gunnar Olsson.

The X files – Writhing with Olsson

> It is always in points of intersecting lines that genuine understanding is concentrated. Only such points are worthy of study. (Olsson, 1991, p. 187)

It is arguably Gunnar Olsson who has done more than any other geographer to 'diagram' the 'lines of power' that structure the metaphysics of presence's alchemical syntheses, and to probe the limits of their hold on 'thought-and-action.' As an indication of his absorption in this matter, Olsson (1991, p. 169) claims that "the story of the straight line contains everything I know and everything I have not yet understood." Simplifying to the extreme, the 'line' to which he refers is first and foremost a *relation*. Sometimes the relation is a contingent conjunction of two previously self-sufficient things (such as when a bat strikes a ball – A,B); sometimes it is their condition of possibility (such as when a man and a woman *become* husband and wife – A:B); at other times it is a relation of negation (such as when something is defined through a constitutive lack – A/not-A). In whatever form they are posited, relations are always engaged in 'ontological transformations.' This is exemplified for Olsson in the braiding of signification: figured as the drunkenness of the Saussurean bar separating signifier and signified, and refigured in the asymptotic imbrication of meaning and matter (cf. Gren, 1994). Nevertheless, Olsson (1991, p. 49) reminds us that, typically, "What is highlighted is *what* is being related. Left in darkness is the relation itself." This is a damaging lacuna, for all of the reasons outlined above. Such an oversight can be put down to the fact that "relations are by necessity invisible ... inaudible ... untouchable ... [and] there is consequently a strong tendency to do away with relations by thingifying them" (Olsson, 1991, p. 99). Accordingly, "Rather than questioning the relations we are talking *in*, we stare ourselves blind on what we are talking *about*." For many, then, "What counts are countable things. What is taboo are totemic relations" (Olsson, 1991, p. 117).

Anyone familiar with postpositivist social theory will no doubt recognize the force of Olsson's tirade against disowning the relation in the name of the relata. What is striking for me in Olsson's work is his attempt to mount "an exhibition of invisible lines" (Olsson's, 1991, p. 3). This leads him to adopt "Mallarmé's example [which] was to paint not the thing but the effect it produces" (Olsson, 1991, p. 181). Such an emphasis on the performative aspect of the work means that Olsson's exhibition is not so much *about* something; it *is* that something. It aspires to become an event in the universe it inscribes (cf. Baudrillard, 1987a). In keeping with this sublime strategy of presenting the unpresentable his "studies are experiments performed on straight lines, themselves serving as objective correlates of abstract relations" (Olsson, 1991, p. 24). Specifically, Olsson aims to render visible three images of thought that have dominated thought-and-action. Whether this is a manifestation of a geometric fixation remains a moot point (cf. Gregory, 1994a; Philo, 1984, 1994).

To cut a long story short, Olsson (1991, p. 24) tells us that "The first lines are the '=' of the equal sign ... The second line is the '/' of the unnameable in-between, another name for the void ... The third line is the '—' of the Saussurean bar." And to put a little flesh on this skeletal framework, he adds that:

> While '=' demarcates what is identical to what and '/' stands for the penumbra of a mutual relation, the '—' is the rendezvous of signifier and signified. While '=' has its roots in logic and '/' comes from dialectics, '—' is central to semiotics. Regardless of these differences, however, the three signs are all possessed by the same kind of mimetic desire; what stands on one side of the line wants to merge with what stands on the other. (Olsson, 1991, p. 169)

Consequently, these three copulatory images of thought express the recurrent figure of parallelism – specifically: the parallels of identity, dialectics, and semiotics – and, when "Viewed together, the lines themselves get cornered into points of power. From the turning and twisting of these correlates emerges a set of figures hitherto unseen" (Olsson, 1991, p. 24). These figures are composed of curves, loops, and spirals, which are themselves highly reminiscent of Deleuze's (1993b) unfolding of the Baroque, Derrida's sliding partitions, and Irigaray's touching lips (see, for example, Olsson, 1993). Whilst it is beyond the scope of the present discussion to retrace Olsson's ingenious twisting and turning of parallelism in any detail, suffice to note that what he seems to want to achieve is a twisting free of thought-and-action from the strictures of parallelism. Consider his remark that "Since the circle has neither beginning nor end, neither up nor down, it carries within itself a hint of a world without categories, perhaps even of a geography without time or space" (Olsson, 1991, p. 151). Or again: "It is to the demateriaized point of abstractness that this volume aspires" (Olsson, 1991, p. 8). Finally, he asks: "Is this geography?" and elicits from himself the following response, which suggests a radicalization of the geometric fixation of spatial science, rather than a clear-cut, epistemological break or a continuation of orthodox spatial science by unconventional means (cf. Olsson, 1984):

> Of course it is! For what is geography, if it is not the drawing and interpretation of lines. The only quality that makes my geography unusual is that it does not limit itself to the study of visible things. Instead it tries to foreshadow a cartography of thought. To practice this art, however, is incredibly difficult, for any attempt must face the challenge of being abstract enough. (Olsson, 1991, p. 181)

Despite the force of Philo's (1994) dismay at the attempt to catch both thought-and-action and the entire-real-history-of-the-world in such a course, angular, and inflexible net, I am not entirely persuaded by the thrust of this charge. For it seems to me that Olsson's fondness for all manner of copulating lines does not simply reflect a continuation of his love affair with the geometrical and cartographic fixations of spatial science – the '=' of identity thinking, the '/' of dialectics, the '—' of semiotics, the '∩' of thought-and-action, and the unpresentable, dematerialized point of abstractness. It is true that Olsson's texts ooze signs of a geometrical fixation, and his desire to elucidate a "cartography of thought" chimes harmoniously with the final 'blessing' of his 'Sermon of remembrance' for orthodox spatial science: "*And there was an eroticization of Euclid*" (Olsson, 1991, pp. 181 and 25, respectively). But in ogling these lines it is easy to miss Olsson's distortion and contortion of space and spacing. His work is not messy, to be sure, but that does not make it anally retentive and obsessively ordered. Rather, his work goes round the twist – and it is this that I love. It splays out multiplicity, heterogeneity, and incommensurability much more successfully than any amount of multiplication, proliferation, or fragmentation.

Gregory (1994a, p. 73), for example, discerns an attempt "to deconstruct spatial science by invoking 'a world where lines are taken to their limits.'" Similarly, Philo sees a continuation of the 'geometric turn' in a new garb – i.e. an 'exploding,' 'fuzzy,' and 'eroticized' spatial science of the immaterial worlds of you-and-me and thought-and-action:

> For all that Olsson claims to 'dematerialize' his geometries and to think beyond the limitations of Euclidean space, I am sure that some readers will *not* detect such a radical break between the attempt to 'fit' social life

into the iron cages of (say) 'central place theory' or distance-decay models and Olsson's attempt to 'fit' it into the specifications of his 'torpedo of human action.' I think that there *are* important differences, but that there would still be some justification for suggesting that both retain a modernist ambition of translating the 'ordinary languages' (or 'stories') of social life into a more 'formal language' where the empty spaces of geometrical diagrams remain empowered by the legacy of Reason's obsession with simplification, elegance, and order ... Olsson presumably reckons himself to be deconstructing this obsession from within, to be producing an exploding geometry with fuzzy edges undermining the crisp lines of Euclid ... but my own response to the diagrams ... is – I would have to admit – a certain dismay at their starkness which speaks to me more of machinery than of human beings. Perhaps the situation is akin to the well-known response of Buttimer (a humanistic geographer) to the web diagrams of time geography, which she saw as mapping a *dance macabre* whose angular and unbending lines struck her as wholly alien to the much more twisting, changing, and unpredictable paths ... that 'real' human beings beat through the clutter of their everyday lives. (Philo, 1994, p. 236)

I think that these suspicions are misplaced. Olsson's experimentation with unencumbered thought-and-action has nothing to do with imposing a template onto events and bodies in order to make them fit. Rather than shaping things up, his gymnastic contortions seek to suspend the usual – i.e. habitual – fitness regimes that are forced onto thought-and-action. His gymnasium does not impose discipline; it recalls the naked (*gumnos*) exercise of thought-and-action unburdened by instrumental imperatives and routinized habits. Furthermore, there are serious problems with the separation and valorization of 'ordinary' languages over and against 'formal' languages, with notions of 'fit' and 'translation' that remain wedded to the discourses of representation and misrepresentation, and with the distinction between the 'cleanliness' of abstract systems of thought-and-action on the one hand and the 'messiness' of everyday life on the other hand. More significantly, whilst it is true that Olsson's work is articulated through all kinds of geometric motifs – points, lines, surfaces, curves, helices, etc. – this is not where the work takes place. It takes place in the differential (s)pacing that (s)plays itself out between these motifs. To read Olsson as a geometric reductionist is to focus only on what is drawn and expressed and to ignore its drawing and expression. For when all is said and done, Olsson's machinations do not amount to a *geometrical analysis* but to a *rhythm* or *spectral analysis*. He cites Mallarmé approvingly: 'NOTHING WILL HAVE TAKEN PLACE EXCEPT THE PLACE.' So, it is not for nothing that Olsson, like Derrida, repeatedly instructs us (in how) to read between the lines, and to compose an 'algebra of silence' attuned to the 'social space of silence:'

"And there was a long silence" (Olsson, 1991, p. 53). It is not, therefore, that in recent times Olsson has begun to bend his lines, making them more flexible and supple, but that the space around them has always been curved and disadjusted. It is the lineaments of the geographical tradition that bend to the s(ed)uctive and sublime force of the difference that a curved space-time makes. Whether straight or crooked, it is always a matter of thinking, writing, and acting under a certain suspension.

In the wake of Olsson's remarkable experiments in spacing, I want the final part of this book to pick up on Deleuze's (1997a, p. 227) deceptively simply insistence that "There are no straight lines, neither in things nor in language." Neither the pointillism of identity, nor the parallels of homology, nor the zigzag of dialectics, nor the braided bars of semiotics. Hereinafter, it simply will not be possible to determine with respect to the arrangement of terms "which are consistent, which are ambiguous, which are coherent, and, most importantly, which dualisms cannot be aligned in parallel without contradiction" (Sayer, 1991, p. 285). Such is the harsh law of spacing: everything is disadjusted and dis-located; everything is (s)played out according to the contingent folding, unfolding, and refolding of the figure schiz. It is this harsh law that I want to pick up on in the final part of the book through the work of Derrida on the one hand and Deleuze and Guattari on the other.

Now, although I engage with the theoretical-practices of Derrida, and Deleuze and Guattari as if they were two directions traversing the same Möbius strip – in the manner of a difference-producing repetition – it may be useful to differentiate between them. Thus far I have sought to demonstrate how events are splayed out in a manner that exceeds our every attempt at calculation, anticipation, and constriction. There is always some accursed share soliciting our holding formations and expressions of relative consistency. Hence our need for other calculi of identity and difference, and other geometries of space and spacing. I have also suggested that there is a politics and an ethic specific to the affirmation of othering: "My law, the one to which I try to devote myself or to respond, is *the text of the other*" (Derrida, 1992c, p. 66). Given such an aleatory state of affairs, I have found Derridean deconstruction to provide an exemplary basis for mapping out each event under suspension. It rigorously and obsessively opens out the folds of what is typically occluded and occulted by those approaches that would wish too hastily to force – i.e. feign – a decision, resolution, and destination. "This lifting or simulacrum of a lifting of repression, a simulacrum which is never neutral and without efficacity, perhaps hangs on this being-suspended" (Derrida, 1992c, p. 56). By contrast, it seems to me that Deleuze and Guattari, like Lyotard, are exemplary in their setting to work of such a counter-actualized, virtualized, and singular suspension: the mapping of the differential relations is itself suspended in favour of their situational activation (the pick-me-up of pop philosophy). Nevertheless, on the Möbius strip such a distinction between mapping and activation does not hold, least of all in terms of two distinct phases: there are just action re(s)plays that redistribute libidinal energy and affects. In a way that recalls the polymorphous perversion of Chapter 1, the ethic of cancer of Chapter 2, and the origami that is still to come in Chapter 7, Derrida (1992c, p. 64) argues that

> the *jeu* ['play,' 'give,'], not simply in the sense of the ludic, but also in the sense of that which, by the spacing between the pieces of an apparatus, allows for movement and articulation ... is sometimes what allows the machine to function normally, but sometimes the same word designates an articulation that is too loose, without rigor, the cause of an anomaly or a pathological malfunctioning. The question is always one of an economic evaluation: what makes the 'best play'?

It is to this splaying out of events according to the folding, unfolding, and refolding of indefinite, undecidable, and suspended hinges that I now turn. Once again it will call for a rhythmanalysis and schizoanalysis.

Part III

Poststructuralist geography

Voyage in place: that is the name of all intensities, even if
they develop in extension.
Gilles Deleuze and Félix Guattari, *A Thousand Plateaus*

Space hesitates about its identity.
Jean-François Lyotard, *Duchamp's* TRANS/*formers*

In the beginning is Repetition.
Henri Michaux, *Spaced, Displaced*

CHAPTER 6

Sliding signs – deconstruction and the quantitative revolution

The security of each point arrested in the name of the law is hence blown up. (Derrida, 1981b, p. 26)

Another way of working with *numbers*, dissemination sets up a pharmacy in which it is no longer possible to count by ones, by twos, or by threes. (Derrida, 1981b, p. 24)

Taking stock

Strictly speaking, it is really scandalous that science has not yet clarified the nature of number. It might be excusable that there is still no generally accepted definition of number, if at least there were general agreement on the matter itself. However, science has not even decided on whether number is an assemblage of things, or a figure drawn on the blackboard by the hand of man; whether it is something psychical ... or whether it is a logical structure; whether it is created and can vanish, or whether it is eternal. It is not known whether the propositions of arithmetic deal with those structures composed of calcium carbonate or with non-physical entities. There is as little agreement in this matter as there is regarding the meaning of the word 'equal' and the equality sign. Therefore, science does not know the thought content which is attached to its propositions; it does not know what it deals with; it is completely in the dark regarding their proper nature. Isn't this scandalous? (Frege, quoted in Plotnitsky, 1994, p. 63)

The various strands of the first two parts of this book all converge on a difficulty that can be stated quite simply. Space takes place: points, lines, surfaces, volumes (are what) deconstruct. Through the difference that space makes, integrity and pointillism are rendered unbecoming: they are ill-mannered and lack consistency. What takes place is fractured, fissured, and fractal: events are cracked open. Such is "the impossibility of a *position* which is not already a *relation*, an ex-position to something (someone?) other" (Kamuf, 1991, p. xv). This is the sense in which place is necessarily splayed out. It is always already 'stretched,' 'distanciated,' and 'disembedded,' to borrow the phraseology of Giddens (1984, 1990). Place and space are always already everywhere perverted, plasticized, and deconstructed. Poststructuralist geography affirms the disadjusted movements *in* place and not merely *around* place (cf. Thrift, 1990, 1991, 1993). In the first part of this book I attempted to *open up* poststructuralism to an ethic of cancer and perversion. In the second part I endeavoured to *open up* geography to schizoanalysis. In this part I want to *open up* space itself: once through Derridean deconstruction; and again through Deleuzoguattarian origami.

The force of deconstruction emerges from a recognition that the points of space do not hold. They are set in motion, like hinges or pivots. The task for a poststructuralist geographer is "to put oneself there where the disparate itself *holds together*, without wounding the dis-jointure, the dispersion, or the difference, without effacing the heterogeneity of the other" (Derrida, 1994b, p. 29). This may sound like preaching to the converted since most geographers will already be familiar with the disintegration and incoherence of 'absolute' notions of space (and time), with the unseemly characterization of space as an emptiness into which various things can be placed. Most of contemporary human geography takes its point of departure from the repudiation of absolute space and the affirmation of 'relative' or 'relational' space. Accordingly, the integrity of space is no longer simply given, but is instead a contingent and local effect of pinning down the differential network of traces within which spatialization is inscribed. It is the holding formation of this networked integrity that deconstruction brings into question. The resulting dislocation and perturbation goes all the way down to that 'vital bottom integer:' one. How easily this figure comes to mind: one, one and one are two, one and two are three, etc. One can always be counted on. Yet each of us endured a massive dose of socialization in order to extract an array of neatly spaced out 'ones' from the continuous variation of intensities and affects. One, two, three, four ... Red, orange, yellow, green ... Me, you, us, them ... Second, minute, hour, day ... Here, there, elsewhere, nowhere ... And on(e) and on(e) and on(e). Divide and rule(r). It is always a matter of painting by numbers, of thinking by numbers, and of spacing by numbers. However, every time some 'one' is called upon, with or without the appearance of the full array of which it is merely a part, there is also a release of undecidability and incalculability.

As I have endeavoured to show in the foregoing chapters, every 'one' is a pack-animal: each carries the innumerable number within its folds. All of those qualities that are usually added on to the simplicity of some 'one' – multiplicity, complexity, structurality, networking, etc. – are there from the off (cf. Derrida, 1982b). "Subjected to this force – the force of the innumerable number – the numerable number ... loses its grip," writes Derrida (1981b, p. 363). "The innumerable does not simply come to exceed or bound the numerical order along its border, from the outside. It works through it from the inside ... Number is always just beyond or just short of itself, in the 'deviation' or the 'spread.'" To deconstruct, then, is to affirm such a disadjustment. No more of one number, one place, one position, one event or one (con)text. To deconstruct is to intervene within an apparently unified and sealed context, prizing open such a scene of (forced) enclosure and stabilization, thereby releasing the hold or grasp of the controlling context for the possibility of supplementary grafts. Deconstruction entails

> the dismantling of conceptual oppositions, the taking apart of hierarchical systems of thought which can then be *reinscribed* within a different order of textual signification. Or again: deconstruction is the vigilant seeking-out of those 'aporias', blindspots or moments of self-contradiction where a text involuntarily betrays the tension between rhetoric and logic, between what it manifestly *means to say* and what it is nonetheless *constrained to mean*. To 'deconstruct' a piece of writing is therefore to operate a kind of strategic reversal, seizing on precisely those unregarded details (casual metaphors, footnotes, incidental turns of argument) which are always, and necessarily, passed over by interpreters of a more orthodox persuasion. For it is here, in the margins of the text, that deconstruction discovers those unsettling forces at work. (Norris, 1987, p. 19)

In this chapter I want to experiment with how the innumerable disarranges the yearning for whole 'ones:' how the difference that space makes deconstructs the integrity of pointillism by forcing its command posts, cornerstones, hinges, and pivots out of joint. By drawing out and activating such moments of deformation and scission in the Order of Things, we will be brought to the (s)play of folding that is the subject of the final chapter. Meanwhile, the one of integrity, the two of metaphysical thinking, and the three of dialectics – although Žižek (1991) insists on its 'quadruplicity' – will become subject to an unruly fourth element that sets the whole series in motion. Such is the swaying and solicitous force of deconstruction. It *affirms* what takes place. It *affirms* that which opens (in) the event. However, since most geographers and spatial scientists – even those of a poststructuralist bent – have come to know only unbecoming and unsavoury characterizations of deconstruction (e.g. Barnett, 1993; Dear, 1986, 1988; Marden, 1992; Scott and Simpson-Housley, 1988), which are overwhelmingly nay-saying, reactive, and nihilistic, it will be necessary to undertake a palaeonomy of the word deconstruction itself. Specifically, it will be necessary to recover what has often been occluded in the rush to figure deconstruction in architectonic terms, and to derail the characterization of it as a negative de-construction, which is at best a laborious dis-mantlement and at worst wanton destruction. Fortunately, not all geographers have been so unbecoming in their engagements with deconstruction (e.g. Hannah and Strohmayer, 1991, 1992, 1993; Olsson, 1991; Strohmayer, 1997a, 1998; Strohmayer and Hannah, 1992).

Not 'One' – palaeonomy and undecidability

Deconstruction is not what you think. (Bennington, 1989a, p. 84)

And should I now write it several times, loading the text with quotation marks, with quotation marks within quotation marks, with italics, with square brackets, with pictographed gestures, even if I were to multiply the refinements of punctuation in all the codes, I wager that at the end the initial residue would return. (Derrida, 1988c, p. 19)

Derrida has referred to 'deconstruction' as "an ugly and difficult word," "a word I have never liked and one whose fortune has disagreeably surprised me" (Derrida, 1992b, p. 7 and Derrida, 1983, p. 44, respectively). Elsewhere, he has noted how the word "imposed itself," adding not only that it "has interest only within a certain context," but also that he does "not think ... it is a *good word*. It is certainly not elegant" (Derrida, 1991a, pp. 270 and 275). Part of the difficulty is that the word 'deconstruction' bends to many different beats, the vast majority of which lead only towards 'false exits.' This is why it is necessary to undertake a palaeonomy of the word 'deconstruction' itself. "I use the word 'palaeonomy' to explain the way we should use an old word," writes Derrida (1989b, p. 224), "not simply to give up the word, but to analyze what in the old word has been buried or hidden or forgotten. And what has been hidden or forgotten may be totally heterogeneous to what has been kept." Yet it is important to bear in mind that palaeonomy is not simply polysemy. Whereas polysemy amasses the many meanings of a word, palaeonomy strikes at the holding formation within which certain aspects are valorized whilst others are repressed.

Where should one begin a palaeonomy of deconstruction? Perhaps by noting Derrida's (1986a, p. 15) insistence that "If I had to risk a single definition of deconstruction, one as brief, elliptical, and economical as a password, I would say simply and without overstatement: *plus d'une langue* – both more than a language and no more of *a* language." Bearing this in mind, one should not begin with the question: 'What is deconstruction?' since all statements of the type 'deconstruction is (not) such and such' miss the point. For "Deconstruction is first and foremost a suspicion directed against just that kind of thinking – 'what is ...?'"

(Derrida, 1989d, p. 73). As Lyotard recommended, one must strive to become incapable of *anticipating* the 'What' of the 'It happens.' For this reason, one cannot approach deconstruction head-on; one cannot encounter it in and of itself, in its right and proper place, in its essence. Wraithlike, deconstruction is otherwise than being.

> I would say that deconstruction loses nothing from admitting that it is impossible; also that those who would rush to delight in that admission lose nothing from having to wait. For a deconstructive operation possibility would rather be the danger, the danger of becoming an available set of rule-governed procedures, methods, accessible approaches. The interest of deconstruction, of such force and desire as it may have, is a certain experience of the impossible. (Derrida, 1991a, p. 209)

So, one will have to approach deconstruction obliquely, through a disseminating series of elliptical, enigmatic, and stop-gap figures: supplements, grafts, folds, undecidables, quasi-concepts, special effects, traces, etc. Yet all of these encryptions are irreducibly faulty. They work by breaking down, disintegrating, and haemorrhaging meaning and sense in all directions. "There you are, forewarned: it is the risk or chance of that fault that fascinates or obsesses me at this very moment, and what can happen to a faulty writing, to a faulty letter" (Derrida, 1991a, p. 409). Deconstruction dis-semenates and defamilializes. Perhaps these faulty words should be either quarantined in gnathic scare quotes (') or else put under erasure (X). Either way, an experience of deconstruction can only gather p(l)ace, then, by means of a series of words – such as *différance*, supplement, *parergon*, graft, hymen, and trace – that are all faulty and screwed up. Inasmuch as this gathering is riven with faults it can be drawn into a series of interruptions, hiatuses, and chiasmata, a *series* of enchained *erasures*, which Derrida (1991a, p. 424) dubs "the *seriasure*," or *sériature*, with all of the associated connotations of seismology, spectrography, and transpar(t)ition. If deconstruction were anything, it would be less an interpretative strategy and more an experience of dissemination and *seriasure* that traverses and sets in motion everything that it encounters. By ceaselessly deforming and scrambling the expected propagation of familiar and familial terms, I am reminded of all of those perverse, immaculate conceptions and carcinogenic difference-producing repetitions that I spun out in the opening portion of the book. As I mentioned in Chapter 2, deconstruction is clonal, carcinogenic, and viral:

> All I have done, to summarize it very reductively, is dominated by the thought of a virus, which could be called a parasitology, a virology, the virus being many things ... The virus is in part a parasite that destroys, that introduces disorder into communication. Even from the biological

standpoint, this is what happens with a virus; it derails a mechanism of
the communicational type, its coding and decoding. On the other hand,
it is something that is neither living nor nonliving; the virus is a microbe.
And if you follow these two threads, that of a parasite which disrupts
destination from the communicative point of view ... and which on the
other hand is neither alive nor dead, you have the matrix of all that I have
done since I began writing. (Derrida, 1994c, p. 12)

Through this matrix of parasitism and undecidability, deconstruction
leans towards the solicitation (from the Latin, *sollus*, 'entire,' and *citus*,
'set in motion') of the founding philosophemes of Western metaphysics.
It attunes itself to the rumbling, shaking, trembling, and vibration of
the taut surface that is spread over the splayed out constellation of
(op)positions. By emphasizing from the start the solicitous character of
deconstruction, it should be apparent that deconstruction resists any
simple architectural reduction whilst foregrounding an irreducible concern with the sexualization of spatiality. Deconstruction is not just
de-construction. It is also sonorous and resonant.

Disembedding deconstruction

Secure housing is the greatest risk of deconstructive discourse. It is always
possible to rearrange the stones of the house without, in the end, disturbing
its capacity to house. (Wigley, 1994, p. 211)

I need to proceed with caution because, on the one hand, I want to avoid
reducing deconstruction to an architectural de-(con)struction, and, on
the other hand, the "all-too-obvious, all-too-literal link" between architecture and deconstruction "cannot be discarded in the interests of a
more nuanced reading of deconstruction without effacing a critical
dimension of Derrida's work" (Wigley, 1994, p. 207). To begin recovering what has been occluded in the reduction of deconstruction to an
architectural moment of de-construction and dismantlement, it is important to recall Derrida's (1989d, p. 74) insistence that "Deconstruction
is *not* negative, is not nihilistic." It does not mean "destroy or dissolve
or cancel" (Derrida, 1992b, p. 7). Likewise, the come-uppance of deconstruction "is not the void, it is not the gaping and chaotic remainder,
the hiatus of destruction" (Derrida, 1989c, p. 69). Deconstruction is
neither negative nor nihilistic (zeroed/neutralized). Deconstruction is
affirmative, although it is not the positivity that comes about by way of
a double negative (−.− = +), since "even if there is some naïveté, and
irreducible naïveté, to deconstruct does not consist in denouncing or
dissolving naïveté, in the hope of escaping it completely: it would rather
be a certain way of resigning oneself to it and taking account of it"
(Derrida, 1992c, p. 57).

Deconstruction, then, has something to do with a structural/strictural solicitation and a rethinking of inhabitation: "Structures were to de undone, decomposed, desedimented," recalls Derrida (1991a, p. 272). Yet if it were simply the dismantlement of a prefabricated structure into its constituent parts, disclosing how the structure was constructed and maintained, then it would do nothing more than clear the ground and recover the resources for another cycle of (re)construction. Furthermore, de-construction, even if pushed into destruction pure and simple through a certain deregulated death drive, would still be both productive and constructive; its apparent negativity and nihility would do nothing to problematize "the cumulative logic of building (ground-foundation-structure-ornament) that plays such a decisive role in organizing discourse in our culture" (Wigley, 1994, p. 210). De-construction would be little more than the 'terrible labour of the negative,' which Rosen (1987, p. 51) describes as "the posttheistic version of salvation," played out for the profit of an architectural regime of expanded reproduction. This is why transgression, opposition, and resistance so often lead into false exists. "To attempt an exit and a deconstruction without changing terrain, ... by using against the edifice the instruments or stones available in the house, ... one risks ceaselessly confirming, consolidating, *relifting* [*relever*] at an always more certain depth, that which one allegedly deconstructs," warns Derrida (1982a, p. 135). Inasmuch as this workfare regime of expanded reproduction knows how to conserve its losses, and how to invest in and profit from negativity, one could call it a *restricted economy*, a zombified version of Being-towards-death (cf. Derrida, 1993b). The logic of building, like that of modernity, is not so much one of an incremental and progressive accumulation, as one of an insatiable appetite for 'creative destruction' (cf. Berman, 1982; Harvey, 1985a, 1985b). The terms in the matrix of expanded reproduction – destruction, construction, deconstruction, reconstruction – are not opposed, but enchained. They are interdependent and mutually constitutive. Each provides an alibi (elsewhere) for the safe-keeping of the others. So, one should perhaps read deconstruction as (de)construction: "The placing in parentheses of the 'de' ... signifies that one must not hear it ... as a negativity affecting an originary and positive constitution" (Derrida, 1989f, p. 17). Deconstruction affirms. It affirms the (de)constitutive (s)playing out of undecidability, solicitation, and dissemination. And yet, "the negative appearance was and remains much more difficult to efface than is suggested by the grammar of the word (de-), even thought it can designate genealogical restoration [*remonter*] rather than a demolition," cautions Derrida (1991a, p. 272). "That is why this word, at least on its own, has never appeared very satisfactory to me ... and must always be girded by an entire discourse."

Architecture against itself

> Contrary to appearances 'deconstruction' is not an architectural metaphor.
> (Derrida, 1989c, p. 69)

So, if deconstruction should not be confused with the metaphysical and
dialectical hinge that unites and divides the creative destruction of
expanded reproduction – programmatically: construction/de-construc-
tion/re-construction – then what should one make of its 'all-too-obvious'
and 'all-too-literal' architectural significations? Deconstruction necessitates an altogether different modality and experience of building,
dwelling, and thinking (Grosz, 1995a; Krell, 1997; Papadakis, Cooke,
and Benjamin, 1989; Tschumi, 1994; Wigley, 1993). It is no longer
(s)paced out and (s)played out according to the synthesized beat of the
terrible labour of the negative.

> Now the concept of deconstruction itself resembles an architectural meta-
> phor. It is often said to have a negative attitude. Something has been
> constructed, a philosophical system, a tradition, a culture, and along comes
> a de-constructor and destroys it stone by stone, analyses the structure and
> dissolves it. Often enough this is the case. One looks at a system –
> Platonic/Hegelian – and examines how it was built, which keystone, which
> angle of vision supports the authority of the system. It seems to me,
> however, that this is not the essence of deconstruction. It is not simply
> the technique of an architect who knows how to de-construct what has
> been constructed, but a probing which touches upon the technique itself,
> upon the authority of the architectural metaphor and thereby constitutes
> its own architectural rhetoric. (Derrida, 1986c, p. 18)

In Heidegger's (1982, p. 22) approach '*Destruktion*' is "a critical process in which the traditional concepts, which at first must necessarily
be employed, are de-constructed [*kritischer Abbau*] down to the sources
from which they were drawn … Construction in philosophy is necessarily destruction." As I previously argued with respect to destabilizing
jetties, the "forces of 'ruin' are not negative, they participate in the
productive or instituting force of the very thing they seem to be tormenting" (Derrida, 1992c, p. 53). *Destruktion*, as architecture against
itself, is not a negative labouring between one phase of construction
and another, nor is it a collapsing of structures and the abandonment
of building. One has no choice but to work as a transformer, as a
transducer of special affects. So, Derrida employed the neologism '*déconstruction*' to translate Heidegger's *Destruktion* and *Abbau*. From its
send off, then, *déconstruction* is halved together and spliced together
(*X*), and it effects "a perpetual withholding operation" and "a permanent
process of disordering order" (Megill, 1985, p. 271, and Derrida, 1989b,

p. 223, respectively). It picks up on what has been forgotten, dissimulated, and repressed in architectural thought-and-practice (palaeonomy), and renders undecidable what has been set up as inside and outside architecture (dissemination). Consequently, rather than seek out "the basis, the original soil, the ultimate foundation," Derrida (1989c, p. 69) insists on the need to develop "the baseless ground of a 'deconstructive' and affirmative architecture." And "Like the vital bottom integer in a serial, when that goes, the whole serial universe goes up in smoke. It never existed" (Burroughs, 1988, p. 7). The deconstruction of a structure, system or architecture does not regress towards a fundamental particle or a simple origin – such as a ground, a foundation or an ineluctable presence. It releases and affirms solicitation, becoming swept up by that which is set in motion.

Home interiors

It is not for nothing that Derrida makes much of the metaphoric exchanges between the household (*oikos*) and the proper (*oikeios*) so that 'simple and immediate presence' – of Being – becomes refracted through a chain of 'spatial' metaphors modelled on the house. For the metaphysics of presence, the house is the primal shelter; it is the exemplary interior (and one that usually rests upon a traditional notion of sexual difference). By contrast, what is beyond the threshold of the house – the street, the city, the wilderness, the desert, etc. – is figured as exteriority itself, as 'homelessness' writ large. This is a homelessness that under conditions of modernity has come to penetrate the grounds, foundations, and interior of the house itself (cf. Mugerauer, 1994). The house, then, serves as the model for differentiating between home and homelessness, proper and improper, authentic and inauthentic, proximal and distal, familial–familiar and alien, presence and absence, and so forth. But the house is not simply one model amongst others. It is what enables one to think in terms of inside and outside, of interiority and exteriority, and of the properties, proprieties, and privileges that home-ownership confers.

Significantly, Derrida has sought to deconstruct the oppositions that are split off according to the structure of the house by reworking the long-standing antagonism between, *on the one hand*, thinking (as un-mediated self-presence) and speech (its most immediate, spontaneous, and therefore proper expression), and, *on the other hand*, the dangerous supplement of writing, which is suspect largely because it is detached from a singular context and removed from authorial and titular control:

> Uprooted, anonymous, unattached to any house or country, this almost insignificant signifier is at everyone's disposal, can be picked up by both

the competent and the incompetent, by those who understand and know
what to do with it ..., and by those who are completely unconcerned with
it, and who, knowing nothing about it, can inflict all manner of imper-
tinence upon it. (Derrida, 1981b, p. 144)

Writing is a disembedding mechanism, which not only facilitates communication between contexts, and across space and time, but which also
opens the possibility for corruption, perversion, quotation, dissemination, and forgetting. This is why writing is a dangerous supplement, an
ambivalent and undecidable *pharmakon* (remedy, cure, recipe, magic
potion, drug, poison). Writing relieves presence: it aids memory and
memorialization, facilitates circulation and distanciation, and acts as a
stock(piler) for the State, but it also begets an occlusion of presence. In
short: "There is no such thing as a harmless remedy" (Derrida, 1981b,
p. 99). For Plato, writing is an occult and diabolic power, which therefore
should be excluded from the *socius*. Suffice it to say that Derrida's
deconstruction of this dispensation amounts to demonstrating how the
pharmakon is an integral (and therefore disintegral), rather than a dispensable, aspect of the House of Being. The supposed supplemental and
disintegrative qualities of writing – as the exemplary and archetypal form
of exteriority – turn out to go 'all the way down' into speech, thinking,
and presence themselves. Such is the aporetic basis for the neo-Platonic
folly of the dispossession of those qualities most intimately bound to
place by new forms of spatialization and temporalization. The taking
place of space is always already. Place never comes to be. It is perpetually
in process, endlessly other than what it will have been.

Despite appearances, then, a supplement is not simply an add-on,
like a superfluous appendage. It is also the addition of what is *missing*
in the original. A supplement remedies a deficiency in the original. It
is therefore a necessary and essential element without which the original
would remain incomplete and lacking. In short, the supplement can
only be added because the original – whose historical and conceptual
priority must now be placed in question and under erasure (X) –
anticipates, expects, and awaits its arrival. The original solicits its supplement: punctum as punter. So, the suppletion that makes repetition
necessary does not return a whole 'one' – as origin, identity, presence,
etc. – ; it returns the disturbing portion (e.g. holes, rifts, gaps, and
lacunae) that punt what appears fully given and wholly integrated outside
of itself: "If it is nothing, it's a nothing which *counts*, which in my view
counts a lot" (Derrida, 1992c, p. 73). Suppletion activates the differentials that are invariably occluded in the tightly knit and seemingly
seamless folds of the same. Such are the cancerous difference-producing
repetitions that endless swerve away from the Hell of the Same. There
is therefore an iterative, disseminative, and undecidable fissure in the

region of the one; there is a (w)hole in the O zone. And so "The origin is still lacking at the beginning," says Hollier (1989, p. 5). Indeed, it is the eternal recurrence of this 'spectral effect' that has led Derrida to conjure a 'logic of the ghost,' which he dubs 'hauntology,' in order to solicit and disturb the 'baseless ground' of ontology. Presence is what deconstructs. "If ... tangible certainty and solidity corresponds to ontology, then ... how to describe what literally undermines it and shakes our belief?" asks Jameson (1995, p. 86).

> Derrida's mocking answer – hauntology – is a ghostly echo if there ever was one, ... which promises nothing tangible in return; on which you cannot build; which cannot even be counted on to materialize when you want it to ... all it says ... is that the living present is scarcely as self-sufficient as it claims to be; that we would do well not to count on its density and solidity.

Hence Derrida's (1986b, p. 210) diabolical challenge to artisans of spatial science: "Regard the holes if you can."

Accordingly, with respect to the habitual architecture of the metaphysics of presence, or of the domesticity of the proper, deconstruction

> identifies structural flaws, cracks in the construction that have been systematically disguised, not in order to collapse those structures but, on the contrary, to demonstrate the extent to which the structures depend on both these flaws and the way that they are disguised. That is, it identifies the structural role of what traditional philosophy would identify as structural flaws and, in so doing, displaces rather than dismantles that philosophy. (Wigley, 1994, p. 207)

These 'structural cracks' – which cut across everything and all the way down, hence their abyssal and fractal quality – are not imperfections or discrepancies that could be summed up, accounted for, and resolved. They are undecidables rather than contradictions. The structure is irreducibly disadjusted and out of joint. The series of oppositions modelled on the house is therefore far from secure since it rests on a forced stabilization of the originary solicitation. When one *affirms* such a solicitation everything is (once again) set in motion.

> It is not enough to say that writing is conceived out of this or that series of oppositions. Plato thinks of writing, and tries to comprehend it, to dominate it, on the basis of *opposition* as such. In order for these contrary values (good/evil, true/false, essence/appearance, inside/outside, etc.) to be in opposition, each of the terms must be simply *external* to the other, which means that one of these oppositions (the opposition between inside and outside) must already be accredited as the matrix of all possible opposition. And one of the elements of the system (or of the series) must

also stand as the very possibility of systematicity or seriality in general. And if one got to thinking that something like the *pharmakon* – or writing – far from being governed by these oppositions, opens up their very possibility without letting itself be comprehended by them; if one got to thinking that it can only be out of something like writing – or the *pharmakon* – that the strange difference between inside and outside can spring; if, consequently, one got to thinking that writing as a *pharmakon* cannot simply be assigned a site within what it situates, cannot be subsumed under concepts whose contours it draws, leaves only its ghost to a logic that can only seek to govern it insofar as logic arises from it – one would then have to *bend* [*plier*] into strange contortions what could no longer even simply be called logic or discourse. (Derrida, 1981b, p. 103)

The *pharmakon*'s ambivalence constitutes the milieu in which forces are polarized, in which opposites are opposed. It illustrates how "At a certain place in the system, one of the elements of the system ... no longer knows what it should do. More precisely it knows that it must do contradictory and incompatible things," writes Derrida (1992a, p. 7). "Contradicting or running counter to itself, this double obligation thus risks paralyzing, diverting or jeopardizing the successful conclusion of the ceremony."

As a double agent and duplicitous architect, deconstruction traces the reversible torque of a Möbius spiralling that turns, folds, and ploughs the inside into the outside, and the outside into the inside. The borders of the whole are neither closed nor open: "if the whole is not giveable, it is because it is the Open, and because its nature is to change constantly, or to give rise to something new" (Deleuze, 1986, p. 9). Such is the double invagination of thresholds and limits, of framing and embedment, and of intervals and (w)holes.

Every model of classical reading is exceeded there at some point, precisely at the point where it attaches to the inside of the series – it being understood that this excess is not a *simple* exit *out* of the series, since that would obviously fall under one of the categories of the series. The excess – but can we still call it that? – is only a *certain* displacement of the series. And a certain *folding back* [*repli*] ... of opposition within the series, or even within its dialectic. (Derrida, 1981b, p. 104)

As an aphoristic slogan, then, "*there is nothing outside the text* [*il n'y a pas de hors-texte*]" (Derrida, 1976, p. 158) neatly blocks any naive appeal to the domestic scenes of metaphysics and dialectics. For as Derrida (1977, p. 198) reminds us: "The context is always already *in* the place and not merely *around* it." The haemorrhagic drift of the general text cannot be contained. Yet one should add that there is nothing inside the general text either. For if one is to broach a text it must have an edge. But this limit, beyond which the textuality of the text would not run, is precisely what a text in general can never possess. Thus, the limit between text and context, and between inside and outside, (is what) deconstructs; the threshold "is shown to turn itself inside out" (Llewelyn, 1986, p. xiii). So:

> In a certain sense it is true to say that 'deconstruction' is still in metaphysics. But we must remember that if we are indeed *inside* metaphysics, we are not inside it as we might be *inside* a box or a milieu. We are still *in* metaphysics in the special sense that we are *in* a determinate language. Consequently, the idea that we might be able to get outside of metaphysics has always struck me as naive. So that when I refer to the 'closure' (*clôture*) of metaphysics, I insist that it is not a question of considering metaphysics as a circle with a limit or simple boundary. And as soon as we acknowledge that the limit-boundary of metaphysics is divisible, the logical rapport between inside and outside is no longer simple. Accordingly, we cannot really say that we are 'locked into' or 'condemned to' metaphysics, for we are, strictly speaking, neither inside nor outside. (Derrida, 1984c, p. 111)

Hereinafter, "the outside is the inside" and vice versa (Derrida, 1981b, p. 44). The threshold is halved together, criss-crossed, twisted, and contorted by undecidable transportations (X). Such is the polymorphous perversion and metamorphotic deformation of a Möbius strip. The deconstructive chiasmus (X) is not simply a 'crossing out' of the threshold since it recalls the two-fold tripping, snagging, and ravelling of deconstruction as a palaeonomic reversal and a disseminating reinscription. In addition, the four seriffed barbs hook into the dissimulated frame, the 'empty square.' Moreover, the point of intersection and bifurcation between the two strokes of the chiasmus – the chiasma – is not simply the centre of a quadrangular surface or the apex of a pyramidic structure; it is not simply an anchorage point for presence, Being, and existence. Not only may the bisection be an optical illusion effected from a certain point of view, but this point also alludes to the vanishing point of perspectival representation, which thereby *displaces* the centre and command post 'along the angle of a certain re-folding' and disjointure. To be 'in' the frame recalls the Old English *in, inn*, as an adverb with verbs of motion, just as to be 'in' the tradition is in a certain sense to set it in motion. In short, "writing on the frame" engenders "a certain repeated dislocation, a regulated, irrepressible dislocation, which makes the frame in general crack, undoes it at the corners in its quoins and joints" (Derrida, 1987b, p. 73). The vanishing point of intersection is the point that flees visual control. Through "the absolute withdrawal of an invisible center or command post," adds Derrida (1993a, pp. 3–4), "a secret power ensures from a distance a kind of synergy. It coordinates the possibilities of seeing, touching, and moving." Accordingly, the chiasmus (X) also indicates that the centre, the structure, and the frame are all out of joint: "The center is, paradoxically, *within* the structure and *outside it*. The center is at the center of the totality, and yet, since the center does not belong to the totality (is not part of the totality), the totality *has its center elsewhere*" (Derrida, 1988d, p. 109).

To deconstruct a structure, then, "is to disclose how it functions as desire, as a search for presence and fulfilment which is interminably deferred" (Derrida, 1984c, p. 126). Yet this desire does not emanate from the invisible centre or the panoptical command post. It comes from a dissimulated distance, from the four corners of an open frame, into which the four points of the chiasmus withdraw. Thus, the barbs of deconstruction and dissemination are not so much oriented towards the interiority of the structure, as they are directed towards its margins, edges, and quoins. So:

> One first locates, in an architectonics ... the 'neglected corners' and the '*defective* cornerstones,' that which, from the outset, threatens the coherence and the internal order of the construction ... The best spot for efficiently inserting the deconstructive lever is a cornerstone. There may be other analogous places but this one derives its privilege from the fact that it is indispensable to the completeness of the edifice. A condition of erection, holding up the walls of an established edifice, it also can be said to maintain it, to contain it, and to be tantamount to the *generality* of the architectonic system, 'of the entire system.' (Derrida, 1986a, p. 72)

Deconstruction, then, is not hinged between two phases of construction: it is folded into itself. Deconstruction is set in motion: it voyages in place and thereby declines settling into position. "And you can take this as a rule," writes Derrida (1989d, p. 75), "that each time Deconstruction speaks through a single voice, it's wrong, it is not 'Deconstruction' any more." Or again: "Duplicity, the being-double ..., cannot be added up as a 1 + 2, but on the contrary hollows itself out in an infinite abyss" (Derrida, 1992a, p. 8). Once again we are brought to the need for a re-spatialization of numbers.

Two into three – oppositional and integral illusions

> Metaphysics, from its inception, leans toward its decline, tends to fallibility, begins in decline, as decline. A pseudo-beginning, the stalling of the startled start. (Berezdivin, 1987, pp. 45–50)

The integrity of a whole one that is simply given in and of itself has been found unbecoming and wanting. But what about those discourses that seem to take account of a certain criss-crossing of thresholds, such as the metaphysical rule of two (with its agonistic oppositions) and the dialectical rule of three (with its sublatable contradictions)? To what extent can the matrix of opposition and the movement of contradiction integrate the accursed share and disturbed portion of undecidability, dissemination, and solicitation? Through a fuller deconstruction of the apparent integrity of metaphysical opposition and dialectical contradiction I will hope to demonstrate the 'harsh law of space' by which such perturbation and destabilization escape domestication. In its wake comes "the desire to escape the combinatory itself, to invent incalculable choreographies" (Derrida, 1995a, p. 108). For despite the best efforts of the dialectic to set what is in motion to work – for example, through the terrible labour of the negative – other movements are taking place.

Take two

Whereas the metaphysical imaginary posits *difference as versus*, the dialectical imaginary posits *difference as contradiction*. The metaphysical imaginary considers differences – such as those between identity and difference, presence and absence, essence and appearance, and truth and error – to be always already constituted and irreducible. It is based on a system of binary oppositions that are assumed to be pre-given, clear-cut, and therefore precluding of any intermediary terms. Moreover, every metaphysical opposition implies not merely the face to face of mutually exclusive terms, but "a hierarchy and an order of subordination" (Derrida, 1982a, p. 329). There will always be at least two (op)positions, providing the diacritical resources for discussions, controversies, and traditions. Yet as I have sought to demonstrate, there remains "an undecidability over what is inside and what is outside, over thresholds" (Llewelyn, 1986, p. xi). The solicitations of palaeonomy, undecidability, and dissemination cannot be contained within the matrix of an oppositional structure. However, this setting in motion does not necessarily result in a collapse of the purportedly rigid spatialization.

> Every concept that lays claim to any rigour whatsoever implies the alternative 'all or nothing.' ... To this oppositional logic ... I oppose nothing, least of all a logic of *approximation* [*à peu près*], a simple empiricism of difference in degree; rather I add a supplementary complication that calls for other concepts, for other thoughts beyond the concept and another form of 'general theory', or rather another discourse, another 'logic' that accounts for the impossibility of concluding such a 'general theory'. (Derrida, 1988a, pp. 116–17)

This logic can be 'other' to the point of overturning a good many habits and comforts. It can lead us to complicate – distinctly – the logic of binary opposition, and to a *certain use* of the value of distinction attached to it ... But that leads neither to 'illogic' nor to 'indistinction' nor to 'indeterminacy.' (Derrida, 1988a, pp. 126–7)

By invoking an 'other' logic to that of binary opposition, Derrida has brought the discussion around to a place that is very close to the 'enveloping resources' of Hegelianism. Here, the danger would not only be that the deconstructive solicitation might be domesticated within the closed architecture of the house (cf. Marden, 1992; Strohmayer and Hannah, 1992), but also that its affirmative force might be swept up by the terrible labour of the negative and turned into a moment of creative destruction, "a noisy declaration of the antithesis" (Derrida, 1991a, p. 370). Little wonder, then, that Derrida should orient deconstruction and dissemination towards an effective intervention in the restricted economy of Hegelianism, which has arguably the most sophisticated shock absorbers for dampening the impact of what sets it in motion (cf. Žižek, 1991).

Dialectical machinations

> We will never be finished with the reading and rereading of Hegel, and, in a certain way, I do nothing other than explain myself on this point. (Derrida, 1981a, p. 77)

> Everything is metamorphosed into its inverse in order to be perpetuated in its purged form. (Baudrillard, 1983b, p. 37)

If deconstruction strives to foster another 'logic' that accounts for the impossibility of concluding a 'general theory' there is nevertheless a 'logic' dead set on forcing such a conclusion: dialectics. Unlike the metaphysical imaginary, the dialectical imaginary does not content itself with the irreducibility of binary opposition. These oppositions are not rejected by dialectics; they are enclosed, swallowed, and consumed by it. Rather than conceiving of difference as an irreducible meeting of opposing forces, Hegelianism conceives of difference as contradiction, thereby opening it up to the possibility of a resolution in a synthetic third term. For the dialectician, one cannot decide between the contradictory positions because both turn out to be inadequate and malformed when they are allowed to stand alone – motionlessly – as a thesis and antithesis, a position and its contrary. In striving for a resolution of contradiction – and recall that to resolve, from the Latin *resolvere resolut*, is to unfasten again and to release back into circulation – the Hegelian dialectic is not static, but dynamic: it is always already set in motion. Hence Derrida's difficulty in distinguishing between deconstruction and

dialectics, and his recourse to duplicitous strategies and stratagems. For
the dialectician, the momentary resolution of stabilized oppositions
arrested in the name of the Law will on reflection beget further contradictions and higher resolutions *ad infinitum*. In retrospect, there is always
some 'excess' that has not been properly taken into account. This excess,
which accompanies every position and negation like an uncanny shadow,
is the driving force of sublation. It necessitates the thirst for a total
resolution of contradiction: for it to be wholly set in motion. This drive
to integrate all excess – to permit of no outside – is what disturbs: it
disturbs those who would wish to integrate all, setting them in motion;
it disturbs those who would wish to affirm otherness, setting them in
motion; and it disturbs these latter since the drive to integration haunts
their own resolve. Even though terms are irreducibly fractured and set
on edge, the dialectical helices remain dominated by a thirst for integrity.
Such is its violence. It will never let alterity and undecidability be. "This
letting beyond essence, 'more passive than passivity,' hear it as the most
provocative thought today," maintains Derrida (1991a, p. 424).

By including dispersal and polysemy within the life of the concept,
by making dis-semenation work to the profit of the generative idea,
dialectics takes account of (i.e. excludes) all loss, all chance productivity,
and every aneconomic gesture. So, "negativity must be counted twice,"
insists Žižek (1991, p. 3) in his own quadratic enclosure of the dialectic.
This double negative should not be confused with the other double
negative (the sublating negation of the negation). The first double negative comes between the original positivity and its negation (whereupon
this latter becomes the third, rather than the second, term in the series).
To negate the original position, engendering its external opposite and
contrary term one must also negate the 'inner negation' by which the
original position moves towards its own essential form. Before the facing
off of contradictory forces, the original position purges itself. Žižek
gives the example of capitalism-in-itself (position) and capitalism-as-
opposed-to-communism (negation), between which is capitalism-
negated-from-within: Fascism. This supplementary negation prior to
the negation of opposition is supposed to mop up any 'excess' that may
be swilling around in the system in order to pre-empt and foreclose
the possibility of discerning a non-dialecticizable excess that might blow
the dialectic apart. Were this successful there would no longer be room
for a deconstructive experience.

Whether threefold or fourfold, the dialectic is driven by a desire for
resolving a generalized motility that would integrate all excess. In so
doing it unfolds according to the beat of negation, and is expressed
through the transducing plasticity of that

term that comes in order to *aufheben*, to deny while raising up, while idealizing, while sublimating into an anamnesic interiority (*Errinnerung*), while *interning* difference in self-presence ... [Hegelianism] determines difference as contradiction only in order to resolve it, to interiorize it, to lift it up (according to the syllogist process of speculative dialectics) into the self-presence of an onto–theological or onto–teleological synthesis. (Derrida, 1981a, p. 44)

Consequently, the determination of difference as opposition/contradiction is not at all to fix two distinct, self-sufficient, and immutable terms in a polarized antagonism. Difference as opposition/contradiction is destined and designed for the erasure – which should not be confused with the *seriasure* – of difference. "The dialectical opposition neutralizes or supersedes ... the difference," says Derrida (1995a, p. 101). "However, according to a surreptitious operation that must be flushed out, one ensures ... mastery under the cover of neutralization every time." The dialectical result, then, is not fashioned through a symmetrical and balanced treatment of contradictory positions. Its resolutions do not come to rest in the middle like a consensus or compromise. Each resolution refracts one force through the transformative medium of another. The resolve of the dialectic is to drive towards totality through an helical negativity. It is processive and expansive. The dialectic amounts to more than merely seeing "a world in a grain of sand," a granularity through which "everything hangs together with everything else" (Olsson, 1991, p. 158). The Hegelian dialectic of *Aufhebung* is not microscopy or the philosophical version of Michelangelo Antonioni's seminal film, *Blow Up* (1966). "What makes [a] logic specifically dialectical," argues Castree (1996, p. 351), "is that it is a logic of internal contradiction. What makes [a] logic systematic is that the insufficiency of each ... form *necessarily* propels the analysis forward to seek more sufficient forms that deal with the prior contradictions." On this account, both the specificity and the systematicity of the dialectic rest on a distinction between an interiority that is contradicted to the core (fractured, fractal) and an exteriority into which this schizoid interiority is driven. The outside *relieves* the inside: it is the open whole within which the strains engendered in the material by an arbitrary limitation and a partial circumscription may find redress and resolution. Whether idealist or materialist in complexion, it is as if the dialectic were propelling itself forward by creating a vacuum in front of itself. Like a jet-engine, the dialectic sucks itself off. It seduces and solicits itself. Dialectical thought does not suffer from distension. It does not swell up from internal pressure. To the contrary, it is drawn towards totality (cf. Arthur, 1993; Ollman, 1993). This is why both Baudrillard's art of seduction and Deleuze's 'schizo stroll' risk falling back under the sway of the dialectical resolve for integration. Perhaps the schizoid and nomadic taste for adestination and the deconstructive liking for suspension will suffice to frustrate this sweeping up operation. One will have to wait and see.

Now, not only does the German *Aufhebung* "unite the affirmative *raise* with the negative *remove*, as does Latin *tollere*, but the affirmation already contains the negation: to raise is to preserve (*erhalten*), and 'in order to preserve it, something is removed from its immediacy and so from an existence which is open to external influences' (Hegel)" (Lyotard, 1988a, p. 92). Like sponging, to *aufheben* is to raise up, subl(im)ate, and resolve whilst both cancelling and maintaining the difference: one takes the difference into the fabric of the same. This double movement of over-coming and preservation is achieved through a negation of a negation, which is the third moment of a trimerous helix. However, whereas for classical logic the negation of a negation would simply return one to the original position (A = not non-A), the dialectical negation of the negation does not (A ≠ not non-A). To the contrary, the dialectic evolves towards a more inclusive synthesis. The discrepancy turns on whether each position is a full and stable one – something to which one *could* return – , and whether the balance of forces between positions – such as a thesis and its antithesis – is equitable, symmetrical, and reversible.

It should now be clear why Derrida refers to the Hegelian dialectic of *Aufhebung* as 'discourse itself,' since it engulfs and digests all oppo-sitions, contradictions, and controversies; it appropriates, introjects, and consumes not only the outside, the exteriority, and the other, but also the limits, boundaries, and partitions that have been erected between the one and the other. As soon as one employs (op)positions in a dialectical manner, then one has always already committed difference to cancellation and an expansive homogenization. Little wonder, then, that Bataille and Sartre, like Deleuze and Derrida, should caution against acquiring a taste for 'digestive philosophy.' Yet "since *one must* eat," the imperative is "*how* for goodness sake should one *eat well?*" (Derrida, 1991c, p. 115; cf. Derrida, 1989a). This is why deconstruction requires a double strategy and a double agency.

So, the shadow of Hegel poses serious problems for any thinker of anomie, infraction, and transgression, of difference, otherness, and al-terity. This is because the *Aufhebung* of digestive philosophy admits of no 'outside.' The outside is only the outside *of* the inside. Indeed, philosophy has taken as its object its own limit and outside. To that extent, terms such as 'outside,' 'limit,' 'heterogeneity,' 'difference,' 'otherness,' and 'alterity' can never serve as the means through which philosophy's border could be overrun and overflowed. This overexten-sion is its object, its un-*thought*, and its *Ur*-thought. "Philosophy has always insisted upon this: thinking its other. Its other: that which limits it, and from which it derives its essence, its definition, its production." "*To insist* upon thinking *its other* ... In thinking it *as such*, in recognizing it, one misses it. One reappropriates it for oneself, one disposes of it, one misses it, or rather one misses (the) missing (of) it, which, as concerns the other, always amounts to the same" (Derrida, 1982a, pp. x and xi–xii, respectively).

This is why digestive philosophy wields an apparatus of capture that is finely attuned to the task of interning the 'outside' and the 'other' within its spheres of influence, jurisdiction, and control. For whatever philosophy places 'outside' and thereby disavows, this 'outside' is still 'inside' the gnathic reach of philosophy, since philosophy places it 'outside,' and expels it from the domestic interior of the proper. Hereinafter, the outside belongs to the inside, although the House of Being is haunted by the tomb (*oikésis*) of the repressed and its pyramid (*X*) (cf. Dooley, 1996; Llewelyn, 1986). Little wonder, then, that Derrida should caution against the "immense enveloping resources of Hegelianism," which "regularly change transgressions into 'false exits'" (Derrida, 1978, p. 251 and Derrida, 1982a, p. 135, respectively). Such an appropriating reduction is always already in place from the moment that philosophy considers the other to be *its* other, the outside to be *its* outside, and the limit to be *its* limit: "the general scheme is *its*. That's why I would insist on another dimension, that is philosophy and another which cannot be *its* other, which resists philosophy as totally heterogeneous and, resisting philosophy, provokes philosophy into new moves, a new space in which philosophy does not recognize itself" (Derrida, 1989b, p. 215).

Like the dialectic, deconstruction counters the dominant metaphor of conceptualization – grasping and holding (*Begriff*) – by releasing the grip of a retaining context. But whereas the dialectic holds onto this release (often teleologically), deconstruction attempts to release such a resolve. As Burroughs (1988) reminds us: the hardest thing is learning how to let go – not to fall, but to become swept up. "The principles of dialectical enquiry ... *should* generate a perpetual state of motion in our concepts and our thoughts," suggests Harvey (1995, p. 11) moments before being seized by a thirst for permanency and rigidity. Unlike metaphysics and dialectics, which are locked onto position (such as being drawn into a matrix of given possibilities or being directed towards an infinitely receding horizon), deconstruction risks *not holding (onto) a position*; "the very desire for a thesis needs to be attacked," says Megill (1985, p. 285). "It is in his failure to 'state a truth,' to 'get to the point' – his failure to write the book that he is interminably prefacing – that Derrida evades the maw of the dialectic" (Megill, 1985, pp. 272–3). Hereinafter: "Reading ... is free to play" (Schrift, 1990a, p. 109). It embodies an irreducible degree of dislocation, disadjustment, and disjointure. In the wake of our resolve as would-be web-masters comes the driftwork of dissemination, schizoanalysis, and

polymorphous perversion. Beyond the power of the metaphysical two
(2^n) and the dialectical three (3^n) comes the deforming force of the
innumerable number: the fourth element as accursed share. Nevertheless, it still may be

> possible to recognize a certain serial law in these points of indefinite
> pivoting: they mark the spots of what can never be mediated, mastered,
> sublated, or dialecticized through any *Erinnerung* or *Aufhebung* ... Insofar
> as the text depends upon them, *bends* to them, it thus plays a *double scene*
> upon a double stage. It operates in two absolutely different places at once,
> even if they are only separated by a veil, which is both traversed and not
> traversed, *inter*-sected. (Derrida, 1981b, p. 221)

Becoming-animal

> Who is ignorant of the fact that wolves travel in packs? Only Freud. Every
> child knows it. Not Freud. (Deleuze and Guattari, 1988, p. 28)

Deconstructive duplicity does not oppose the digestive bent of dialectics.
Instead, it suspends its resolve in manifold undecidability. Like schizoanalysis, deconstruction does not follow Freud in his 'reductive glee'
at subtracting the pack from the only number that counts: one and one
and one etc. (e.g. mum and dad and me). For Freud "it is always a
question of bringing back the unity or identity of the person or allegedly
lost object ... The wolves will have to be purged of their multiplicity."
In stark contrast to the occlusive violence of individuation, Derrida and
Deleuze return these stragglers and loners to the lycanthropic packs
from whence they came. They never stop drawing our attention to the
fact that the smallest element is the manifold (X) and not the period
(.). It is all the stranger, then, that Deleuze should so gleefully reduce
Hegel to a *single* figure – the master-thinker of identity – and dialectics
to a *single* movement – the unremitting sublation of difference. By
reducing Hegel-the-manifold-pack-animal to *only one* Hegel, "Doesn't
Hegel become the 'bow-wow' of contemporary philosophers, the ab-
horred victim of the pack of the thinkers of difference, and their absolute
enemy?" (Malabou, 1996, p. 117). Hegel is excluded from the pack so
that he may act as a limit or running border against which the pack can
constitute itself, precisely, as a variable pack. For the sake of consistency
even Hegel must be allowed to 'become-animal.' Even the master-thinker
of identity runs with a pack and is open to difference-producing repetitions. Even Hegel stutters (cf. Deleuze, 1994a; Deleuze and Guattari,
1986). In this regard, it is perhaps Derrida who has done most to maintain
Hegel as part of the pack.

No more than any other, the Hegelian text is not made of a piece. While respecting its faultless coherence, one can decompose its strata and show that it *interprets itself*: each proposition is an interpretation submitted to an interpretative decision ... In interpreting negativity as labor, in betting on discourse, meaning, history, etc., Hegel has bet against play, against chance. He has blinded himself to the possibility of his own bet, to the fact that the conscientious suspension of play ... was itself a phase of play ... Since no logic governs, henceforth, the meaning of interpretation, because logic is an interpretation, Hegel's own interpretations can be reinterpreted – against him ... Reinterpretation is a simulated repetition of Hegelian discourse. In the course of this repetition a barely perceptible displacement disjoints all the articulations and penetrates all the points welded together. A trembling spreads out which then makes the entire old shell crack. (Derrida, 1978, p. 260)

Never is there only one Hegel. The familiar and the familial become (again) a teeming milieu of undecidability, iterability, and dissemination, of experimentation, invention, and drift. Even Hegel expresses polymorphous perversity, although it invariably manifests itself through 'secret discharges' (Derrida, 1986b; cf. Deleuze, 1977a). Likewise with the case of the pack-Plato, from whom many have forcibly extracted the solitary figure of Plato along with a secure corpus: Platonism.

Platonism would mean ... the thesis or the theme one has extracted by artifice, misprision, and abstraction from the text, torn out of the written fiction of 'Plato.' Once this abstraction has been supercharged and deployed, it will be extended over all the folds of the text, of its ruses, overdeterminations, and reverses, which the abstraction will come to cover up and dissimulate ... but this effect is always turned back against the text ... The forces that are thus inhibited continue to maintain a certain disorder, some potential incoherence, and some heterogeneity in the organization of the theses. They introduce parasitism into it, and clandestinity, ventriloquism, and, above all, a general tone of denial. (Derrida, 1995b, pp. 119–21)

Folding is what gives and takes consistency: the twofold of metaphysics, the threefold of dialectics, and the fourfold of deconstruction. This is why the '*dé-*' of *déconstruction* and *désistance* is not simply negative or nihilistic. It is by way of the re-fold that the fourth side of the dialectic comes into play. It comes into play not through negativity, but through affirmation. By opening the dialectical triangle to its fourth side it gets a chance to escape from itself along a multifarious line of flight. "Since it is a certain *sliding* that is in question ... what must be found, no less than the word, is the point, the *place in the pattern* at which a word drawn from the old language will start ... to slide and make the entire discourse slide" (Derrida, 1978, pp. 263–4). Accordingly:

> It has been necessary to analyze, to set to work, ... certain marks ... that by *analogy* (I underline) I have called undecidables, that is, unities of simulacrum ... that can no longer be included within philosophical (binary) opposition, but which, however, inhabit philosophical opposition, resisting and disorganizing it, *without ever* constituting a third term, without ever leaving room for a solution in the form of speculative dialectics. (Derrida, 1981a, p. 42)

This process of sliding and suspension, which frustrates the integrating drive of metaphysics and dialectics, is what Derrida calls dissemination. "Dissemination *displaces* the three of ontotheology along the angle of a certain re-folding [*re-ploiement*]," says Derrida (1981b, p. 25). "A crisis of *versus*: these marks can no longer be summed up or 'decided' according to the two of binary oppositions nor sublated into the three of speculative dialectics ... They 'add' a fourth term the more or the less." Such is the fourth as a disturbed and disturbing element. It is not an integer – least of all the place of non–sublatable excess – or a facilitator of integration, but a carrier of the innumerable and the incalculable: the more or the less.

> Dissemination endlessly opens up a *snag* in writing that can no longer be mended, a spot where neither meaning, however plural, nor *any form of presence* can pin/pen down [*agrapher*] the trace. Dissemination treats – doctors – that *point* where the movement of signification would regularly come to *tie down* the play of the trace, thus producing (a) history. The security of each point arrested in the name of the law is hence blown up. (Derrida, 1981b, p. 26)

Having given due consideration to the 'almost absolute proximity' of the setting in motion of deconstruction and the setting in motion of dialectics, I want briefly to pick up on the movement of deconstruction itself. This will provide a suitable context for the origami that is to come in the final chapter.

The choreography of deconstruction

> The deconstructive dance is improvisational, its movement is 'abstract,' offering variations on the 'original' choreography, often transformed to such an extent that the audience finds it difficult to recognize what dance is being performed. Yet, for all its strangeness ... [one] gets the sense that this new version *fits*. (Schrift, 1990a, p. 118)

One of the characteristic features of Derrida's style has been its eschewal of a general theoretical metalanguage. "There will be no 'upshot'" warns Rorty (1989, p. 130) "– nothing to carry away ... once one has finished reading it." In other words, there is no 'portable Derrida' that could be routinely whipped out and applied from context to context. One is compelled to engage in improvization and experimentation (cf. Brannigan, Robbins, and Wolfreys, 1996; *Imprimatur*, 1996). Nevertheless, the Derridean style is not without a certain regularity of step, although just as dissemination entails the risk of not holding (onto) a position, deconstruction risks not taking a step (*pas, ne pas*). It risks losing its t(h)read and footing in a simulacrum of movement; it opens itself – through undecidability, iterability, and dissemination – to adestination and *désistance* (Derrida, 1987a, 1989f). Hereinafter, "I abandon this reading to you," writes Derrida (1988c, p. 25): "polysemia or even dissemination drags it far from any shore, preventing what you call an event from ever arriving. Let the net float, the infinitely tortuous play of knots and links which catches this sentence in its drawing."

Quite simply, "if there is a problem about application it is not because deconstruction is too pure to be applied; it is because it is always already applied" (Culler, 1988, p. 140). Moreover, Derrida (1990, p. 85) insists that "Deconstruction is neither a theory nor a philosophy. It is neither a school nor a method. It is not even a discourse, nor an act, nor a practice." For Derrida, deconstruction is an *event*. It does not consist in anything. It has a certain *désistance* that does not so much negate a stance, as uproot the whole series of stances, standings, and stanzas. "Read in the gap, it never comes to be" (Derrida, 1981b, p. 353).

Where to begin a chor(e)ography of deconstruction? "I remember having looked to see if the word 'deconstruction' ... was good French," recalls Derrida (1991a, p. 271). "I found it in the *Littré*: The grammatical, linguistic, or rhetorical senses [*portées*] were found bound up with a 'mechanical' sense [*portée machinique*]." Perhaps unsurprisingly, then, it is this mechanical sense that has provided the most popular steps for performing deconstruction. These steps move to the beat of 'reversal and reinscription' and of 'extracting, grafting, and extending.' It provides for a kind of automotive dance movement (cf. Schwartz, 1992). "I am seeking the good metaphor for the operation I pursue here," says Derrida (1986b, p. 204). "I would like to describe my gesture, the posture of my body behind this machine ... a sort of dredging machine."

Accordingly, the most common operationalization of deconstruction is in terms of a deceptively simple programme. Take the circuitry of some ready-made oppositions, whether metaphysical (valvular) or dialectical (transistorized) in organization, and perform two subroutines on them: a reversal and a reinscription. Whilst the *reversal* of polarity amounts to a transvaluation of established values, such that one inverts the given dissymmetry of folded force stabilized in the hierarchical arrangement of terms, the *reinscription* of terms amounts to a full-blown short circuit. In electronics, there is a circuit if a conductor connects two points of potential difference. This is shorted when either the two points are placed in direct contact or when they are joined by another conductor of much lower resistance. What the two subroutines of reversal and reinscription amount to is an effective shorting of metaphysics and dialectics. It demonstrates how each 'point' is criss-crossed by other 'points,' and that the closed, insular, and integrated circuitry of any particular (con)text is similarly criss-crossed by the superconductivity of other (no less deconstructable) circuits.

Programmatically, then,

> we proceed: (1) to the extraction of a reduced predicative trait that is held in reserve, limited in a given conceptual structure (limited for motivations and relations of force to be analyzed), *named X*; (2) to the de-limitation, the grafting and regulated extension of the extracted predicate, the name X being maintained as a kind of *lever of intervention*, in order to maintain a grasp on the previous organization, which is to be transformed effectively. Therefore, extraction, graft, extension: you know that this is what I call, according to the process I have just described, *writing*. (Derrida, 1981a, p. 71)

This two-fold strategy leaves a dislocating trace in an apparently stabilized context by extracting, grafting, and extending the deforming force of all of those traits that have been repressed by the current arrangement of folded forces. Deconstruction "is not *neutral*. It *intervenes*," and so one must always "underline the necessity of reinscription rather than denial" (Derrida, 1981a, pp. 93 and 94, respectively). An effective intervention in the metaphysical and dialectical reserve cannot be a mere inversion or reversal since this would leave the oppositional *structure* of reactive forces intact. This is why deconstruction seeks a general disjointure and displacement of the system: "Let us space," says Derrida (1986b, p. 75). Thus, the two subroutines or steps of deconstruction – reversal and reinscription – are dissymmetrical. Whilst reversal remains within the polarized circuitry of the restricted economy, reinscription attempts a breakthrough into the general economy without reserve. Furthermore, the two steps are not successive, but simultaneous. On the basis of dissymmetry and simultaneity, Derrida deploys the pictogram '*X*' to diagram how deconstruction is halved together: this 'in-the-same-stroke' or '*du-même-coup*' of the two contrary operations suspends the would-be cutting through to a decision in the iterable and solicitous (s)play of the undecidable. The twofold force of deconstruction (fold, unfold; step, no step) inscribes a strategic twist into the logic of reversal and disarrangement. It intervenes within the regulated matrix of apparently static and mobile terms in order to thwart their gearing as a restoration of the place of the proper and of essence (Haar, 1992). "What this does destroy is a *facade of unity*, a certain presumption about what a text is, or should be helped to be," notes Wood (1990, p. 58). "But equally it could be said to *bring to life* in the text the forces active in its construction. The text ceases to be a thing containing a meaning, but becomes (again) a struggle between order and chaos, a desperate attempt to exchange its own materiality for a transparency."

In this way, deconstruction plays a vital part in prizing open the insulated and integrated circuits of innumerable contexts governed by regimes of forced stabilization. It is less a way of reading a (con)text, than one of writing (on) a (borderless) (con)text. Such is the drift from representation to transformation. Once again the notion of a cancerous overextension comes to mind.

Through the (s)playing out of deconstruction and dissemination in this chapter it should have been apparent that spatial science requires a chor(e)ography irreducible to points, identities, and presence. As I will try to demonstrate in the final chapter, this other chor(e)ography is exemplified in the art of folding, unfolding, and refolding. On this basis pointillism gives way to origami, and schizoanalysis becomes rhizomatic. From an initial setting in motion of a controlling context, then, I have arrived at what Derrida (1992c, p. 45) aptly calls the "play of foldings." I could pursue this further via Derrida, but I have found the work of Deleuze and Guattari to be much more remarkable in this regard. It is to this 'play of foldings' as the harsh law of space and the diabolical art of poststructuralist spatial science that I finally turn.

CHAPTER 7

Neighbourhood of infinity – spatial science after Deleuze and Guattari

The model for the sciences of matter is the 'origami,' as the Japanese philosopher might say, or the art of folding. (Deleuze, 1993b, p. 6)

One does indeed find folds everywhere. (Deleuze, 1995, p. 156)

Each infinity – an inf(l)ection of the fold (X)

It is because we act and we live in infinitude that the responsibility with regard to the other (*autrui*) is irreducible ... I owe myself infinitely to each and every singularity ... And this is why undecidability is not a moment to be traversed and overcome. (Derrida, 1986d, pp. 86–87)

Never miss a twist or a fold. (Derrida, 1989f, p. 10)

The playing out of deconstruction in the preceding chapter culminated in the notion of folding. In this chapter I want to round off my consideration of poststructuralist geographies by pursuing origami as the exemplary art of spatial science. In this context I have found the work of Deleuze and Guattari to be exemplary. The art of folding bends to every occasion. It is pliancy pure and simple. It complicates everything. Bereft of transcendent rules or final solutions, a folded thing always opens up to (an experience of) infinity. Hence the fact that Deleuze and Guattari (1988, p. 350) joyfully declare that they "have no system, only lines and movements." Accordingly, an actual fold is inseparable from the virtual unfold that accompanies it, like a *différantial* shadow. The one is an expression of the multiple. As Deleuze (1993b, p. 3) reminds us: "The multiple is not only what has many parts but also what is folded in many ways." The holding formation and apparent identity of the folded material belies its interminable complication, relentless variation, and ceaseless differentiation. Disadjustment is the condition of folding. The individuation of a molar aggregate – such as a thing, person, place, concept, or animal – takes on consistency by way of a regulated practice of folding: "Subjectivation is created by folding" (Deleuze, 1988a, p. 104).

Poststructuralist geography (un)folds events. Hence its transformative and experimental character: "any creative work is a new way of folding adapted to new materials" (Deleuze, 1995, p. 158). It splays out the spacing and timing of an event's holding formation and consistency, opening the event to the deforming force of difference-producing repetitions. What appears to have been given once-and-for-all in actuality is returned to the variable pack from whence it came: real multiplicity, real virtuality, real chaosmosis. Poststructuralist geography picks up on the *différantial* tropology and Möbius spiralling of the infinitely disadjusted and variable whole that is (the) Open. A Möbius strip is a one-sided surface, topologically equivalent to a circle, with only one boundary curve that separates points locally, but not globally. If there is no integrative *Totality* $= X$, then it is because this figure $- X -$ splays out. Matter is always moving out of place, to misquote a catchphrase from Sibley (1988). It never quite 'holds together,' no matter how much force and binding are applied. Such is the "world ... of folding and unfolding. The whole thing is a crossroads, a multiple connectedness" (Deleuze, 1995, p. 155). For example, Deleuze (1986, 1989) argues that post-Second World War cinema shifted away from the integrative 'movement-image' towards the 'time-image' of a pure "crystal where time scintillates" (Ropars-Wuilleumier, 1994, p. 260; see also Rodowick, 1997). "The model of the whole, of an open totality, presupposes that there are commensurable relations and rational cuts between images, in the image itself, and between image and whole ... If postwar cinema breaks with this model, it's because it sets up all sorts of irrational cuts and incommensurable relations between images" (Deleuze, 1995, p. 63). In effect, "There's no totalization any more, because time no longer derives from motion and measures it, but manifests itself directly" (Deleuze, 1995, p. 64).

Folding deforms and disadjusts. There is no avoiding its power of metamorphosis. A body is defined neither by (the constancy of) its form nor by (the regularity of) its functions (habit), but by the folding of forces that affect its composition and render it affective in its turn. A body becomes what it can do: to affect and be affected – hence the ethic of the event: to be worthy of one's encounters and affects (cf. Doel, 1995; Fraser, 1997; Massumi, 1992a; Philo, 1992). For Bachelard, metamorphosis is a force that challenges all form, signification, and referentiality. It is not simply a movement from one being to another. It is a becoming that takes on a consistency and a rhythm all of its own. Most assume that their materials are elastomers, which return to approximately their original form after being stressed, whereas I seek out materials that are more plasticky than elasticated. Within their elastic limits elastomers have an inalienable form. The strain in the material completely disappears when the stress is removed (hysteresis notwithstanding). By contrast, plastics do not return to the same – except under duress. Elastic materials absorb stressful forces. Plasticky materials absorb form. As Bachelard, Barthes, and de Man note, the metamorphotic play of plasticity knows no bounds. Like origami, the plasticization of metamorphosy should not be reduced to a static transfer of affects from one being to another, as is so often the case with metaphor. It is a becoming with an immanent consistency all of its own, rather than a mere imitation or exchange of forms (cf. Buttimer, 1982, 1993; Cresswell, 1997a; Mikkonen, 1996).

Intermission

> You will not arrive at a homogeneous system that is not still worked on by immanent, continuous, and regulated variation. (Deleuze, 1993a, p. 210)

In the first chapter of this book I offered a sketch of the theoretical-practices of Derrida and Deleuze, employing the motif of perversion as my recurring image of thought. I then took up their twisted thoughts-and-actions in relation to other poststructuralist authors, such as Lyotard, Irigaray, and Baudrillard, before carrying their disarranging force into the warped spaces of academic Geography. A couple of things are worth emphasizing. First, since every point is splayed out, the minimal element is not the point but the fold. Whatever consists does so by way of a regulated (s)play of folding. To that extent, the art of spatial science is more akin to origami than it is to the pointillism that has hitherto dominated the geographical tradition. Second, since every point is splayed out, everything is fractured. The (s)play of folding takes place by way of the Open, which is not so much a finite totality, as the event horizon of infinite disjointure. "It is the horizon itself that is in movement," say Deleuze and Guattari (1994, p. 38). When one takes the fold to infinity, as Deleuze, Derrida, Foucault, and Michaux encourage us to do, one becomes embroiled in incalculable choreographies. For

> there are always many infinite movements caught within each other, each folded in the others, so that the return of one instantaneously relaunches another in such a way that the plane of immanence is ceaselessly being woven ... Diverse movements of the infinite are so mixed in with each other that, far from breaking up the One-All of the plane of immanence, they constitute its variable curvature, its concavities and convexities, its fractal nature as it were ... Every movement passes through the whole of the plane by immediately turning back on and folding itself and also by folding other movements or allowing itself to be folded by them, giving

rise to retroactions, connections, and proliferations in the fractalization of this infinitely folded up infinity. (Deleuze and Guattari, 1994, pp. 38–9)

The composition of folds is not what something is, but rather what it is in the process of becoming, its becoming-other, and its ceasing to be. Each act of folding creates a distinct singularity whilst expressing an incalculable multiplicity. This is why one must insist on the indefinite article – *a* folded piece of paper. For the event of origami, of folding, is neither the actual composition of relations that lends the apparent something consistency – *a* frog, *a* boat, *a* box, *a* bird, etc. – , nor the virtual multiplicity of all possible compositions that is held in abeyance on the plane of immanence. Deleuze (1997b, p. 5) puts it beautifully: "This indefinite life does not itself have moments, however close together they might be, but only meantimes (*des entre-temps*), between-moments." An event passes between the folds: it is a becoming real without being an actual state of affairs, and it floats on the surface of things in a kind of suspended animation.

The event of folding has neither beginning nor end, neither origin nor destination. It is only (just) in the middle, in the duration of becoming. An event is "the part that eludes its own actualization in everything that happens" (Deleuze and Guattari, 1994, p. 156). It has "kept the infinite movement to which it gives consistency;" it is a "virtual that is real without being actual, ideal without being abstract." And since an event is only ever 'meanwhile,' it should now be clear why Deleuze (1986, p. 1) insists that "you cannot reconstitute movement with positions in space or instants in time: that is, with immobile sections." Rather, one must strive to express 'real movement' and 'concrete duration.' Such is the fold. It neatly expresses Nietzsche's (1968) formula for the will to power: whatever you will, will its eternal return (Deleuze, 1983b). What returns amidst the events of folding, then, is not more of the same – such as a perpetual present (constancy, being) – , but rather the differentiation of the chaosmos (variability, becoming). By way of the fold, "it is *the returning that returns*" (Wood, 1988, p. 42). With respect to becoming, pointillism is the affliction, and origami is the *pharmakon*. "In this constructivism the concept now serves the event instead of essence, and as such employs a capacity for articulating a circumstance or case: how, why, when" (Millett, 1997, p. 54). Becoming-other unfolds across the surface of bodies. It is 'otherwise than being,' to borrow a phrase from Levinas (1981). If the minimal element is indeed the fold, rather than the point, then the fold is always at least twofold. "Folds are in this sense everywhere, without the fold being a universal. It's a 'differentiator,' a 'differential'" (Deleuze, 1995, p. 156). It is in this sense that the fold is a differential calculus of intervals.

Since a folded figure is not a being but a way of being, the event of folding is a matter of style, mannerism, and comportment. It is a matter of expression and articulation, and not of imitation, resemblance or representation: expressionism, not essentialism. The event "is not the object as denoted, but the object as expressed or expressible, never present, but always already in the past and yet to come" (Deleuze, 1990a, p. 136). For example: 'to cut.' No matter how close one gets to the instance of cutting, the surface is either about to be cut, or else it has been cut, but the cutting *itself* eludes the present. An event is both that which has happened (*absolute past*) and that which is about to happen (*absolute future*), but never that which is happening – and yet *it* cuts. "An event is neither substance, nor accident, nor quality, nor process; events are not corporeal. And yet, an event is certainly not immaterial; it takes effect, becomes effect, always on the level of materiality" (Foucault, 1982, p. 231; see also Derrida, 1994a). Finally, an haecceity is the quality that makes something unique or describable as 'this (one).' "We must think of hecceities as absolute singularities, as indescribable somethings whose very indescribability is the source of their power" (May, 1993, p. 6).

A fold is always at least twofold. Sometimes it functions as a line of rigid or supple segmentation, which effectively partitions and territorializes the plane of immanence into a plane of organization. Sometimes it acts as a line of flight, which unfolds and deterritorializes the plane of organization. In short: "We need both to cross the line, and make it endurable, workable, thinkable ... we have to manage to fold the line and establish an endurable zone in which to install ourselves, confront things, take hold, breathe – in short, think," says Deleuze (1995, pp. 110–11). Or again: "Bending the line so we manage to live upon it, with it: a matter of life and death. The line itself is constantly unfolding at crazy speeds as we're trying to fold it to produce 'the slow beings that we are.'" Such is life on "the plane of immanence: multiplicities fill it, singularities connect with one another, processes or becomings unfold, intensities rise and fall" (Deleuze, 1995, pp. 146–7). Accordingly, "The One (*L'Un*) is not the transcendent which can contain everything, even immanence, but is the immanent contained in a transcendental field. 'A' (*Un*) is always the index of a multiplicity: an event, a singularity, a life ..." (Deleuze, 1997b, p. 5). Or again: "Pure immanence is A LIFE, and nothing else," insists Deleuze (1997b, p. 4): "the indefinite article understood as the index of the transcendental." It is transcendental to the extent that *a* life is never fully actualized, but endures as a real virtuality, as a real multiplicity, even though it is nevertheless coterminous with the passing moments of a certain life. The pure immanence of *a* life entails a transcendental empiricism, rather than the simple empiricism of a subject experiencing given sensations. "Only empiricism knows how to transcend the experiential dimensions of the visible without falling into Ideas" (Deleuze, 1990a, p. 20). Or again: "Empiricism knows only events," note Deleuze and Guattari (1994, p. 48). But only *"on the condition that the event is not confused with its spatio-temporal realization in a state of affairs"* (Deleuze, 1990a, p. 22). And if an event is never simply given, since it is both virtual and incorporeal, it is likewise never given to a subject that would appropriate it as an object of representation. Accordingly, the force of empiricism "begins from the moment it defines the subject: a *habitus*, a habit, nothing but a habit in a field of immanence, the habit of saying I" (Deleuze and Guattari, 1994, p. 48: cf. Bourdieu, 1990; Derrida, 1988b; Massumi, 1992a). To get a sense of such immanence, it may be worth lingering over the notion of becoming.

Metamorphosy, becoming, and other transformers

A correspondence of relations does not add up to a becoming ... But neither is it resemblance, an imitation, or, at the limit, an identification. (Deleuze and Guattari, 1988, p. 237)

Some things, bodies, and events are obviously in a dynamic state of becoming. One state becomes another. Indeed, becoming is always a becoming-other. Some wood becomes a table. A boy becomes a man. The sky becomes grey. There is a beginning, a middle, and an end. Two beings and one becoming. On this account, becoming is one-dimensional, insofar as it is bounded by two points. However, not every imaginable becoming can be realized and actualized. One must distinguish between real and illusory becomings. For example, one can really become taller, but a base metal cannot become gold.

So far so good, except that Deleuze and Guattari refuse to conceive of becoming in such a way. First, they affirm the reality of the most unlikely of becomings, such as a becoming-woman, becoming-animal, and becoming-inhuman for every body. Second, a becoming may well have a beginning, middle, and end, but it need not necessarily unfold in that order (*à la* Godard). Third, a becoming is not one-dimensional, it is not bounded by points. To the contrary, a becoming is always at least twofold and is invariably manifold. Fourth, a becoming does not transform one thing into another. It unfolds in a direction perpendicular to that of commonsensical becomings. Fifth, becoming is always a becoming-unlimited. It is not merely a localized event that can be contained within a given state of affairs. Becoming opens onto (an experience of) infinity. It is metamorphosy in a pure state. Hence both Deleuze's (1977b, pp. 206–7) comment that "Representation no longer exists; there's only action," and Foucault's (1977, p. 172) assertorial suggestion that "The philosophy of representation – of the original, the first time, resemblance, imitation, faithfulness – is dissolving; and the arrow of the simulacrum released by the Epicureans is headed in our direction. It gives birth – rebirth – to a 'phantasmaphysics.'" Sixth, even though becoming is always unlimited, it is nevertheless 'singular,' 'molecular,' and 'minoritarian.' Singularity should not be confused with its commonsensical meanings of oneness, singleness, and individuality. It is neither 'one (of a kind),' nor a 'whole (one).' Rather, singularity should be understood in its mathematical usage: as a break-point, such as when a function takes on an infinite value or when matter becomes infinitely dense (Clarke, Doel, and McDonough, 1996). "Singularity is never one-off [*ponctuelle*], never closed by a point or a fist [*poing*]. It is a mark [*trait*], a differential mark, and different from itself: different *within itself*" (Derrida, 1992c, p. 68). It is the fractal singularity of the iterability of a non-saturable event horizon (i.e. a context). It marks the taking place of the event: how it goes off. Seventh, becomings may sweep up individuals, but they are no less impersonal and collective for that. Eighth, even though becomings are always real, they are nevertheless incorporeal events that frolic on the surface of things, rather than penetrating the depths of beings. Yet since depth is an effect of folding, the force of becoming unfolds through the entirety of a body or state of affairs, no matter how voluminous and labyrinthine it may be. Nineth, "Becomings belong to geography, they are orientations, directions, entries and exits" (Deleuze and Parnet, 1987, p. 2). Or again: "Philosophy is becoming, not history; it is the coexistence of planes, not the succession of systems" (Deleuze and Guattari, 1994, p. 59). I will pause at ten, the big One-Nothing, partly because a becoming cannot be fixed between given limits. Becoming is fractal: it frustrates the calculi of differentiation and integration.

Given this at least tenfold departure from commonsensical notions of becoming, it should be understandable why many commentators are incredulous with respect to Deleuze and Guattari's seemingly miraculous becomings (cf. Braidotti, 1994, 1997; Miller, 1993; Probyn, 1996). Each of the ten departures seems to be questionable. Yet rather than waste effort detailing the obvious and not-so-obvious counterpoints to this odd characterization of becoming, and then strive to overturn these counterpoints in their turn, let me simply outline the 'new' image of thought that gives it consistency before taking up one apparently miraculous instance of becoming: werewolves.

Deleuze denounces dialectics for being a 'false movement' that oscillates from one abstract concept to the other, guided only by imprecision. Deleuze (1991, pp. 44–5) is adamant that "The combination of opposites tells us nothing; it forms a net so slack that everything slips through." Such an exchange of point for point is found in most notions of representation, imitation, metaphor, and becoming. It is this kind of pointillistic exchange that Deleuze and Guattari's becoming declines and swerves away from. Whether dialectical or not, the golden triangle of, say, metaphor acts "as a structure that would merely yoke together two things in order to make a third" (Mikkonen, 1996, p. 311). For example: a boy, a rat, a rat-boy. But is it a *real* becoming-rat of the boy, or only a localized transfer of affects, an illusory becoming-rat – analogy, similarity, semblance, imitation, complementarity, etc.? However, "It is quintessential to metamorphosis that a sense of an event or an act is always introduced into this figure" of metaphor, argues Mikkonen (1996, p. 311). For "if something metamorphoses, time must intervene: one needs a *before* and an *after*. Metaphoric relationship is atemporal." Metamorphosy expresses the pulse of time and space in accordance with its own duration and intension. Verbs in the infinitive are excellent examples: to run, to walk, to grow, to cut ... The open fold of metamorphosis short-circuits and overruns the boundary points of metaphor. Becoming is not continuous between two points; it is discontinuous in and of itself. Becoming is an event: *it* rains ... On this 'new' image of thought, points are not given – as boundaries, origins, way-stations, destinations, typicalities, ideals, etc. – they are infinitely declined. Beings are not assured in advance. They are the localized effects of fold upon fold. Everything that 'is' emerges as a certain regularized comportment of 'ands.' Paradoxically, then, becoming is that which does not move – pure speed, absolute deterritorialization, infinite metamorphosy, unlimited plasticity, etc. To that extent nomad thought should not be confused with travelling theory (cf. Rojek and Urry, 1997). 'Betweenness' is neither juxtaposition, nor fusion, nor resolution, nor averaging. It is not a static Result. Rather, becoming is an ongoing process that belongs neither to the one, nor to the other, but to the movement of becoming that takes flight between them, "carrying away the one *and* the other, a stream without beginning or end, gnawing away at its two banks and picking up speed in the middle" (Deleuze and Guattari, 1983, p. 58). In such a situation, each becomes endlessly other. "In the rumbling that shakes us today," noted Foucault (1989, p. 61), "perhaps we have to recognize the birth of a world where the subject is not one but split, not sovereign but dependent, not an absolute origin but a function ceaselessly modified."

Instead of adopting the circulation of (op)positions as a founding moment and regulative principle, Deleuze and Guattari employ blocks of becoming, intervals that dislocate all, nomadic encounters, and haphazard conjunctions. Their philosophy works through a synthetic and contingent principle: encounters, conjunctions, haecceities, and events. Such an immanent theoretical-practice could be called 'nomad thought,' a 'discourse of the *and*' (Boundas, 1993), and a 'transcendental empiricism' (Baugh, 1993). By dwelling on change, becoming, and consistency, rather than on fixity, being, and constancy, it should be clear why Boundas and Olkowski (1994, p. 3) refer to Deleuze as a "*Stutterer, thinker of the outside*." For in making theoretical-practice stutter, stability is discharged through variation. Hereinafter, there is nothing left but the play of joints (and ... and ... and). Accordingly, getting swept up within a blind zone of undecidability could be called 'molecularization,' 'deterritorialization' or 'becoming.' One could equally call it rhythmanalysis, schizoanalysis, or rhizomatics, even origami, hang-gliding, or surfing. For becoming does away with all integral, molar, and majoritarian categories; it resolves the question of rigidity and turgescence by re-releasing continuous variation. A becoming cannot be summed up as a one plus one. It is not a one into two or a two into three. It is a twofold – a one-dimensional line of flight that traverses and unfolds the two-dimensional surfaces and three-dimensional volumes of things. It is no coincidence, for example, that in the *Logic of Sense*, Deleuze (1990a) opens up the three dimensions of the proposition – denotation (which links the proposition to a state of affairs), manifestation (which links the proposition to an enunciator), and signification (which links the proposition to concepts) – along its fourth dimension: *sense*. Sense is the fourth side that both supports the triangulation of denotation, manifestation, and signification, and carries the event away into delirium. "Nonsense is not the absence of sense," notes Colwell (1996, para. 9); "it is sense that fails to result in denotation or signification or manifestation." Moreover, a becoming neither progresses nor regresses; it involutes, running its own line 'between' things. The involuted movement of such a line weaves a block – a smooth space – that comes to occupy all of the dimensions previously made available to the system of points – a striated space. Furthermore, through involution the line-block of becoming has only a middle, from which it grows and takes flight.

Owing to the reality of becoming, one should always seek consistency, and never constancy. For whilst everything that consists is real, the real is never constant. Consistency is what remains when the illusory constancy is discharged through becoming. At the limit of this discharge, becoming deterritorializes constancy into the consistency of "a completed aberrance" (Welchman, 1992, p. 154). Hereinafter, "being [is] obliquely swept away by the verbs" (Deleuze, 1993a, p. 41). A line-block does not begin and does not end, but is always in the middle of things; it is an inter-being, a becoming, and an *intermezzo*. In the wake of an arboreal filiation, the rhizomatic line-block ushers in a succession of contingent alliances. For whilst the tree establishes the verb 'to be,' the rhizome is halved together through conjunctions: 'and ... and ... and.' In nomad thought, then, the destabilizing jetties of the interval, joint, and fold take all; they halve together and interlace any line in the rhizome with any other. This is the sense in which consistency is a plane – but only on condition that all of the available dimensions are given expression.

Accordingly, the Deleuzoguattarian encounter exemplifies what it is to 'come between' and to 'take place.' It releases "anti-oedipal forces – the schizzes-flows – forces that escape coding, scramble the codes, and flee in all directions: *orphans* (no daddy-mommy-me), *atheists* (no beliefs), and *nomads* (no habits, no territories)" (Seem, 1988, p. xxi). Bauman is wary of the nomad as an exemplary figure of our postmodernity (cf. Cresswell, 1997b; Miller, 1993). "Unlike the settlers, nomads are on the move. But they circle around a well-structured territory with long invested and stable meaning assigned to each fragment" (Bauman, 1993, p. 240). He prefers the vagabond, who "is a pilgrim without a destination; a nomad without an itinerary. The vagabond journeys through an unstructured space; like a wanderer in the desert . . . Each successive spacing is local and temporary – episodic" (Bauman, 1993, p. 240). Yet Deleuze and Guattari adopt the nomad because its smooth space sets the striated spaces of State philosophy and sedentary thought into continuous variation. As for the vagabond, they prefer the model of a schizophrenic out for a stroll (Deleuze and Guattari, 1984). Such an encounter takes flight through continuous variation, and the line-block that it weaves is without intrinsic properties, only situational ones. On this basis, there is a Deleuzoguattarian encounter in the same way that *it* rains. There are a plethora of strokes, movements, and traces, and there are modulations of stroke, deviations of movement, and traces of traces – "nothing left but the world of speeds and slowness without form, without subject, without face. Nothing left but the zigzag of a line, like 'the lash of the whip of an enraged cart driver' shredding faces and landscapes" (Deleuze and Guattari, 1988, p. 283). Hereinafter, *it* is an haecceity, a singularity, and an event.

Becoming-other, -indiscernible, and -unlimited stretches across the surface of bodies. It unfolds by way of "the open, the whole which is not a closed ensemble but the interstitial passage from one ensemble to another, from one border to the other," notes Martin (1996, p. 21). "It is this suspended passage that Deleuze calls transversality. A type of infinite declension which, from one edge of the rift to the other, relinks all ... by opening each to the other through a transversal connection which affirms their breaks and distances." This is why I think that Hallward (1997) misconstrues Deleuze's attempt to give consistency to a becoming that would not be limited by the need to relate one given being and another.

For Hallward, Deleuze's project is to become-immediate. "Unlimited and *therefore* inclusive ... 'a world without others' – a world of one singularity-multiplicity, a world beyond worldly mediation or relation altogether" (Hallward, 1997, p. 7). By occluding the differential element that traverses the unlimited, open fold, it is indeed possible to conclude that Deleuze's philosophy is given over to "ontological univocity; a critique of its repression or mis-representation; its restoration (redemption) declared through an escape from worldly mediation; dissolution of the subject (or equation of subject and object); a consequent insistence upon the literal and immediate. Always, Deleuze tries to break out of a Given situation (positioned, related, specified, mediated, figured) towards a situation in which 'everything divides, but into itself'" (Hallward, 1997, pp. 7–8). Of course, everything hinges on the topological nature of this 'itself:' the extent to which it holds together – and apart. Everything divides not into some One, but into the Open. The Open alludes to "a monism that is also a pluralism," (Schrift, 1990b, p. 108).

Drawing on Deleuze's (1988a) reading of Foucault, Hallward (1997, p. 9) notes how

> the Real requires an archaeologist. Its original immediacy must be uncovered and reconstructed through its Given fragments … '… all reality is manifestly present', but it is nevertheless 'not *given* in … a manifest way' … *To become-Real is to be extracted from the Given.* This 'extraction' of virtual from actual is the process which *eliminates a situated specificity or context*, which makes the Real independent of context or scale, on the fractal model. It is achieved through annihilation, explosion, or paralysis of the Given.

Becoming has a consistency all of its own. There is only a becoming, and not a being to which the becoming (be)comes. There is nothing beyond betweenity. There is nothing outside of the relation. "Deleuze and Guattari's simple technique is to replace conjugations with connections," says Goodchild (1996, p. 150). One enters into 'pacts' with some others – animals, molecules, machines, discourses. In this way the boundary folds that stabilize, compact, and stratify can be unfolded into a line of flight that enacts a relative deterritorialization and transformation in the direction of the limiting horizon that is now open. "The other for Deleuze is … a moving horizon of perpetual becoming, towards which the split and nomadic subject … moves" (Braidotti, 1996, p. 5). One never becomes alone, but only on the outskirts of a pack. "Events are like crystals, they become and grow only out of the edges, or on the edge," says Deleuze (1990a, p. 9). To become is "no longer to sink" into the depths of the pack, "but to slide the whole length in such a way that the old depth no longer exists at all, having been reduced to the opposite side of the surface."

Shape-shifting

> Theology is very strict on the following: there are no werewolves, human
> beings cannot become animals. That is because there is no transformation
> of essential forms; they are inalienable and only enter relations of analogy.
> The Devil and the witch, and the pact between them, are no less real for
> that. (Deleuze and Guattari, 1988, p. 252)

There is much force invested in the conviction that one essential form
cannot really be transformed into another: whatever is, is. Just so. Any
apparent transformation of inalienable forms turns out to be the work
of the *imagination* (as if it were the case that what is is not), *miraculation*
(the inexplicability of divine artifice), or *imitation* (the localized transfer
of affects). Becomings are the illusory effects of visions or spells: not
really metamorphic (becoming-other) but merely anamorphic (the deformation wrought upon things from a certain parallactic point of view).
Little wonder, then, that so many onto-theologians should caution us
against dabbling in the occult arts of metaphor and metamorphosis: a
warning that is all the more ironic when it comes from those who profess
their anti-essentialist credentials. For example, no sooner are we coaxed
into acknowledging the production of space, into experimenting with
the art of spacing, than we are warned of the dangers of spatial metaphors
lest we be led astray from what spatial constructivism really means (i.e.
literally, in essence). Meanwhile, for those who no longer believe in
essential and inalienable forms – least of all with respect to space – but
only in immanent, accidental, and constructed ones, the world proves
to be one of becoming. It will have been (*post modo*). However, it is
important to note that becoming does not necessarily beget a change in
form or function. Our world does not *move* from one form to another,
nor does it *change* from one form into another. Rather, our world is
suspended between forms: "the world is always in the middle of things"
(Haraway, 1991, p. 304). It is only whilst something (= X) is in suspension that events unfold and becomings take place. As I demonstrated in
the opening chapter, with Deleuze, one is always taken and screwed
from behind, when one's back is turned. Becoming does not belong to
a subject or an I: it is an impersonal and collective process, intensive,
collective, and untimely. As with Bataille (1982), the metamorphosy of
becoming always goes by way of an upturned eye and an upturned I
(Doel and Clarke, 1997a). Meanwhile, the world is on tenterhooks, but
insofar as these hooks are deconstructive (X), the stretching out and
splaying out of an event sets it in motion. I am reminded of the body
hangings undergone by Stelarc discussed in Chapter 2. By suspending
his body from hooks, the form, function, articulation, and comportment
of the body that are set through the routines and habits of everyday life

give way to an immanent experimentation with what a body can do. Under suspension a body (without organs) must be made. With this notion of becoming suspended between forms (the motionless trip that will have been), the exemplary becoming comes to the fore: lycanthropy. Werewolves do not change form: they become. Rather than possessing two or more forms, werewolves shed forms. They are neither multiform nor formless. They are deforming.

During the sixteenth and seventeenth centuries, Franche-Comté, a province of the Holy Roman Empire, appears to have had an unusually large number of witches and werewolves (Oates, 1989). On Oates' account, their trials were mostly in secular courts, with the Inquisition's role being rather limited, and she argues that the decline of accusations and trials against suspected werewolves was because of "the magistrates' increasing caution with regard to evidence in such cases rather than their disbelief in the reality of werewolves" (Oates, 1989, p. 331). As with other events of becoming, the case against a suspected werewolf did not so much turn on the essential status of a particular body, but on the nature of the relations into which that body formed a pact. Some, however, did believe in the *reality* of a human becoming a wolf. Indeed, many mediaeval sources suggest that werewolves should be pitied as a sort of 'anomalous nature,' insofar as their shape-shifting was beyond their control (involuntary, monomorphic metamorphosis). Be that as it may, Jean "Bodin was quite exceptional in arguing that the human body could be physically transformed into that of an animal" (Oates, 1989, p. 319), just as nature itself was capable of many seemingly miraculous transformations. One thinks of hybridization, the conversion of iron into steel or the metamorphosis of a caterpillar into a butterfly. Unlike Bodin, most rejected the reality of a human becoming a wolf: "the human being, created by God in His own image, was immutable unless God Himself decided otherwise" (Oates, 1989, p. 317). There were no real werewolves, but the trials continued nevertheless.

Werewolves: there are no such *things*. But if there were such *events*, then they would be truly diabolical. Without going into the ins and outs of a complex network of discourses on the diabolical pacts between bodies, animals, and demons, suffice to say that werewolves were by and large considered to be *illusory* transformations 'in ecstasy,' conjured by a demon working on one or more bodies, with or without the complicity of those bodies, in order to produce *real* effects. Rather than being an anomalous nature, the pacts between bodies and demons were suspected of being the work of witchcraft (voluntary, polymorphic meta-morphosis).

With respect to werewolves there are a number of possibilities: (1) there are no werewolves, despite all of the apparent evidence and proofs to the contrary (primacy of ideal form over expressive matter); (2) there are werewolves, in the sense that one body is capable of assuming two forms (primacy of plastic materials over contingent forms); (3) werewolves are illusory – the signs, powers, and affects properly attributed to two inalienable bodies are here misappropriated: a wolf is taken to be human or vice versa (dissemblance, misrecognition, imitation, etc.); and (4) werewolves are illusory but they nevertheless have material effects (representation teeters on the verge of the simulacrum). There is a fifth possibility, which is that of Becoming in the Deleuzoguattarian sense: although there are no werewolves in essence, nor any transcendent force that dissembles real bodies and their effects, becoming is perfectly real, producing effects, without ever being actualized in a given state of affairs. Clearly, it is the difference between these last two possibilities that interests me: *either* werewolves are 'ecstatic transformations' motivated by the pact of a given body with the Devil (a bout of witchcraft that dissimulates the transference of affects from one body to another), *or* werewolves are real becomings carrying one form into another.

To square it with the Christian doctrine of inalienable forms given by God, the notion of illusory transformations and dissimulated transfers of effects lifted metamorphosis to the surface of a body. For whilst there could be no '*substantial transformation*' of a body in its essence, many argued that there could be an '*accidental transformation*' of those parts that were not essential to the essence of a body – such as the ageing of skin, the greying of hair, the physical symptoms of illness – and an '*apparent transformation*' of a body owing to an interference with the faculties of perception and judgement. Without enacting a substantial transformation of the Human and Wolf forms, werewolves could still take shape: as real wolves possessed by demons or imitating humans; as real humans who 'resemble' a wolf through physiognomy, expression, gesture, comportment, imitation or a melancholic illness such as *lycanthropia*; as a hallucination caused by drugs, misrecognition or insanity; as an illusion conjured by witchcraft and demons, which may or may not involve the transference of wounds and affects from one body to another (repercussion); and so on and so forth. Nevertheless, even though werewolves have risen to the surface, they are still limited by His essentialism – by the given and inalienable depth of a body. God remains sovereign. "The Devil is a transporter; he transports humours, affects, or even bodies ... But these transports cross neither the barrier of essential forms nor that of substances or subjects" (Deleuze and Guattari, 1988, p. 253). However, when this inalienable depth is recognized as being merely the special effect of a certain regulated play of folding, then werewolves take on a real consistency all of their own, which is distinct from the accidental forms of a 'human-being' and a 'wolf-being.' Hereinafter, real becomings run amok betwixt and between 'major' or 'molar' forms.

Accordingly, "all becomings are already molecular," insist Deleuze and Guattari (1988, p. 272). "That is because becoming is not to imitate or identify with something or someone. Nor is it to proportion formal relations." Werewolves and other such becomings know only of immanent and accidental forms, which have no consistency or reality beyond the event horizon (virtuality, multiplicity) of the open context in which they are (un)folded. Henceforth, "no Aristotelian definition through species, genus and difference is possible: only a map, where various lines suggest a rather fuzzy shape" (Lecercle, 1985, p. 182). Becoming necessitates a schizoanalysis and a rhythmanalysis (Perez, 1990).

So, let me be crystal clear on the following point. Hybridity is not becoming: "one does not reach becoming or the molecular," declare Deleuze and Guattari (1988, p. 293), "as long as a line is connected to two distant points, or is composed of two contiguous points." Hybridization is a mixing or splicing that is integrative and which produces an end result (two pass into three: the one, the other, and the halfling that comes between). Becoming is immanent and produces neither integration nor a result. Motifs of resemblance, imitation and representation are just as unbecoming. This is why Miller (1993, p. 11) is mistaken to argue that: "'Becoming,' for Deleuze and Guattari, means becoming caught up in a process of osmosis (not metaphor) with *de-anthropologized* and *de-identitized* entities – women, infants, animals, foreigners, the insane – in order to resist the dominant mode of representation represented by the majority." Miller frets about the purity of the ingredients and their mixture: the 'utopian' Becoming-x's and the 'real' Being-x's. THE becoming-nomad as distinct from real nomads. THE becoming-woman as distinct from real women. THE becoming-animal as distinct from real animals. The worry is that Deleuze and Guattari not only idealize the heterogeneity of real 'somethings = x,' but that such a manoeuvre feeds off these others. "Becoming woman, becoming animal, becoming minoritarian and 'third world' is a masquerade invented expressly for white male majoritarian humans to play; it is a form of exoticism" (Miller, 1993, p. 23). Likewise, Braidotti (1994, p. 124) notes the "tension between images and man-made representations of '*Woman*' and the experiences of real-life women in their great diversity." And echoing *chora*, Jardine wonders whether 'becoming woman' continues the phallomorphic desire to render women obsolete: "There would remain only her simulacrum: a female figure caught in a whirling sea of male configurations. A silent, mutable, head-less, desireless spatial surface necessary only for *his* metamorphosis" (Jardine, 1985, p. 217; see also Jardine, 1984). The fear is that "the appropriation of the metaphorics of 'becoming woman'" is nothing more than "a new label for male self-expansion," as Grosz (1994a, p. 161) puts it, that "women are still the vehicles, the receptacles of men's becomings, their machinic conditions" (Grosz, 1994a, p. 182). All of these concerns rest on a misconstrual of becoming. They remain yoked to a pre-deconstructive onto-theology that conceives of becoming as a real or imagined exchange of positions. Becoming is not to take on another('s) form, but to unfold a 'molecular' line of deformation and flight between 'molar' forms. Space takes place.

On the one side, the 'x' of a becoming-x does not belong to the molar form that is designated by that name: a becoming-woman does not belong to the molar woman any more than a becoming-animal belongs to the plane of organization of animality. A becoming-x is not a molar-x. Meanwhile, on the other side, the becoming of a becoming-x does not belong to the molar form out of which the becoming is unfolded. Take a molecular becoming-child and a molar adult, the molecular becoming-woman and a molar woman, or a molecular becoming-wolf and a molar wolf. Only an *it* becomes – *it* is an event or haecceity, rather than a state of affairs, a way of being rather than a being. The reality of becoming-animal "resides not in an animal one imitates or to which one corresponds but in themselves, in that which suddenly sweeps us up and makes us become – a *proximity, an indiscernibility* that extracts a shared element from the animal far more effectively than any domestication, utilization, or imitation could" (Deleuze and Guattari, 1988, p. 279).

Between a human form and an animal form on the molar plane of organization runs a twofold becoming on the molecular plane of consistency: a man, a dog, a becoming. Some body, with its habits and comportment, does not get from one form to the other and reciprocally through the bypath of a miraculous becoming. To the contrary, *it* becomes through the unfolding of a molecular-man from the molar-man, a molecular-dog from the molar-dog, and connecting the two molecular-fluxes such that a zone of consistency – a Body without Organs (BwO) – is unfolded on the plane of immanence. *It* is a real abstraction – an abstraction of the virtual from the actual. Therefore: "Eliminate ... everything that roots each of us (everybody) in ourselves, in our molarity," announce Deleuze and Guattari (1988, pp. 279–80). To have done with all forms of pointillism. To take points into the fold. "For everybody/everything is the molar aggregate, but *becoming everybody/everything* is another affair, one that brings into play the cosmos with its molecular components. Becoming everybody/everything (*tout le monde*) is to world (*faire monde*), to make a world (*faire un monde*)." This is why Deleuze and Guattari (1988, p. 279) tell us that the "imperceptible is the immanent end of becoming, its cosmic formula." What is it to become imperceptible? – "to be like everybody else." Take *it* to infinity: make a becoming of every body on the One-All of the infinitely (un)folded fold. As the trailer puts it for *Terminator 2: Judgment Day* (1991: James Cameron) – "*It*'s nothing personal."

So, where to begin? Always in the middle of a given state of affairs. Deterritorialization and becoming are always situational, molecular, and minority affairs – irrespective of the 'mass' of bodies involved. "We can be thrown into a becoming by anything at all, by the most unexpected, most insignificant of things. You don't deviate from the majority unless there is a little detail that starts to swell and carries you off" (Deleuze and Guattari, 1988, p. 292). Or again: "That is how we sorcerers operate. Not following a logical order, but following alogical consistencies or compatibilities. The reason is simple. It is because no one, not even God, can say in advance whether two borderlines will string together ... No one can say where the line of flight will pass" (Deleuze and Guattari, 1988, p. 250), or what will happen to it. Case by case. Body by body. Rhizome by rhizome. Nothing is given, except the necessity of habit, expression, and consistency.

> An example: Do not imitate a dog, but make your organism enter into composition with *something else* in such a way that the particles emitted from the aggregate thus composed will be canine as a function of the relation of movement and rest, or of molecular proximity, into which they enter ... it can be the animal's natural food (dirt and worm), or its exterior relations with other animals (you can become–dog with cats, or become–monkey with a horse), or an apparatus or prosthesis to which a person subjects the animal (muzzle and reindeer, etc.), or something that does not even have a localizable relation to the animal in question ... If we interpret the word 'like' as a metaphor, or propose a structural analogy of relations (man–iron = dog–bone), we understand nothing of becoming ... You become animal only molecularly. You do not become a barking molar dog, but by barking, if it is done with enough feeling, with enough necessity and composition, you emit a molecular dog. Man does not become wolf, or vampire, as if he changed molar species ... Of course there are werewolves and vampires, we say this with all our hearts; but do not look for a resemblance or analogy to the animal, for this is becoming-animal in action, the production of the molecular animal (whereas the 'real' animal is trapped in its molar form and subjectivity). (Deleuze and Guattari, 1988, pp. 274–5)

It is not that the *ideal* of becoming gets mixed up with or imposed upon *actual* beings (cf. *chora*), but that each is differentiated by way of the open fold that constitutes its plane of immanence and consistency. "When immanence is no longer immanent to something other than itself," conclude Deleuze and Guattari (1994, p. 47), "it is possible to speak of a plane of immanence." One constructs it by declining the temptation to fix upon 'something-or-other = x.' Something transpears "as a result of contingency rather than necessity, as a result of an ambience or milieu rather than an origin, of a becoming rather than a history, of a geography rather than a historiography, of a grace rather than a nature" (Deleuze and Guattari, 1994, pp. 96–7). Accordingly, the werewolf is not a halved together form: the human and the wolf forms integrated into one shape-shifting body. It is the expression of an immanent life. A body may or may not want to be sealed up in an inalienable form, but its composition and articulation of relations will not cease varying for that (cf. Deleuze, 1983c; Shaviro, 1993). "The BwO howls! 'They've made me an organism! They've wrongfully folded me! They've stolen my body!' The judgement of God uproots it from its immanence and makes it an organism, a signification, a subject."

Under suspension, the immanence of becoming demonstrates why "Bodies are defined not by their genus and species, nor by their origins and functions, but by what they can do, the affects they are capable of, in passion as in action" (Deleuze and Parnet, 1987, p. 60). A body takes on consistency through the splaying out of its folds. "'To be' is to be coming into a relation, to be a becoming, to produce a new affect, relation, or modification between terms that are themselves modifications" (Goodchild, 1996, p. 40). It is not that "it's one or the other, or that one becomes the other, becomes two. Because multiplicity is never in the terms, however many, nor in all the terms together, the whole. Multiplicity is precisely in the 'and,' which is different in nature from elementary components and collections of them" (Deleuze, 1995, p. 44). To that extent, the judgement of God that tries to force inalienable and immutable forms onto bodies necessitates a sorcerous and diabolical ethic of becoming. Such an ethic would amount to an "uncapping of the multiplicities dissimulated by the principle of the 'self'" (Millett, 1997, p. 54). The ethical response is to open a given fold of the body to infinity: not to break the play of folding, but to delimit it; to return it to its immanent consistency (cf. Goodchild, 1997; Lyotard, 1993).

Consistency

> Everything is brought together; in this way, Deleuze and Guattari's thought resembles a garbage tip. *Multiplicity*, embracing heterogeneous terms, is the first element of the immanent relation. Yet intensity will not be produced by a group of sterile objects lying alongside each other. Secondly, they need to interact and affect each other – they need to acquire *consistency*. (Goodchild, 1996, p. 3)

A non-totalizable multiplicity of strewn out part-objects that needs to be set to work. That is how Goodchild paraphrases Deleuze and Guattari's take on the immanent relations that express social space: multiplicity, consistency, creation, machinery, and desire. Desiring-machines lend consistency to the multiplicitous ruins of our world. "We live today in the age of partial objects, bricks that have been shattered to bits, and leftovers," declare Deleuze and Guattari (1988, p. 42). "We no longer believe in a primordial totality that once existed, or in a final totality that awaits us at some future date ... We believe only in totalities that are peripheral. And if we discover such a totality alongside various separate parts ... it is added to them as a new part fabricated separately." On the basis of this declaration, one may be tempted to infer that Deleuze and Guattari believe that our world is one of fragmentation and lack, whereupon folding would become an expedient device for suggesting that the disarray of strewn out bits and pieces resists a final resolution. However, this may occlude the essential element, which is the fold, rather than the point. "An approach based on part-objects ... is the approach of a demented experimenter who flays, slices, and anatomizes everything in sight, and then proceeds to sew things randomly back together again. You can make any list of part-objects you want: hand, breast, mouth, eyes ... It's still Frankenstein," insist Deleuze and Guattari (1988, p. 171). So, "What we need to consider is not fundamentally organs without a body, or the fragmented body," that is to say elements without a totality, "it is the body without organs, animated by various intensive movements." A body without organs (BwO) is a zone of immanence and intensity that opens onto the *full* BwO, the infinitely (un)folded fold, the *plane* of immanence and consistency: the whole that is open. "The BwO is what remains when you take everything away" (Deleuze and Guattari, 1988, p. 151). What remains is precisely that which maintains the different detached pieces in their disjointure – "*consistency*: the 'holding together' of heterogeneous elements" (Deleuze and Guattari, 1988, p. 323). What remain are the differentials and not miniaturized integers, the folds and not that which is folded, the relations and not the relata.

The requirement is to take on consistency without occluding the infinite dissimilation into which it plunges. This is why it is not so easy to make a BwO. As with film, the taking on of consistency requires one to "discover the right running speed," as Martin (1996, p. 19) so aptly puts it. It is always a matter of spacing and pacing, of speed and slowness, of contrast and exposure. Consistency is forged through "catatonic states and periods of extreme haste, of suspensions and shootings, coexistence of variable speeds, blocks of becoming, leaps across voids, displacements of a centre of gravity on an abstract line, conjunctions of lines on a plane of immanence, a 'stationary process' at dizzying speed which sets free particles and affects" (Deleuze and Parnet, 1987, p. 95). From the perspective of consistency everything comprises an immanent and double articulation of speed and slowness (*longitude*), and of intensities and affects (*latitude*).

Inscribed on the plane of consistency are *haecceities*, events, incorporeal transformations that are apprehended in themselves; *nomadic essences*, vague yet rigorous; *continuums of intensities* or continuous variations, which go beyond constants and variables; *becomings*, which have neither culmination nor subject, but draw one another into zones of proximity or undecidability; *smooth spaces*, composed from within striated space. (Deleuze and Guattari, 1988, p. 507)

By creating concepts one constructs a zone of clarity, a region of consistency, and a neighbourhood of infinity on the plane of immanence. "The concept is not paradigmatic but *syntagmatic*; not projective but *connective*; not hierarchical but *linking* [*vicinal*]; not referential but *consistent*" (Deleuze and Guattari, 1994, p. 91). On this basis, poststructuralist geography draws out a line of flight fit for the becomings of nomad thought and the diabolical art of spatial science. Such a line is as much in points as between them. This line is much more than a mere relation between terms. It cracks them open and splays them out.

Stringiness

Lines aren't things running between two points; points are where several lines intersect. Lines never run uniformly, and points are nothing but inflections of lines. More generally, it's not beginnings and ends that count, but middles ... So a multilinear complex can fold back on itself with intersections and inflections ... As though these are so many twists in the path of something moving through space like a whirlwind that can materialize at any point. (Deleuze, 1995, p. 161)

Picking up on my earlier 'defence' of Olsson against those who find his images of thought-and-action too regular and petrified, violently reducing the infinite variability, singularity, and contingency of our multiplicitous world to a *very* small set of relations that are always closed in on themselves, let me just add two things. First, from a certain point of view Olsson's figures are shut tight: a point of infinite density takes in the entirety of thought-and-action; a triangulation of the equal sign of identity (=), the solidi of dialectics (/), and the bars of semiotics (—); an empty square – initially static, then in rotation; a torpedo; an 'American football;' a double helix; a Möbius strip; etc. (Olsson, 1980, 1991, 1993). Closure is everywhere in Olsson's figuration of thought-and-action. However, as these figures are made more supple through folding, unfolding, and refolding, it becomes increasingly evident that they always remain open. Olsson has succeeded in giving a certain consistency to literally *elliptical* images of thought-and-action (cf. Nancy, 1992). Ellipse as the trace of a regular oval, and ellipse as ellipsis, omission, and disjointure. Olsson's images of thought-and-action are neither closed nor open. They work anamorphically by folding in on themselves and closing down (onto the 'dematerialized point of abstractness,' for example) and metamorphically by unfolding out of themselves onto other registers (the 'dematerialized point of abstractness' as worm-hole, for example). Olsson (1993, p. 288) conveys the incommensurability of this double agency beautifully: "I now return to the picture of the American football. I cannot really explicate how and why, but when I look at this peculiar image with my eyes closed, I see that the shell of the oval consists of a set of tightly packed threads, sometimes shaped as a double helix, sometimes as a Moebius band." Not only does the metamorphosis of one folded figure into another take place within interleaved ellipses, the metamorphosy itself is inexplicable (i.e. diabolical, and therefore the source of great pleasure, laughter, and *jouissance*). No matter how close the folds seem to be together in space and time, innumerable others unfold them, splay them out, and sweep them away.

Given time, it would be nice to play off the open fold in Olsson against string theory and superstring theory in physics (Davies and Brown, 1988; Peat, 1991). In both cases, a certain 'stringiness' emerges as a likely contender for resolving many of the conceptual and mathematical difficulties that arise from conceiving of elementary particles as point-like entities without extension. While stringiness in physics is supposed to get rid of the problem of nonsensical infinities, stringiness in poststructuralist spatial science opens every figure to (an experience of) the deforming force of infinite metamorphosy. Likewise, the 'super' of superstrings refers to the search for a super*symmetry* in all of the ten-plus dimensions of space-time, whereas in poststructuralist spatial science, stringiness begets dissymmetry, dissimilitude, and disadjustment. Nevertheless, these strings do not have fixed or ideal forms, and attributes such as mass vary according to the way in which the strings oscillate, as do their tension and compaction.

Unzipping parallactic space-time

No more certainties, no more continuities. We hear that energy, as well as matter, is a discontinuous structure of points: punctum, quantum. Question: could the only certainty be the *point*? (Tschumi, 1994, p. 219)

I don't like points. (Deleuze, 1995, p. 161)

What does the differential (s)play of folding and stringiness suggest about space and time? Many have assumed that the co-joining and integration of the three (reversible) dimensions of space and the one (irreversible) dimension of time solves most, if not all, of the fundamental difficulties associated with conceiving of space and time in isolation. Yet this four-dimensional space-time, figured most frequently as a box in motion, replicates the initial imprecision: space-time is assumed to be integral, homogeneous, and divisible, and events are assumed to take place 'in' this continuous space-time matrix. The rigidity of this image of thought clearly precludes folding. Such are the dangers of a *certain* (pointillistic) spatialization of thought, which is only able to express differences of degree to the extent that it corresponds to a quantitative homogeneity. Consequently, whatever shape-shifter one takes up as one's image of thought for the disadjusted dimensions of space-time, one should note that the notion of a 'space-time *continuum*' does not amount to an addition of space and time ($3 + 1 = 4$). By insisting on the folding of space-time one cannot so easily fall back onto taken-for-granted and pre-critical understandings of space and time. The dimensions of space-time are a special effect of folding, and each fold opens up a discontinuity – or complementarity – in space-time itself (cf. Plotnitsky, 1994, 1997). "Thus a continuous labyrinth is not a line dissolving into independent points, as flowing sand might dissolve into grains, but resembles a sheet of paper divided into infinite folds or separated into bending movements, each one determined by the consistent or conspiring surroundings" (Deleuze, 1993b, p. 6). These notions come to the fore in many films that take a certain relativization of space-time as their theme. In what follows I will pick up only a few of them.

The *Back to the Future* trilogy of films (1985, 1989, 1990: Robert Zemeckis) aptly refer to the devices for shifting one's relative position in the four-dimensional 'space-time continuum' as 'flux capacitors,' although unlike *Bill and Ted's Excellent Adventure* and *Bogus Journey* (1988: Stephen Herek; 1991: Peter Hewitt), one can only use such devices to move in the one dimension of time and not in the three dimensions of space. In the *Back to the Future* trilogy movement is one dimensional. What counts is the direction: forward or backward. However, because the films assume that space-time is a homogeneous and uniform, spatialized sequence of self-identical, integrative, and contiguous instants ($t_0 \leftrightarrow t_1 \leftrightarrow t_2 \ldots t_n$), when the 'flux capacitor' shifts relative position it can only cut into a *given* space-time continuum. To go forward or backward in (a) time: that is the only possibility. For one can only cut into the past and future of that which culminates in and departs from the *present* moment in space-time. Yet whilst the past and future of a particular present are always already given in advance, one can nevertheless change the present by undertaking a differential action in 'its' past, and then returning to what will have become an alternative future for the present. There is nothing very surprising in all of this. Most people tend to think of space-time in terms of a fixed and unchanging line of events that culminates in what is 'now,' and from which a series of possible futures bifurcate. As time progresses the

spread of possibilities collapses into a given line, although new possibilities ceaselessly open up with each given action. The future is indeed
de-differentiated and zipped up. Miraculously, it seems to close by way
of a sliding presence that leaves nothing of itself in its wake. So, what
makes films like the *Back to the Future* trilogy interesting is the fact
that they allude to the un-zipping of past times, reanimating all of the
world's potential once more. By moving in two directions at once they
enable an apparently stable space-time to exfoliate a block of parallel
space-times. By revoking the surety of 'now' the integral formation of
space-time all but falls apart, and what (only just) holds things together
is the particular point of view according to which it is traversed. Once
those points of view become relativized in their turn only the 'flux
capacitors' can facilitate communication between the incommensurable
portions of space-time. Yet as the films repeatedly warn, the parallel
processing while criss-crossing of incompossible space-time continua
always risks a catastrophic short-circuiting.

The two *Terminator* films are based on the same logic as that played
out in the *Back to the Future* trilogy. In *The Terminator* (1984: James
Cameron) the forces of humanity wish to maintain the possibilities of
the future by preserving the integrity of the present (if a given boy
lives, then his grown-up persona may defeat the machines of the future),
whilst in *Terminator 2: Judgment Day* (1991: James Cameron) the forces
of humanity wish to close-off *a certain* future by altering the charac-
teristics of the present (if a line of research can be blocked-off, then a
particularly unpleasant future will no longer be able to take place). Were
this deterrence of the future of the event to succeed, however, this
future would no longer bear on this present and the apparently closed
loop of space-time would become splayed out, giving risk to an undecidable, ontological flicker (cf. the fading in and out of people in
photographs carried in the *Back to the Future* trilogy). Indeed, such
undecidability will have been ramified to infinity. In a curved space-time,
the parallels of Euclidean geometry interlace, and aporia reigns. "It is
necessary from this standpoint to conceptualize the contemporaneous-
ness or coexistence of the two inverse movements, of the two directions
of time ... as if the two waves that seem to us to exclude or succeed
each other unfolded simultaneously in an 'archaeological,' micropolitical,
micrological, molecular field." For example, one tries to ward off something: illness, sex, writing ... Without yet existing, the warded-off limit
nevertheless acts on and solicits the present. The manifold future sets
the manifold present in motion once again. I am reminded of Ts'ui
Pên's pullulated labyrinth of time: "I leave to various future times, but
not to all, my garden of forking paths" (Borges, 1985, p. 89).

More generally, the *Back to the Future* trilogy and *Groundhog Day*
(1992: Harold Ramis) exemplify the extrema of this conception of space-

time. Whilst the latter demonstrates the infinite variability within the closed loop of a given portion of space-time (the difference-producing repetition of a day that never ends), the former demonstrates the simultaneity of parallel tracts of space-time that communicate through departures from a given presence. And despite the naivety of this conception, at least it should alert one to the fact that singular points are both multiplicitous and disadjusted in and of themselves.

> Singularities are the precise points at which all of the variations in (of) the field are copresent, from a certain angle of approach, *in potential*. That copresence in potential is '*in*tension' as opposed to extension ..., closer to a 'virtuality' ... *absolutely real*. It is absolute in that it is nowhere in the space-time coordinates of extension, and yet it is perspectival, because the variation of the field is ever on the approach, from a certain angle, to a singularity of its own copresence. It is real, yet incorporeal. (Massumi, 1996a, p. 397)

Fractals, chaosmos, and dustiness

> I don't believe in things. (Deleuze, 1995, p. 160)

In prolonging this image of thought, Massumi makes much of these 'singular' point-folds, or 'bifurcation points,' where the *in*-tensity of pure virtuality – the whole, open multiplicity – gives way to the *ex*-tensive unfolding of actual occurrences. This is an expression of the chaosmos, although it significantly departs from conventional depictions of chaos. Typically, chaos is presented as that which occurs beyond a certain threshold, such as when a laminar flow becomes a turbulent swirl. Through the compounding of discrepancies, periodicity may become chaotic: "small initial errors grow exponentially until they 'dominate' any regular motion" (Schroeder, 1991, p. 25). Sometimes this is driven by 'repulsive points' or *repellors*, which lead the initiator to generate a divergent explosion. Sometimes it is driven by 'basins of attraction' or *strange attractors*, which may converge onto a Cantor-like set of infinitely scissile points. Chaos begets fractals – curves that cannot be differentiated. Yet what underlies them is symmetry: self-similarity, self-affinity, rotation, periodicity, and invariance against change or scaling. Chaos is not the opposite of symmetry, of the well-proportioned and the well-ordered. To the contrary, chaos is the alibi of symmetry.

To generate fractals, one often need only repeat a very simple operation, like folding, cutting, hollowing or erasing. Take the Mandelbrot set, Hilbert curve, or the Sierpinski gasket. Or consider the simple folding that produces the snowflake-like Koch curve. Take a segment of a straight line and raise an equilateral triangle out of its middle third. The length of this figure has grown by one-third. Repeat this process on the four resulting segments, and then on the resulting sixteen. Now, repeat to infinity. As the curve takes shape its length extends to infinity, and although it is continuous, there is no point at which it could be differentiated. Moreover, since the curve is infinitely long, it is not reducible to a one-dimensional object, such as a line. Yet by the same token, since the Koch curve does not enclose a region of a plane, it is not a two-dimensional area, such as a surface. It is neither one thing nor the other – but there is nothing 'vague' or remotely 'messy' about it. Its between-ness has a precision all of its own, with a Hausdorff dimension of 1.26. What this demonstrates is the need for us to re-consider what we expect of such things as points, lines, surfaces, and volumes, and of their similarities and differences. Most of these expectations are unbecoming. For example, we usually assume that a line has a higher resolution than a point or that a surface has two dimensions and a volume three. Something as simple as a Hilbert curve is enough to cast such assumptions into doubt. A Hilbert curve is a line that asymptotically fills up a surface. Its Hausdorff dimension is 2. Hence the seemingly miraculous ability to translate an area into a line without any loss of detail. This goes against the grain of commonsensical notions of dimensionality based on extension, such that a one-dimensional line has zero-dimensional points at its extremities (the two ends of a rope ...), a two-dimensional surface has one-dimensional lines for its boundaries (the four edges of a square ...), a three-dimensional volume is bounded by two-dimensional surfaces (the six faces of a die ...), a four-dimensional entity is bounded by three-dimensional volumes (the n regions of space-time ...), etc. It is difficult enough to comprehend dimensionality beyond one's own lived experience – as Abbott (1944) shows in his witty account of a Flatlander's intrusion into first Lineland, and then Spaceland – without losing the surety of discrete dimensions as well. Perhaps, as Klein suggested, what appears to be "a point in three-dimensional space is in reality a tiny circle going round the fourth space dimension. From every point in space a little loop goes off in a direction that is not up, down, or sideways ... The loops are not *inside* space, they extend space ... The fifth dimension can still be *there*, but nothing gets very far by going through it" (Davies, 1984, pp. 159–60).

Now, whilst some fractals take continuity to infinity, others take discontinuity to infinity. For example, consider the so-called 'middle-third-erasing' Cantor set. To generate one, simply wipe out the middle third of a line, and then wipe out the middle thirds of the two remaining segments. Carry on erasing middle thirds indefinitely. After infinite iterations, the total length of the set is zero, but "the leftover 'dust' still contains infinitely many, in fact *uncountably* many, 'points'" (Schroeder, 1991, p. 16). With a Hausdorff dimension of 0.63, the "Cantor dust is more (a lot more!) than just a point (dimension 0) and

much less than a length of line or curve (dimension 1)." The dust is
infinitely porous and "totally discontinuous – yet infinitely divisible,
just like a continuum" (Schroeder, 1991, p. 162). Without intervals or
points, this dust consists of nothing but holes, and holes within holes –
and nothing but traces, and traces of traces. Although the dust of the
middle-third-erasing Cantor set is embedded in one dimension, one can
obviously take this dustiness into two, three, four ... n embedding
dimensions. It is not for nothing that Deleuze (1993b, p. 94) suggests
that one sees "the fold of things through the dust they stir up." Nevertheless, other fractals are much more 'solid,' such as the Cantor gasket
in two embedding dimensions (holey surface), and the Cantor cheese
or Menger sponge in three (holey volumes). These fractals have
Hausdorff dimensions of 1.89, 2.97, and 2.73, respectively.

Now, in contrast with the typical fixation on symmetry, similarity,
repetition of the same, and extensive thought-and-actions, Massumi's
(1992a, 1996b) take on chaos, fractals, and dustiness is given over to
dissymmetry, dissimilation, difference-producing repetitions, and intensive thought-and-action. A

> singular point is when a system enters a peculiar state of indecision, where
> what its next state will be turns entirely unpredictable. The unfolding of
> the system's line of actions interrupts itself. The system momentarily
> suspends itself. It has not become inactive. It is in ferment. It has gone
> 'critical.' This 'chaotic' interlude is not the simple absence of order. It is
> in fact a super-ordered state: it is conceived as the literal co-presence of
> all of the possible paths that the system may take, their physical inclusion
> in one another ... It has folded in on itself, becoming materially self-ref-
> erential – animated not by external relations of cause-effect, but by an
> intensive interrelating of versions of itself ... The self-referentiality of the
> critical system is indeed in excess over the actual. The possible futures
> are present, but only in effect – incipient effect (resonance and interference,
> vibration and turbulence, unfoldable into an order). (Massumi, 1996b, no
> pagination)

On this basis, Massumi is able to distinguish between possibility,
which is "analytically thought-out into a combinatoric, to predictable
effect," and potential, which is "pragmatically, impossibly re-infolded
in continual experimental variation." One appears to (s)pace oneself
from one point to another. However, such a movement only takes on
consistency from a very precise parallactic and anamorphic point of
view that is itself open to other passages. Between one point and another,
everything (else) takes place. So, each modality of distancing – nearness,
farness, closeness, proximity, presence, absence, distanciation, etc. –
will have to take into account the fact that it is worked over by in-tensive
refolding. Hereinafter, space-time is not only relativized from each

particular point of view, it is infinitely disadjusted in and of itself. The real is actual and virtual, extensive and intensive, unfolded and enfolded, serial and parallel. The real demands 'double duty' and 'double agency' from its thoughts-and-actions. Both too much and too little, too soon and too late, too fast and too slow. Presence is only half-formed through being halved together. If "the fixation of one line of actualization ... stabilizes and freezes the event, shifting us from the uncertainty of the becoming of the event to the safety of the being of the referent," as Colwell (1996, para. 33) puts it, then the redemptive task is to counter-actualize this fixation and to re-eventize the actual. It is to take the real to infinity. However, the infinite is not accomplished; it is open. Such is the nature of the fold, which pulls in two directions at once. Or rather: the fold expresses a manifold pullulation.

Folding space and time

> The issue is not one of relation, but of 'fold-in,' or of 'fold according to fold.' (Deleuze, 1993b, p. 135)

To the extent that the film *Dune* (1984: David Lynch) plays with the notion of 'folding space,' rather than merely moving in a given block of space-time continua, it is much more apt than either the *Back to the Future* trilogy, the *Terminator* films, or *Groundhog Day*. Nevertheless, whilst there are many allusions to the general relativity of space-time in *Dune*, the dominant figure is one of cubism: a superimposition of multiple perspectives, interlocking movements, and geometrical forms, exemplified in the block-like electromagnetic body-armour. As for the folding of space-time itself, one might usefully contrast *Dune* with the *Star Trek* series (1979+). Whilst trekkies can only 'beam about' at the speed of light – a high-tech version of particulate or pointillistic travel – , those in *Dune* travel faster than light – taking an instantaneous, motionless trip. Rather than moving from one point *in* space-time *to* another, and to the extent that space-time is as much 'in' its observation as the observation is 'in' space-time, the required location is actualized through a perspectival and relativized refolding of space-time's virtuality. One does not travel faster than light: one travels faster than another's space-time. Take Einstein's relativity. Two observers moving past each other experience time and space differently: each senses time passing more slowly for the other; and each experiences the other as being fore-shortened in the direction of motion. Or take Heisenberg's uncertainty principle in quantum theory. Not only can one not *know* both the position and momentum of elementary particles, such particles *do not possess* both properties 'at one and the same space-time.' And whilst it is conventional to confine the significance of such relativity and uncertainty to speeds approaching that of light, this is to display a profound ignorance of both the material and experiential nature of everyday space-time. For example, consider the foreign-exchange dealers 'hooked on speed' and wired into the global-local nexus of the money markets, and the cleaners who linger over the surface of things. Their incommensurable (but evidently compossible) worlds collide over such things as smudges on a screen, debris on a desktop, and telephones left off the hook (Allen and Pryke, 1994). Everywhere it is a matter of speed and slowness, of territorialization and deterritorialization, and of foreshortening and elongation. Relativity is not just significant for extreme events: it also works through the quotidian. Think of the dilation of time and space as one endures the slow-motion catastrophe of a car crash. Likewise, every second of boredom can swell to eternity, just as every night of raving can vanish into a blink of the eye.

Relatively speaking, then, one takes a motionless trip in somebody else's space-time. One never travels alone, but always in relation to another. For "every point of view is a point of view on variation. The point of view is not what varies with the subject ... it is, to the contrary, the condition in which an eventual subject apprehends a variation (metamorphosis), or: something = x (anamorphosis)" (Deleuze, 1993b, p. 20). Through folding, Euclidean space and perspectival space are splayed out and deconstructed. "Space can no longer be regarded as a homogeneous void, but as a plurality of 'local geometries'" (Marks, 1995, p. 67). Or again: "There is no longer either invariable form or variable point of view on to a form. There is a point of view which belongs so much to the thing that the thing is constantly being transformed in a becoming identical to the point of view" (Deleuze, 1989, p. 147).

Through a change of register space-time shifts. It contracts and dilates. It folds, unfolds, and refolds. In *Dune*, another space-time comes to you. Movement, no movement, just a folding (of, in) space. And this is why the pleonasm of 'folding space' jars: 'folding' should have sufficed. The invaginal, motionless tripping and destabilization in place does not fold a given planar arrangement; it folds (un)folds. Or rather: "A fold is always folded within a fold ... Unfolding is thus not the contrary of folding, but follows the fold up to the following fold" (Deleuze, 1993b, p. 6). Likewise, it is erroneous to assume, as Urry (1995, p. 30) does, that "although two objects can occupy the same point in time (in different places) therefore [*sic*] they cannot occupy exactly the same point in space" – thus naturalizing the apparent 'finitude' and 'scarcity' of space, along with such things as the 'friction of distance' and the 'drag of space' (cf. Doel and Clarke, 1998b). Such elementary misunderstandings are not helped by *volumetric* and *expansive* notions of space and time. For example, in clarifying why 'spatial relations' such as 'between-ness' represent an abstraction of form from content, Sayer (1985, p. 52) insists that it "is obviously not an abstraction which can be objectified: 'space-as-such', 'form' or 'spatial relations' are literally contentless abstractions." There are no special or general effects of space *per se*, only effects of various entities *in* space. The example of 'between-ness' is not merely fortuitous, then, since the whole exercise amounts to reducing space to the contingent 'infill' or 'stuffing' between Things. Whilst such Things possess due cause, spacing remains a contingently constituted special effect. "Thus space is a set of *relations* between entities and is not a substance," warns Urry (1985, p. 25). "Nevertheless, it does not follow that spatial and temporal relations can be unproblematically *reduced* to the relations within and between social entities."

To the extent that every fold plays its part in the expression of an event and the consistency of a state of affairs, one cannot differentiate between 'necessary' and 'contingent' relations – "in the former the nature of the relata depends on the relation; in the latter it is independent of the relation" (Sayer, 1985, p. 49). Such a distinction would assume that the calculus of difference is the property of substance, rather than of spacing. On this basis, substance would be akin to the virtual dimension – what the (abstract) composition of a body can do – while space would merely become the realm of the actual – what bodies do in given (concrete) contexts of interrelation and interpenetration. As Yeung (1997, p. 67) puts it in a moment of candid reductiveness: "an enactment of causal power ... is subject to time- and space-specific constraints."

Take two bodies: a man and a woman who get married, so becoming husband-and-wife. Initially there is a structural indifference between them: *a* man, *a* woman. This is expressed as a contingent relation since the relata, in their present state, do not depend on a constitutive conjunction between them for the form that they take. However, the two bodies can nevertheless be halved together into 'husband-and-wife,' transforming the initial structural indifference into a necessary relation. This transformation is possible because of the given properties of the two bodies, along with the causal powers of other entities entering into relation with those bodies: church, state, family, media, etc. Given everything that I have said in previous chapters about the deconstruction of integrity and differential spacing, I do not want to labour why I find this account unbecoming of a spatial scientist. For a start, one will never stabilize, isolate or disentangle the composition of 'a' body. Nor will one ever exhaust what a particular body can do (cf. Deleuze, 1988b, 1990b). The integrity of 'a' body only takes on consistency to the extent that it is (s)played out across innumerable contexts in which 'it' is inscribed: principles of becoming, metamorphosis, and the 'sideways glance' of anamorphosis (Doel and Clarke, forthcoming). This is why Deleuze, following Spinoza, renders two questions equivalent: what is the structure of a body? and what can a body do? A body's structure is the composition of its relations, whilst what it can do corresponds to its capacity for affecting and for being affected. "In the first place, a body, however small it may be, is composed of an infinite number of particles; it is the relations of motion and rest, of speed and slowness between particles that define a body, the individuality of a body. Second, a body affects other bodies, or is affected by other bodies" (Deleuze, 1992b, p. 625). Taken together, these two expressions signal a return to the surface from the depths. Such depths now appear only as folds traversed from certain – although by no means all – directions.

The return to the surface

effects of conjuncture (and that is the world) (Derrida, 1994b, p. 18)

Everything now returns to the surface. (Deleuze, 1990a, p. 7)

Critical realism plumbs the depths. It seeks to recover traces of sunken essences from beneath the cover of appearances. Abstraction is its plumbline of choice. For the critical realist, the "purpose of abstraction is to isolate causal mechanisms (the 'real') in relation to a concrete phenomenon," says Yeung (1997, p. 58), to "step towards ... the real essence, power and mechanism of an object;" and "to distinguish external/ incidental/contingent from internal/essential/necessary relations between objects and events." This helps to differentiate between the empirical – a given actuality – and the real – a virtual potential. It also helps to distinguish between objects and thought objects, between actual objects, abstract objects, and concrete objects. An actual object exists as an event, whereas an abstract object is "a one-sided or partial aspect of an object," as Sayer (1981, p. 7) famously put it.

Now, given the generally hazy and chaotic nature of our intuitive knowledge of events, "to understand their diverse determinations we must first abstract them systematically," argues Sayer (1992, p. 87). "When each of the abstracted aspects has been examined it is possible to combine the abstractions so as to form concepts which grasp the concreteness of their objects." In this way, the reciprocal movement of abstraction–concretization has nothing whatsoever to do with 'messiness,' and still less is it undecidable or indiscernible. The need for a double movement of abstraction–concretion arises because the world is dissimulative, parallactic, and complex. Fortunately, however, things remain essentially integral, graspable, and stable. Even though we are part of the real and engaged in a transformative activity grounded in practical adequacy and reflexivity, the real is nevertheless given. It is what it is. So: abstract–polish–combine. This is very different to origami:

fold–unfold–refold. It is also very different to deconstruction: extraction–graft–extension. Nevertheless, all three only ever take on consistency from the vantage of a particular point of view. Abstraction "isolates in thought a *one-sided* or partial aspect of an object" (Sayer, 1992, p. 87). "Concrete objects are constituted by a combination of diverse elements or forces *from* where the abstraction is made," continues Yeung (1997, p. 58). The toing and froing of abstraction and concretization, of reduction and expansion, trace out the continuum of thought as an act of creation. The movement between the concrete and the abstract is not a movement from reality to theory; it is immanent to thought-and-action itself. One must therefore distinguish between two divergent series on a Möbius strip: the twofold of the concrete-in-thought and the abstract-in-thought, and the twofold of the real-concrete and the real-abstract. On the Möbius strip of thought-and-action, each twofold is distinct locally, but indistinct globally (cf. Althusser, 1979; Althusser and Balibar, 1979). And if one can only count in terms of integers, one will no doubt discern various levels or plateaux of abstraction, each with its own quantum state held between thresholds beyond which it jumps to another level. In such an image of thought, the extrema may perhaps be the infinitely complex and quaquaversal concretion on the one side, and the simplest form and the most universal abstraction on the other (being and nothingness, for example).

Owing to the disadjusted logic of supplementarity that I have iterated in the preceding chapters, the difficulties with this double movement of abstraction–concretion should be self-evident. Neither the 'one-sided' nor the 'many-sided' are stable. No amount of cutting and suturing, isolating and combining, or subtracting and suppletion will ever resolve the double invagination that splays the inside out and the outside in. Similarly, the iterative immobilization of the essential from the flux of contingent materiality, of abstracting-cum-compacting the n-dimensional 'reality' of some thing, will not suffice to isolate the special effects of spatialization and temporalization, of spacing and duration. The critical realist's axiomatic dichotomy of causes and effects knows nothing of becoming and geophilosophy. Its irreversible logic of potential causal powers that may be triggered off under certain contingent conditions, thereby realizing various conjunctional effects, knows nothing of how "to emit accelerated or decelerated particles in a floating time that is no longer our time, and to emit haecceities that are no longer of this world: deterritorialization, 'I was disorientated ...'" (Deleuze and Guattari, 1988, p. 283).

Abstraction and concretion are 'chaotic conceptions,' to borrow one of Sayer's ambivalent phrases. To say that something is a 'chaotic conception' is usually an act of malevolence: one denounces the bastard other, whose arbitrariness rests on relations of mere semblance, in order to signal one's allegiance to the good side – the side of 'rational abstractions' and (practically) 'adequate conceptions,' that express 'real,' 'necessary,' 'substantial,' 'causal,' 'constitutive,' and 'essential' relations, without which 'something = x' would be other than it is. The same trait of bad faith usually accompanies the designation of 'superficial conceptions' and 'undecidable conceptions.' Abstraction and concretion are supposed to be the tools for fabricating adequate conceptions in the face of chaos, superficiality, and undecidability. They are the routes by which sound thought-and-action can be kept on track. At this juncture I do not want to go over whether the motifs of abstraction and concretion are most appropriately configured in terms of intuition, commonsense, experience, typicality, iteration, dialectics, or origami. Parenthetically, though, I cannot resist noting that Yeung (1997, pp. 60–1) enumerates no less than nine "stringent conditions" or "useful criteria and guidelines" that a 'good' abstraction should, perhaps, satisfy, and that should, perhaps, filter out "almost contentless abstractions," which otherwise may become "strengthened" or "manipulated" in illegitimate or occult ways. The elements of this apparatus for sieving and grading upwardly-mobile abstractions range from self-consistency to emancipatory potential, by way of explanatory power, degree of precision, scope for suasion, and capacity for prediction. If this ninefold grilling does not suffice "to adjudicate what constitutes an adequate abstraction," then Yeung (1997, pp. 60–1) more or less shrugs, rounding things off with the throw-away line that "simplicity becomes an obvious candidate as the final criterion." Yet to the extent that abstraction and concretion are folded, unfolded, and refolded in many ways, they are, practically speaking, (only just) adequate for opening onto the chaosmos and the plane of immanence. One can no longer oppose the contentless and chaotic to the adequate and rational, since each is the slightly phased refolding of the other. So, just as the outside slides into the inside along the fold of a Möbius strip, and reciprocally, the ebb and flow of abstraction-cum-concretion is both chaotically adequate and adequately chaotic: through ceaselessly falling apart it gives consistency to the infinite variability. Rather than denounce abstractions and concretions that do not appear chaotic enough, one should simply refold them. This is less a sublation of an apparent contradiction than an ablation of a facade (i.e. face) of unity: consistency is what is left when constancy is discharged. "*The face, what a horror,*" insist Deleuze and Guattari (1988, p. 190). Faces are attributed to bodies. They are facilitators of recognition and identification *par excellence*. However, counter-currents of defacialization are always at work, opening up the facade to a labyrinthine complication.

people are constantly putting up an umbrella that shelters them and on the underside of which they draw a firmament and write their conventions and opinions. But poets, artists, make a slit in the umbrella, they tear open the firmament itself, to let in a bit of free and windy chaos and to frame in a sudden light a vision that appears through the rent ... Then come the crowd of imitators who repair the umbrella with something vaguely resembling the vision, and the crowd of commentators who patch over the rent with opinions: communication. Other artists are always needed to make other slits ... This is to say that artists struggle less against chaos (that, in a certain manner, all their wishes summon forth) than against the 'clichés' of opinion ... the page or canvas is already so covered with preexisting, preestablished clichés that it is first necessary to erase, to clean, to flatten, even to shred, so as to let in a breath of air from the chaos that brings us the vision ... Art is not chaos but a composition of chaos that yields the vision or sensation, so that it constitutes, as Joyce says, a chaosmos, a composed chaos – neither foreseen nor preconceived. (Deleuze and Guattari, 1994, pp. 203–4)

The outside is the infinitely (un)folded fold; it "is not a fixed limit but a moving matter animated by peristaltic movements, folds and foldings that together make up an inside" (Deleuze, 1988a, pp. 96–7). Consistency, then, is not just splayed out, it is also played out. Schizo-analysis interlaces with a certain kind of rhythmanalysis.

Rhythmanalysis

the formula of the Body without Organs: the interval is substance. The intervallic, interstitial substance synchronizes all the periods of the milieu components, their rates of synthesis, of transformation. All is metamorphosis, but substance is the enduring interval, lifetime, or Aion. (Canning, 1994b, p. 91)

Tonality is the relationship between the tones of a musical scale or the observance of a single tonic key as the basis of a composition. In traditional musicology, the first note of the scale – the tonic – is privileged as the 'tonal centre' around which a composition will (r)evolve. Five notes up the scale is the second most important note – the dominant. Between these two notes there is a kind of spontaneous force that returns the dominant to the tonic. Likewise for chords formed on these two notes. "Generally, tonality operates ... through a statement of *identity*, a statement of *alterity*, and a final *reassertion* of the *original* identity," writes Sweeney-Turner (1996, p. 228). It is "the structure of the *perfect cadence* – one begins on the *tonic*, moves out to the *dominant*, and achieves *closure* with a *return* to the tonic." While this movement is not strictly speaking dialectical, it does demonstrate how difference can be used to reinforce identity. Within the tonal system, the dominant (difference) is the structural alibi for the expanded reproduction of the tonic (identity). Since they form a compact, "*any* possibility of a centri*fugal* proliferation ... spinning away from a central point is closed off by ... a kind of centri*petal* dialectics which always returns to that centre. In the tonal system, closure is everywhere" (Sweeney-Turner, 1996, p. 228). Difference returns to identity, just as deviation participates in the spread of the norm. Accordingly, in traditional harmonic theory, "the only reason *why* intervallic movement was proposed was to provide a framework for containing it within *an overall schema of closure*," he continues. "One opens the interval between tonic and dominant ... *only in order to close it off*. Effectively, one captures the power of difference only in order to dialectically *reassert* the *original* identity all the more *forcefully* – in tonal music, the origin surrounds the supplement, hems it in, and usurps its force within an overall structural stasis" (Sweeney-Turner, 1996, p. 231). Additionally, the dialectical structuration of tonality resolves the traditional opposition between melody as an arrangement of single notes in a musically expressive succession (a temporalized, diachronic movement in extension) and harmony as a combination of simultaneously sounded notes to produce chords and chord progressions (a spatialized, synchronic arrangement that is intensive). Yet here as elsewhere, the harmonic 'calculus of intervals' fractures and splays out the presumed unity of each note from the off. A note is not so much self-sustained as subtracted from the pack. "Why must we always imagine music simply as note-structures in empty space, instead of beginning from a homogeneously filled acoustical space and *carving out music*, revealing musical figures and forms with an erasure?" asked Stockhausen. "So I composed negative forms as well, to correspond to the positive forms ... holes, pauses, cavities of various shapes" (quoted in Peters, 1997, p. 14).

Just as *a* colour is subtracted from the infinitude of continuously variable colouration, so too with *a* note. Every note is divided and (s)played out in and of itself. The pointillism of melody is always already everywhere criss-crossed by the intervallic spacing of harmony. "This fissure is not one among others. It is *the* fissure: the necessity of interval, the harsh law of spacing," insists Derrida (1976, p. 200). "Spacing is not the accident of song. Or rather, as accident and accessory, fall and supplement, it is also that without which, strictly speaking, the song would not have come into being." What begins to stir in the wake of this sweeping up of pointillism by the calculus of difference is the possibility of soliciting a deconstructive atonality from the closure of dialectical tonality.

The hold of dialectical tonality has been slackened, twisted, and collapsed in many pieces (e.g. through the structurally ambiguous play on the interval of a third, with its relations of tonic-mediant and tonic-submediant). Nevertheless, such a release of atonality may well prove ineffectual since it depends upon tonality for its sense, direction, and motivation. Transgression confirms the Law that it criss-crosses. Perhaps, then, one might conclude that atonal dissemination, as a centrifugal force counteracting the centripetal force of dialectical tonality, is illusory. Atonality may act as an alibi to get the dialectic off the hook (X). After all, it was commonplace in the physical sciences to assume that a centripetal force was balanced by an equal and opposite centrifugal force. This proved not to be the case: no such countervailing force exists. So although Derrida and Deleuze draw upon harmonic theory to enact a "swerve *away* from dialectics," as Sweeney-Turner (1996, p. 231) puts it, such a swerve may be reintegrated into dialectical musicology. It is here that the duplicity and double agency of poststructuralist spatial science once again comes to the fore. What matters is expression: how the intervallic structure is splayed out. This expressionism brings me back to the rhythm and consistency of origami: "One must learn the necessity of a scansion that comes to fold and unfold a thought," Derrida (1989f, p. 3) reminds us. "This is nothing other than the necessity of a rhythm – rhythm itself."

Rhythm concerns the periodical accent and the duration of notes within a musical composition. Since rhythm coordinates the flow of sonic events it is usual to emphasize its unifying and integrative force. Like melody, rhythm would appear to trace the flow of a mobile, sonic presence, driven by protention and retention. Each sonic event is fore-shadowed by the events that precede it and conserved in those that follow. Such is the rhythmic mastery of the event implied by the twin motifs of periodicity and duration. "The death of the instant," through protention and retention, "effectively squeezes alterity out of the instant, sucking it into a seamless temporality," says Peters (1997, p. 13), summarizing Levinas; "each instant is sonically penetrated by the others, thereby destroying the very idea of otherness. Levinas suggests that only the 'wrong note' holds out against melodic extinction by 'refusing to die'; the resulting instantaneous is elsewhere described as a 'diachrony without protention or retention.'" So, the 'rhythm of alterity' and the 'harsh law of spacing' need to eschew the continuity of musical lines and curves. "All the lines are lines of variation, which do not even have constant co-ordinates. The One, the All, the True, the object, the subject are not universals, but singular processes – of unification, totalisation, verification, objectivation, subjectification – present in the given apparatus" (Deleuze, 1992c, p. 162). Such would be rhythm without periodicity and duration. Like Levinas, "Derrida opts for an aleatory method, to break with the dialectical rhythm in which what comes after is represented in what comes before, teleology of goals and expectations fulfilled or disappointed" (Leavey, 1986, p. 127). Surprisingly, perhaps, there is the same aleatory impulse in Althusser (Elliott, 1998). And at the heart of such an 'aleatory materialism' is the event of becoming, singularity, and immanence (Massumi, 1992b).

The event of folding

> And even if there are only two terms, there is an AND between the two, which is neither one nor the other, nor the one which becomes the other, but which constitutes the multiplicity. (Deleuze and Parnet, 1987, p. 34–5)

'And' is not simply a connective, joint, and hinge between two things, it also implies progression (*better and better*), causation (*and then*), great duration (*on and on*), great number (*more and more*), addition (*this and that equals those*), differentiation (*there are writers and there are writers*), variety (*X and Y*), and succession (*walking two and two*). Without the conjunctive 'and,' there would be neither space nor spacing. 'And' enables everything to be put into circulation. Yet for all of its work, 'and' seems to be almost universally reviled. For example, in a review of McNay's (1992) *Foucault and Feminism*, Probyn despairs as 'the ampersand returns.' By reneging on its usual invisibility, clandestinity, and dissimulation, and coming centre-stage, so to speak, she bemoans "the very cleanness of the two distinct categories, Foucault and feminism, [which thereby] renders difficult movement between the two" (Probyn, 1994, p. 510). Such a reaction has become commonplace whenever a relation is posed in the form of *This and That*. It is as if the conjunctive 'and' were assumed to be an impenetrable and impervious partition, wholly out of place in these more nuanced, undecidable, and blurred times of reversibility, rather than rigidity. Now, whilst such rigidity is indeed lamentable, it has nothing whatsoever to do with the conjunctive 'and.' Wherever there is an 'and,' there is never a clean cut separating distinct and immutable terms.

As I have sought to demonstrate throughout this book, 'and' is a little fold that is itself the occasion for the intrusion of innumerable interleaved folds into our world. "Matter thus offers an infinitely porous, spongy, or cavernous texture without emptiness, caverns endlessly contained in other caverns: no matter how small, each body contains a world pierced with irregular passages, surrounded and penetrated by an increasingly vaporous fluid, the totality of the universe resembling a 'pond of matter in which there exist different flows and waves' [Leibnitz]" (Deleuze, 1993b, p. 5). Space is composed of intervals, disadjustments, and folds within folds, and populated solely by conjunctions, infinitives, and partitives. Space, place, things, people, and events are all composed from these 'joints.'

Now, so obsessed are we with establishing and maintaining rigid designators – with pinning down and padding out the most paranoiac and paralysing question of all: What *is* ...? – that we fail to inquire into the nature of the *fixative* that produces something or someone that can be given over for bonding and bondage in the first place. "AND is neither one thing nor the other, it's always in between, between two things; it's the borderline, there's always a border, a line of flight or flow, only we don't see it, because it's the least perceptible of things," notes Deleuze (1995, p. 45). "And yet it's along this line of flight that things come to pass, becomings evolve, revolutions take place ... an AND, AND, AND which each time marks a new threshold, a new direction of the broken line, a new course for the border." The fold – or relay – of a little 'and' disjoins what is held in place, dividing that which is supposedly given and present in and of itself. 'And' sets the event in motion. Such is the "triumph of the conjunction AND (*et*) over the predicative IS (*est*)" (Boundas, 1993, p. 5). Henceforth, one will have to (dis)locate and (up)root 'is' in this gap: the interval takes all; space takes place. Hereinafter, there is nothing outside an ever open and non-saturable context; there is nothing outside – or inside – the play of folding. Hereinafter: "Perhaps it is in the holes that the movement takes place" (Deleuze, 1988c, p. 18, quoted and translated by Hardt, 1993, p. xx).

Throughout this book I have repeatedly insisted on the unbecoming character of pointillism. By contrast, origami affirms the fact that there are only ever degrees of consistency that never stop being worked over by the disarranging force of chaosmotic variation. No beings (*is*s), just becomings (*and*s). Some take it for granted that the '*is*,' as the exemplary motif of the metaphysics of presence and the ontology of immutable being, has a certain phallic value: it stands tall and erect, alone and self-assured, without any recourse to the hand of another. The phallic One has only itself: pure positivity at the source. As I argued in Chapter 3, such a phallic structuration haunts and solicits Western metaphysics: an unseemly and unbecoming characterization of sexual difference animates ontology. Meanwhile, an erection is never simply given. Each is established in specific contexts, according to particular relations of affectation, and endures only so long as that which flows through it is constricted and held under pressure. Indeed, there is no phallogo-centrism that is not worked over by fluids and vapours: a gust of fresh air, a taste of the outside ... As Deleuze (1988a, p. 97) put it in his appreciation of Foucault, one should always think of "The inside as an operation of the outside." Moreover, the phallic term is energized not by auto-affection or auto-eroticism, but by way of this constitutive outside. A battery of flows animate and energize everything that appears phallic, so that every constant moves and trembles according to the rhythm of the flows that surge through it: rhythmanalysis. This is why the phallic '*is*' vibrates. Ontology gives way to vibratology, and in so doing schizoanalysis and nomad thought come to the fore.

> 'Nomad thought' does not lodge itself in the edifice of an ordered interiority; it moves freely in an element of exteriority. It does not repose on identity; it rides difference. It does not respect the artificial division between the three domains of representation, subject, concept, and being; it replaces restrictive analogy with a conductivity that knows no bounds ... It synthesizes a multiplicity of elements without effacing their heterogeneity or hindering their potential for future rearranging. (Massumi, 1992a, pp. 4–6)

So, with regard to all of those '*is*s,' it is not a question of expulsion or exorcism – as if one could have done with the spectre of hauntology! It is not that constancy is bad or wrong. It is simply unbecoming and ill-mannered. Constancy is bereft of consistency: that's all. Ontology should be placed under erasure, to be sure, but real consistency takes place only when '*is*' becomes a deterritorialized term, wrenched from its usual phallogocentric context in order to be (s)played out – once again – as a vibrator, according to the ebb and flow of incalculable '*ands*' that are forever coming and soliciting our affection. For there are multiple becomings in every body: this is what moves the earth and shakes the world. In this way, rhythmanalysis gets swept up by schizoanalysis. Such is the art of spatial science when it truly expresses the differentials that space makes.

> The fissure has become primary, and as such grows larger. It is not a matter of following a chain ..., even across voids, but of getting out of the chain or the association ... It is the method of BETWEEN, ... which does away with all ... of the One. It is the method of AND, 'this and then that,' which does away with all ... of Being ... The whole undergoes a mutation, because it has ceased to be the One-Being, in order to become the constitutive between-two ... The whole thus merges with what Blanchot calls the force of 'dispersal of the Outside' or the 'vertigo of spacing ...' (Deleuze, 1989, pp. 179–80)

The chaosmos that we call a world can be folded, unfolded, and refolded in many ways. It remains for a geographer, for an origamist-cum-spatial-scientist, to take up some folds and experiment with their rhythm and consistency, their intensities and affects. Our duty as geographers is simply to make space for the deforming force of alterity and to open up space to the differential currents of dissimilation, disjointure, and dissemination. Letting space take place. That is the ethic specific to poststructuralist geography. It is the diabolical art of a perverse, carcinogenic, and solicitous spatial science. It is the affirmation of everything that declines integration and swerves away from stabilization. Derrida (1986b, p. 75) put it exquisitely: "Let us space."

Bibliography

Abbott, E. A. (1944) *Flatland: A Romance of Many Dimensions* (Blackwell, Oxford).

Adorno, T. W. (1973) *Negative Dialectics*, trans. E. B. Ashton (Routledge & Kegan Paul, London).

Agnew, J., Livingstone, D. N., and Rogers, D. (eds) (1996) *Human Geography: An Essential Anthology* (Blackwell, Oxford).

Allen, J., and Pryke, M. (1994) "The production of service space," *Environment and Planning D: Society and Space*, 12(4): 453–76.

Althusser, L. (1979) *For Marx*, trans. B. Brewster (Verso, London).

Althusser, L., and Balibar, E. (1979) *Reading Capital*, trans. B. Brewster (Verso, London).

Ansell-Pearson, K. (1997) *Viroid Life: Perspectives on Nietzsche and the Transhuman Condition* (Routledge, London).

Arthur, C. J. (1993) "Hegel's *Logic* and Marx's *Capital*," in *Marx's Method in Capital*, ed. F. Moseley (Humanities Press, Atlantic Highlands, NJ) pp. 63–87.

Augé, M. (1995) *Non-Places: Introduction to an Anthropology of Supermodernity* (Verso, London).

Barnes, T. J. (1993) "Whatever happened to the philosophy of science?" *Environment and Planning A*, 25(3): 301–4.

Barnes, T. J. (1994) "Five ways to leave your critic: a sociological scientific experiment in replying," *Environment and Planning A*, 26: (1653–8).

Barnes, T. J. (1998) "A history of regression: actors, networks, machines, and numbers," *Environment and Planning A*, 30(2): 203–23.

Barnett, C. (1993) "Peddling postmodernism: a response to Strohmayer and Hannah's 'Domesticating postmodernism,'" *Antipode*, 25(4): 345–58.

Barnett, C. (1995) "Awakening the dead: who needs the history of geography?" *Transactions of the Institute of British Geographers*, 20(4): 417–19.

Barth, L. (1996) "Immemorial visibilities: seeing the city difference," *Environment and Planning A*, 28(3): 471–93.

Barthes, R. (1972a) *Critical Essays*, trans. R. Howard (Northwestern University Press, Evanston, IL).

Barthes, R. (1972b) *Mythologies*, trans. A. Lavers (Hill and Wang, New York).

Barthes, R. (1978) *A Lover's Discourse: Fragments*, trans. R. Howard (Hill & Wang, New York).

Barthes, R. (1984) *Image Music Text* ,trans. S. Heath (Fontana, London).

Bassett, K. (1994) "'Whatever happened to the philosophy of science?': some comments on Barnes," *Environment and Planning A*, 26(3): 337–42.

Bassett, K. (1995) "On reflexivity: further comments on Barnes and the sociology of science," *Environment and Planning A*, 27: 1527–33.

Bataille, G. (1982) *Story of the Eye*, trans. J. Neugroschal (Penguin, Harmondsworth).

Bataille, G. (1988) *The Accursed Share: An Essay on General Economy: Volume 1: Consumption*, trans. R. Hurley (Zone, New York).

Baudrillard, J. (1981) *For a Critique of the Political Economy of the Sign*, trans. C. Levin (Telos, St Louis, MO).

Baudrillard, J. (1983a) *In the Shadow of the Silent Majorities*, trans. P. Foss, P. Patton, J. Johnston (Semiotext(e), New York).

Baudrillard, J. (1983b) *Simulations*, trans. P. Foss, P. Patton, P. Beitchman (Semiotext(e), New York).

Baudrillard, J. (1986) "The year 2000 will not take place," in *Future*Fall: Excursions into Post-Modernity*, eds E. A. Grosz, T. Threadgold, D. Kelly, A. Cholodenko, and E. Colles (Power Institute of Fine Arts, University of Sydney, NSW), pp. 18–28.

Baudrillard, J. (1987a) *Forget Foucault*, trans. N. Dufresne (Semiotext(e), New York).

Baudrillard, J. (1987b) *The Evil Demon of Images*, trans. P. Patton, and P. Foss (Power Institute of Fine Arts, University of Sydney, NSW).

Baudrillard, J. (1988a) *Xerox & Infinity*, trans. Agitac (Agitac, London).

Baudrillard, J. (1988b) *America*, trans. C. Turner (Verso, London).

Baudrillard, J. (1988c) *The Ecstasy of Communication*, trans. B. Schutze, and C. Schutze (Semiotext(e), New York).

Baudrillard, J. (1990a) *Seduction*, trans. B. Singer (Macmillan, London).

Baudrillard, J. (1990b) *Cool Memories*, trans. C. Turner (Verso, London).

Baudrillard, J. (1990c) *Revenge of the Crystal: Selected Writings on the Modern Object and Its Destiny, 1968–1983*, eds and trans. P. Foss, and J. Pefanis (Pluto, London).

Baudrillard, J. (1990d) *Fatal Strategies*, trans. P. Beitchman, and W. G. J. Niesluchowski (Pluto, London).

Baudrillard, J. (1993a) *Baudrillard Live: Selected Interviews*, ed. M. Gane (Verso, London).

Baudrillard, J. (1993b) *The Transparency of Evil: Essays on Extreme Phenomena*, trans. J. Benedict (Verso, London).

Baudrillard, J. (1993c) *Symbolic Exchange and Death*, trans. I. H. Grant (Sage, London).

Baudrillard, J. (1994) *Simulacra & Simulation*, trans. S. F. Glaser (University of Michigan Press, Ann Arbor).

Baudrillard, J. (1995) "The virtual illusion: or the automatic writing of the world," *Theory, Culture & Society*, 12(4): 97–107.

Baudrillard, J. (1996a) "Vivisecting the 90s: An interview with Jean Baudrillard," http://www.ctheory.com/a24-vivisecting_90s.html.

Baudrillard, J. (1996b) *The Perfect Crime*, trans. C. Turner (Verso, London).

Baudrillard, J. (1996c) *The System of Objects*, trans. J. Benedict (Verso, London).

Baudrillard, J. (1998) *The Consumer Society: Myths and Structures*, trans. C. Turner (Sage, London).

Baugh, B. (1993) "Deleuze and empiricism," *Journal of the British Society for Phenomenology*, 24(1): 15–31.

Bauman, Z. (1989) *Modernity and the Hololcaust* (Polity, Cambridge).

Bauman, Z. (1990) "Modernity and ambivalence," in *Globalization: Nationalism, Globalization and Modernity*, ed. M. Featherstone (Sage, London), pp. 143–169.

Bauman, Z. (1993) *Postmodern Ethics* (Blackwell, Oxford).

Bauman, Z. (1996) "From pilgrim to tourist – or a short history of identity," in *Questions of Cultural Identity*, eds S. Hall, and P. Du Gay (Sage, London), pp. 18–36.

Beck, U. (1992) "From industrial society to risk society: questions of survival, social structure and ecological enlightenment," *Theory, Culture & Society*, 9(1): 97–123.

Beck, U., Giddens, A., and Lash, S. (1994) *Reflexive Modernization: Politics, Tradition and Aesthetics in the Modern Social Order* (Polity, Cambridge).

Beckett, S. (1958) *The Unnamable* (Grove, New York).

Beckett, S. (1986) "Waiting for Godot," in *Samuel Beckett: The Complete Dramatic Works* (Faber & Faber, London), pp. 7–87.

Bell, D. (1973) *The Coming of Post-Industrial Society* (Basic Books, New York).

Bell, M., Butlin, R., and Heffernan, M. (eds) (1995) *Geography and Imperialism 1820–1940* (Manchester University Press, Manchester).

Benko, G. (1997) "Introduction: modernity, postmodernity and the social sciences," in *Space and Social Theory: Interpreting Modernity and Postmodernity*, eds G. Benko, and U. Strohmayer (Blackwell, Oxford), pp. 1–44.

Bennington, G. (1988) *Lyotard: Writing the Event* (University of Manchester Press, Manchester).

Bennington, G. (1989a) "Deconstruction is not what you think," in *Deconstruction: Omnibus Volume*, eds A. Papadakis, C. Cooke, and A. Benjamin (Academy Editions, London), p. 84.

Bennington, G. (1989b) "L'arroseur arrosé(e)," *New Formations*, 7: 35–49.

Bennington, G. (1989c) "Deconstruction and postmodernism," in *Deconstruction: Omnibus Volume*, eds A. Papadakis, C. Cooke, and A. Benjamin (Academy Editions, London), pp. 85–7.

Bennington, G. (1996a) "X," in *Applying: To Derrida*, eds J. Brannigan, R. Robbins, and J. Wolfreys (Macmillan, London), pp. 1–20.

Bennington, G. (1996b) "Genuine Gasché (perhaps)," *Imprimatur*, 1(2&3): 252–7.

Benvenuto, B., and Kennedy, R. (eds) (1986) *The Works of Jacques Lacan: An Introduction* (Free Association, London).

Berezdivin, R. (1987) "In stalling metaphysics: at the threshold," in *Deconstruction and Philosophy: The Texts of Jacques Derrida*, ed. J. Sallis (University of Chicago Press, Chicago), pp. 47–59.

Berman, M. (1982) *All That Is Solid Melts into Air: The Experience of Modernity* (Verso, London).

Bhabha, H. (1993) *The Location of Culture* (Routledge, London).

Bhaskar, R. (1989) *Reclaiming Reality* (Verso, London).

Blanchot, M. (1993) *The Infinite Conversation*, trans. S. Hanson (University of Minnesota Press, Minneapolis).

Blum, V., and Nast, H. (1996) "Where's the difference? The heterosexualisation of alterity in Henri Lefebvre and Jacques Lacan," *Environment and Planning D: Society and Space*, 14: 559–80.

Bogue, R. (1989) *Deleuze and Guattari* (Routledge, London).

Borges, J. L. (1985) "The garden of forking paths," in *Fictions*, (John Calder, London), pp. 79–92.

Botting, F., and Wilson, S. (1998) "By accident: the Tarantinian ethics," *Theory, Culture & Society*, 15(2): 89–113.

Boundas, C. V. (1993) "Foreclosure of the other: from Sartre to Deleuze," *Journal of the British Society for Phenomenology*, 24(1): 32–43.

Boundas, C. V., and Olkowski, D. (1994) "Editors' introduction," in *Gilles Deleuze and the Theatre of Philosophy*, eds C. V. Boundas and D. Olkowski (Routledge, London) pp. 1–22.

Bové, P. (1988) "Foreword: The Foucault phenomenon: the problematics of style," in G. Deleuze, *Foucault*, trans. and ed. S. Hand (Athlone, London), pp. vii–xl.

Boyne, R. (1990) *Foucault and Derrida: The Other Side of Reason* (Unwin Hyman, London).

Braidotti, R. (1994) *Nomadic Subjects: Embodiment and Sexual Difference in Contemporary Feminist Theory* (Columbia University Press, New York).

Braidotti, R. (1996) "An anti-Oedipal tribute," *Radical Philosophy*, 76: 3–5.

Braidotti, R. (1997) "Meta(l)morphoses," *Theory, Culture & Society*, 14(2): 67–80.

Brannigan, J., Robbins R., and Wolfreys, J. (eds) (1996) *Applying: To Derrida* (Macmillan, London).

Brooke-Rose, C. (1981) *A Rhetoric of the Unreal: Studies in Narrative Structure, Especially of the Fantastic* (Cambridge University Press, Cambridge).

Bryant, C. G. A., and Jary, D. (eds) (1991) *Giddens' Theory of Structuration: A Critical Appreciation* (Routledge, London).

Buck-Morss, S. (1991) *The Dialectics of Seeing: Walter Benjamin and the Arcades Project* (MIT Press, Cambridge, MA).

Buck-Morss, S. (1994) "Fashion in ruins: history after the Cold War," *Radical Philosophy*, 68: 10–17.

Burgin, V. (1996) *In/different Spaces: Place and Memory in Visual Culture* (University of California Press, Berkeley).

Burroughs, W. S. (1988) *The Western Lands* (Picador, Basingstoke).

Butler, J. (1993) *Bodies that Matter: On the Discursive Limits of 'Sex'* (Routledge, London).

Buttimer, A. (1982) "Musing on helicon: root metaphors and geography," *Geografiska Annaler*, 64B: 89–96.

Buttimer, A. (1993) *Geography and the Human Spirit* (Johns Hopkins University Press, Baltimore, MD).

Canning, P. (1994a) "Fluidentity," *SubStance*, 44/45: 35–45.

Canning, P. (1994b) "The crack of time and the ideal game," in *Gilles Deleuze and the Theatre of Philosophy*, eds C. V. Boundas, and D. Olkowski (Routledge, London), pp. 73–98.

Carlstein, T., Parkes D., and Thrift, N. (eds) (1978a) *Timing Space and Spacing Time: Volume 1: Making Sense of Time* (Arnold, London).

Carlstein, T., Parkes D., and Thrift, N. (eds) (1978b) *Timing Space and Spacing Time: Volume 2: Human Activity and Time Geography* (Arnold, London).

Carroll, D. (1987) *Paraesthetics: Foucault, Lyotard, Derrida* (Methuen, Andover).

Carter, P. (1987) *The Road to Botany Bay: An Essay in Spatial History* (University of Chicago Press, Chicago).

Castells, M. (1996) *The Rise of the Network Society: The Information Age: Economy, Society and Culture, Volume I* (Blackwell, Oxford).

Castells, M. (1997) *The Power of Identity: The Information Age: Economy, Society and Culture, Volume II* (Blackwell, Oxford).

Castree, N. (1996) "Birds, mice and geography: Marxisms and dialectics," *Transactions of the Institute of British Geographers*, 21(2): 342–62.

Caygill, H. (1998) *Walter Benjamin: The Colour of Experience* (Routledge, London).

Chambers, I. (1994) *Migrancy, Culture, Identity* (Routledge, London).

Chaney, D. (1994) *The Cultural Turn: Scene-Setting Essays on Contemporary Cultural History* (Routledge, London).

Clarke, D. B. (1997) "Consumption and the city, modern and postmodern," *International Journal of Urban and Regional Studies*, 21(2): 218–37.

Clarke, D. B., and Doel, M. A. (1994a) "The perfection of geography as an aesthetic of disappearance: Baudrillard's America," *Ecumene*, 1: 317–21.

Clarke, D. B., and Doel, M. A. (1994b) "Transpolitical geography," *Geoforum*, 25(4): 505–24.

Clarke, D. B., Doel, M. A., and McDonough, F. X. (1996) "Holocaust topologies: singularity, politics, space," *Political Geography*, 15(6 & 7): 457–89.

Cloke, P., Philo, C., and Sadler, D. (1991) *Approaching Human Geography: An Introduction to Contemporary Theoretical Debates* (Paul Chapman, London).

Colwell, C. (1996) "Deleuze, sense and the event of AIDS," *Postmodern Culture*, 6(2). http://muse.jhu.edu/journals/postmodern_culture/.

Cresswell, T. (1997a) "Weeds, plagues, and bodily secretions: a geographical interpretation of metaphors of displacement," *Annals of the Association of American Geographers*, 87(2): 330–45.

Cresswell, T. (1997b) "Imagining the nomad: mobility and the postmodern primitive," in *Space and Social Theory: Interpreting Modernity and Postmodernity*, eds G. Benko, and U. Strohmayer (Blackwell, Oxford), pp. 360–79.

Critchley, S. (1990) "Writing the revolution: the politics of truth in Genet's Prisoner of Love," *Radical Philosophy*, 56: 25–34.

Critchley, S. (1992) *The Ethics of Deconstruction: Derrida and Levinas* (Blackwell, Oxford).

Culler, J. (1988) *Framing the Sign: Criticism and its Institutions* (Blackwell, Oxford).

Daniels, S. (1992) "Place and the geographical imagination," *Geography*, 77(4): 310–22.

Darnton, R. (1979) *The Business of Enlightenment: A Publishing History of the Encyclopédie, 1775–1800* (Belknap, Cambridge).

Davies, P. (1984) *Superforce: The Search for a Grand Unified Theory of Nature* (Heinemann, London).

Davies, P., and Brown, J. (eds) (1988) *Superstrings: A Theory of Everything?* (Cambridge University Press, Cambridge).

Dear, M. J. (1986) "Postmodernism and planning," *Environment and Planning D: Society and Space*, 4: 367–84.

Dear, M. J. (1988) "The postmodern challenge: reconstructing human geography," *Transactions of the Institute of British Geographers*, 13: 262–74.

Dear, M., and Wassmansdorf, G. (1993) "Postmodern consequences," *Geographical Record*, 83(3): 321–5.

de Certeau, M. (1986) *Heterologies: Discourse on the Other*, trans. B. Massumi (Manchester University Press, Manchester).

Deleuze, G. (1972) "Schizophrénie et positivité du déir," *Encyclopédia Universalis*, vol. 4 (Éditions Encyclopédie Universalis France, Paris).

Deleuze, G. (1977a) "I have nothing to admit." *Semiotext(e)*, 2(3): 111–16.

Deleuze, G. (1977b) "Intellectuals and power," with M. Foucault, in M. Foucault *Language, Counter-memory, Practice* (Cornell University Press, Ithaca, NY), pp. 205–17.

Deleuze, G. (1983a) "Politics," in G. Deleuze, and F. Guattari *On the Line* (Semiotext(e), New York), pp. 69–115.

Deleuze, G. (1983b) *Nietzsche and Philosophy* (University of Columbia Press, New York).

Deleuze, G. (1983c) "Francis Bacon: the logic of sensation," *Flash Art*, 112: 8–16.

Deleuze, G. (1986) *Cinema 1: the Movement-Image*, trans. H. Tomlinson, and B. Habberjam (Athlone, London).

Deleuze, G. (1988a) *Foucault*, trans. S. Hand (Athlone, London).

Deleuze, G. (1988b) *Spinoza: Practical Philosophy*, trans. R. Hurley (City Lights, San Francisco).

Deleuze, G. (1988c) "Signes et événements," *Magazine Littéraire*, 257: 16–25.

Deleuze, G. (1989) *Cinema 2: the Time-Image*, trans. H. Tomlinson, and R. Galeta (Athlone, London).

Deleuze, G. (1990a) *The Logic of Sense*, trans. M. Lester, ed. C. V. Boundas (Columbia University Press, New York).

Deleuze, G. (1990b) *Expressionism in Philosophy: Spinoza*, trans. M. Joughin (Zone, New York).

Deleuze, G. (1991) *Bergsonism* (Zone, New York).

Deleuze, G. (1992a) "Mediators" trans. M. Joughin, in *Zone 6: Incorporations*, eds J. Crary, and S. Kwinter (Zone, New York), pp. 281–94.

Deleuze, G. (1992b) "Ethology: Spinoza and us" trans. R. Hurley, in *Zone 6: Incorporations*, eds J. Crary, and S. Kwinter (Zone, New York), pp. 625–33.

Deleuze, G. (1992c) "What is a dispositif?," in *Michel Foucault: Philosopher*, ed. and trans. T. J. Armstrong (Harvester Wheatsheaf, Hemel Hempstead), pp. 159–66.

Deleuze, G. (1993a) *The Deleuze Reader*, ed. C. V. Boundas (Columbia University Press, New York).

Deleuze, G. (1993b) *The Fold: Leibniz and the Baroque*, trans. T. Conley (University of Minnesota Press, Minneapolis).

Deleuze, G. (1994a) "He stuttered," in *Gilles Deleuze and the Theatre of Philosophy*, eds C. V. Boundas, and D. Olkowski (Routledge, London), pp. 23–29.

Deleuze, G. (1994b) *Difference and Repetition*, trans. P. Patton (Athlone, London).

Deleuze, G. (1995) *Negotiations, 1972–1990*, trans. M. Joughin (Columbia University Press, New York).

Deleuze, G. (1997a) "Literature and language," *Critical Inquiry*, 23(2): 225–30.

Deleuze, G. (1997b) "Immanence: A life ..." *Theory, Culture & Society*, 14(2): 3–7.

Deleuze, G. (1997c) *Essays Critical and Clinical*, trans. D. W. Smith, and M. A. Greco (Minnesota University Press, Minneapolis).

Deleuze, G., and Guattari, F. (1983) *On the Line*, trans. J. Johnston (Semiotext(e), New York).

Deleuze, G., and Guattari, F. (1984) *Anti-Oedipus: Capitalism and Schizophrenia*, trans. R. Hurley, M. Seem, H. R. Lane (Athlone, London).

Deleuze, G., and Guattari, F. (1986) *Kafka: Toward a Minor Literature*, trans. D. Polan (University of Minnesota Press, Minneapolis).

Deleuze, G., and Guattari, F. (1988) *A Thousand Plateaus: Capitalism and Schizophrenia*, trans. B. Massumi (Athlone, London).

Deleuze, G., and Guattari, F. (1994) *What is Philosophy?*, trans. G. Burchell, and H. Tomlinson (Verso, London).

Deleuze, G., and Parnet, C. (1987) *Dialogues*, trans. H. Tomlinson, B. Habberjam (Athlone, London).

Demeritt, D. (1996) "Social theory and the reconstruction of science and geography," *Transactions of the Institute of British Geographers*, 21(3): 484–503.

Derrida, J. (1976) *Of Grammatology*, trans. G. Spivak (Johns Hopkins University Press, Baltimore, MD).

Derrida, J. (1977) "Limited Inc abc," *Glyph*, II: 162–254.

Derrida, J. (1978) *Writing and Difference*, trans. A. Bass (University of Chicago Press, Chicago).

Derrida, J. (1981a) *Positions*, trans. A. Bass (University of Chicago Press, Chicago).

Derrida, J. (1981b) *Dissemination*, trans. B. Johnson (University of Chicago Press, Chicago).

Derrida, J. (1982a) *Margins of Philosophy*, trans. A. Bass (University of Chicago Press, Chicago).

Derrida, J. (1982b) "Sendings: on representation," *Social Research*, 49(2): 294–326.

Derrida, J. (1983) "The time of a thesis: punctuations," in *Philosophy in France Today*, ed. A. Montefiore (Cambridge University Press, Cambridge), pp. 34–50.

Derrida, J. (1984a) *Signéponge / Signsponge*, trans. R. Rand (Columbia University Press, New York).

Derrida, J. (1984b) "No apocalypse, not now (full speed ahead, seven missiles, seven missives)," *Diacritics*, 14: 20–31.

Derrida, J. (1984c) "Dialogue with Jacques Derrida," in *Dialogues with Contemporary Continental Thinkers: The Phenomenological Heritage* (Manchester University Press, Manchester), pp. 105–26.

Derrida, J. (1985) "The time is out of joint," in *Deconstruction is/in America: A New Sense of the Political*, ed. A. Haverkamp (New York University Press, New York), pp. 14–38.

Derrida, J. (1986a) *Mémoires: For Paul de Man*, revised edn 1989, trans. C. Lindsay, J. Culler, E. Cadava, and P. Kamuf (Columbia University Press, New York).

Derrida, J. (1986b) *Glas*, trans. J. P. Leavey, and R. Rand (University of Nebraska Press, Lincoln).

Derrida, J. (1986c) "Architecture where the desire may live," *Domus*, 671: 17–25.

Derrida, J. (1986d) "Remarks on deconstruction and pragmatism," in *Deconstruction and Pragmatism*, ed. C. Mouffe (Routledge, London), pp. 77–88.

Derrida, J. (1987a) *The Post Card: From Socrates to Freud and Beyond*, trans. A. Bass (University of Chicago Press, Chicago).

Derrida, J. (1987b) *The Truth in Painting*, trans. G. Bennington, and I. McLeod (University of Chicago Press, Chicago).

Derrida, J. (1988a) *Limited Inc*, ed. G. Graff, trans. S. Weber, and J. Mehlman (Northwestern University Press, Evanston, IL).

Derrida, J. (1988b) "Interview with Jean-Luc Nancy," *Topoi*, 7 (2): 113–21.

Derrida, J. (1988c) "The truth in painting," in *The New Modernism: Deconstructionist Tendencies in Art–Art / Design Profile*, 8 ed. A. Papadakis (Academy Editions, London), pp. 19–25.

Derrida, J. (1988d) "Structure, sign and play in the discourse of the human sciences," in *Modern Criticism and Theory: A Reader*, ed. D. Lodge (Longman, London), pp. 108–23.

Derrida, J. (1989a) "Biodegradables: seven diary fragments," *Critical Inquiry*, 15 (4): 812–73.

Derrida, J. (1989b) "On colleges and philosophy: Jacques Derrida with Geoff Bennington," in *Postmodernism: ICA Documents*, 4 & 5, ed. L. Appignanesi (Free Association, London), pp. 209–28.

Derrida, J. (1989c) "Fifty-two aphorisms for a foreword," in *Deconstruction: Omnibus Volume*, eds A. Papadakis, C. Cooke, and A. Benjamin (Academy Editions, London), pp. 67–9.

Derrida, J. (1989d) "Jacques Derrida interview by Christopher Norris: discussion and comments," in *Deconstruction: Omnibus Volume*, eds A. Papadakis, C. Cooke, and A. Benjamin (Academy Editions, London) pp. 71–8.

Derrida, J. (1989e) "How to avoid speaking: denials," trans. K. Frieden, in *Languages of the Unsayable: The Play of Negativity in Literature and Literary Theory*, eds S. Budwick, and W. Iser (Columbia University Press, New York,) pp. 3–70.

Derrida, J. (1989f) "Introduction: desistance," in P. Lacoue-Labarthe, *Typography: Mimesis, Philosophy, Politics*, ed. C. Fynsk (Harvard University Press, Cambridge, MA), pp. 1–42.

Derrida, J. (1990) "Some statements and truisms about neologisms, newisms, postisms, parasitisms, and other small seismisms," trans. A. Tomiche, in *The States of Theory*, ed. D. Carroll (Columbia University Press, New York), pp. 63–94.

Derrida, J. (1991a) *A Derrida Reader: Between the Blinds*, ed. P. Kamuf (Harvester Wheatsheaf, Hemel Hempstead).

Derrida, J. (1991b) *Cinders*, trans. N. Luckacher (University of Nebraska Press, Lincoln).

Derrida, J. (1991c) "'Eating well,' or the calculation of the subject: an interview with Jacques Derrida," in *Who Comes After the Subject?*, eds E. Cadava, P. Connor, and J.-L. Nancy (Routledge, London), pp. 96–119.

Derrida, J. (1992a) "Passions: 'An oblique offering'", in *Derrida: A Critical Reader*, ed. D. Wood (Blackwell, Oxford), pp. 5–35.

Derrida, J. (1992b) "Jacques Derrida interview," in *Talking Liberties*, eds D. Jones, and R. Stoneman (Channel 4 Television, London), pp. 6–9.

Derrida, J. (1992c) *Jacques Derrida: Acts of Literature*, ed. D. Attridge, trans. (Routledge, London).

Derrida, J. (1992d) *Given Time: 1. Counterfeit Money*, trans. P. Kamuf (University of Chicago Press, London).

Derrida, J. (1993a) *Memoirs of the Blind: The Self-Portrait and Other Ruins*, trans. P.-A. Brault, and M. Naas (University of Chicago Press, London).

Derrida, J. (1993b) *Aporias*, trans. T. Dutoit (Stanford University Press, Stanford).

Derrida, J. (1994a) "The deconstruction of actuality: an interview with Jacques Derrida," *Radical Philosophy*, 68: 28–41.

Derrida, J. (1994b) *Specters of Marx: The State of the Debt, the Work of Mourning, and the New International*, trans. P. Kamuf (Routledge, London).

Derrida, J. (1994c) "The spatial arts: an interview with Jacques Derrida (P. Brunette, D. Wills)," in *Deconstruction and the Visual Arts: Art, Media, Architecture*, eds P. Brunette, and D. Wills (Cambridge University Press, Cambridge) pp. 9–32.

Derrida, J. (1995a) *Points ... Interviews, 1974–1994*, ed. E. Weber, trans. P. Kamuf and others (Stanford University Press, Stanford, CA).

Derrida, J. (1995b) "*Khora*" in *On the Name*, trans. D. Wood, J. P. Leavey, and I. McLeod, ed. T. Dutoit (Stanford University Press, Stanford, CA), pp. 89–127.

Derrida, J. (1995c) "Archive fever: a Freudian impression," *Diacritics*, 25(2): 9–63.

Derrida, J. (1996) "'As if I were dead': an interview with Jacques Derrida," in *Applying: To Derrida*, eds J. Brannigan, R. Robbins, and J. Wolfreys (Macmillan, London), pp. 212–26.

Descombes, V. (1980) *Modern French Philosophy*, trans. L. Scott-Fox, and J. M. Harding (Cambridge University Press, Cambridge).

Descombes, V. (1993) *The Barometer of Reason: On the Philosophies of Current Events* (Oxford University Press, Oxford).

Dews, P. (1987) *Logics of Disintegration: Post-structuralist Thought and the Claims of Critical Theory* (Verson, London).

Dixon, D. P., and Jones III, J. P. (1996) "For a *supercalifragilisticexpialidocious* scientific geography," *Annals of the Association of American Geographers*, 86(4): 767–79.

Dixon, D. P., and Jones III, J. P. (1998) "My dinner with Derrida, *or* spatial analysis and poststructuralism do lunch," *Environment and Planning A*, 30(2): 247–60.

Doel, M. A. (1992) "In stalling deconstruction: striking out the postmodern," *Environment and Planning D: Society and Space*, 10: 163–79.

Doel, M. A. (1993) "Proverbs for paranoids: writing geography on hollowed ground," *Transactions of the Institute of British Geographer*, 18: 377–94.

Doel, M. A. (1994a) "Deconstruction on the move: from libidinal economy to liminal materialism," *Environment and Planning A*, 26: 1041–59.

Doel, M. A. (1994b) "Something resists: reading–deconstruction as ontological infestation (departures from the texts of Jacques Derrida)," in P. Cloke, M. Doel, D. Matless, M. Phillips, and N. Thrift, *Writing the Rural: Five Cultural Geographies*, (Paul Chapman, London), pp. 127–48.

Doel, M. A. (1994c) "Writing difference," *Environment and Planning A*, 26: 1015–20.

Doel, M. A. (1995) "Bodies without Organs: deconstruction and schizoanalysis," in *Mapping the Subject: Geographies of Cultural Transformation*, eds S. Pile, and N. Thrift (Routledge, London), pp. 227–41.

Doel, M. A. (1996) "A hundred thousand lines of flight: a machinic introduction to the nomad thought and scrumpled geography of Gilles Deleuze and Félix Guattari," *Environment and Planning D: Society and Space*, 14: 421–39.

Doel, M. A. (forthcoming) "Un-glunking geography: spatial science after Dr. Seuss and Gilles Deleuze," in *Thinking Space*, eds M. Crang, and N. Thrift (Routledge, London).

Doel, M. A., and Clarke, D. B. (1997a) "From ramble city to the screening of the eye: *Blade Runner*, death and symbolic exchange," in *The Cinematic City*, ed. D. B. Clarke (Routledge, London), pp. 140–67.

Doel, M. A., and Clarke, D. B. (1997b) "Transpolitical urbanism: suburban anomaly and ambient fear," *Space and Culture*, 1(2): 13–36.

Doel, M. A., and Clarke, D. B. (1998a) "Figuring the Holocaust: singularity, theory, and spatial purification," in *Rethinking Geopolitics*, eds G. Ó. Tuathail, S. Dalby (Routledge, London), pp. 39–61.

Doel, M. A., and Clarke, D. B. (1998b) "Virtual worlds: simulation, suppletion, s(ed)uction, and simulacra," in *Virtual Geographies: Bodies, Spaces and Relations*, eds M. Crang, P. Crang, and J. May (Routledge, London).

Doel, M. A., and Clarke, D. B. (forthcoming) "Dark Panopticon. Or, Attack of the Killer Toma-toes," *Environment and Planning D: Society and Space*.

Dooley, M. (1996) "Playing on the pyramid: resituating the 'self' in Kierkegaard and Derrida," *Imprimatur*, 1(2 & 3): 151–61.

Driver, F. et al. (1995) "Geographical traditions: rethinking the history of geography," *Transactions of the Institute of British Geographers*, 20(4): 403–22.

Eagleton, T. (1986) *Against the Grain: Essays 1975–1985* (Verso, London).

Elliott, G. (1998) "Ghostlier demarcations: on the posthumous edition of Althusser's writing," *Radical Philosophy*, 90: 20–32.

Ellis, J. M. (1989) *Against Deconstruction* (Princeton University Press, Princeton, NJ).

Entrikin, J. N. (1991) *The Betweenness of Place: Towards a Geography of Modernity* (Macmillan, London).

Evans, D. (1996) "Historicism and Lacanian theory," *Radical Philosophy*, 79: 35–40.

Farinelli, F., Olsson G., and Reichert D. (eds) (1994) *Limits of Representation* (Accedo, Munich).

Ferrell, R. (1996) *Passion in Theory: Conceptions of Freud and Lacan* (Routledge, London).

Foucault, M. (1970) *The Order of Things: An Archaeology of the Human Sciences*, trans. from the French (Tavistock, Andover).

Foucault, M. (1977) "Theatrum philosophicum," in M. Foucault, *Language, Counter-memory, Prac-tice: Selected Essays*, ed. and trans. D. F. Bouchard (Cornell University Press, Ithaca, NY), pp. 165–96.

Foucault, M. (1980) "Questions on geography," in *Power/Knowledge: Selected Interviews and Other Writings, 1972–1977*, ed. C. Gordon (Pantheon, London), pp. 63–77.

Foucault, M. (1982) *The Archaeology of Knowledge*, trans. A. M. Sheridan-Smith (Pantheon, New York).

Foucault, M. (1984) "Preface," in G. Deleuze, F. Guattari, *Anti-Oedipus: Capitalism and Schizo-phrenia*, trans. R. Hurley, M. Seem, and H. R. Lane (Athlone, London), pp. xi–xiv.

Foucault, M. (1986) "Of other spaces," *Diacritics*, 16: 22–7.

Foucault, M. (1988) "The concern for truth: interview with François Ewald," in *Michel Foucault: Politics, Philosophy, Culture: Interviews and Other Writings*, ed. L. D. Kritzman (Routledge, New York), pp. 255–67.

Foucault, M. (1989) *Foucault Live (Interviews, 1966–84)*, ed. S. Lotringer, trans. J. Johnston (Semi-otext(e), New York).

Foucault, M. (1990) "Maurice Blanchot: the thought from outside," in M. Foucult, and M. Blan-chot, *Foucault/Blanchot*, trans. J. Mehlman, and B. Massumi (Zone, New York), pp. 7–58.

Fraser, N. (1997) "Feminism, Foucault and Deleuze," *Theory, Culture & Society*, 14(2): 23–37.

Frisby, D. (1985) *Fragments of Modernity: Theories of Modernity in the Work of Simmel, Kracauer and Benjamin* (Polity, Cambridge).

Fuller, J. (1992) "Distillations – a premonitory reading of Deleuze," *Pli: Warwick Journal of Philosophy*, 4(1 & 2): 159–73.

Fyfe, N. (1996) "Review of: *Consuming Places*, John Urry," *Transactions of the Institute of British Geographers*, 21(2): 437–8.

Game, A. (1995) "Time, space, memory, with reference to Bachelard," in *Global Modernities*, eds M. Featherstone, S. Lash, and R. Robertson (Sage, London) pp. 192–208.

Gasché, R. (1986) *The Tain of the Mirror* (Blackwell, Oxford).

Gasché, R. (1994) *Inventions of Difference: On Jacques Derrida* (Harvard University Press, Cambridge, MA).

Genet, J. (1989) *Prisoner of Love*, trans. B. Bray (Pan, London).

Giddens, A. (1984) *The Constitution of Society: Outline of the Theory of Structuration* (Polity, Cambridge).

Giddens, A. (1990) *The Consequences of Modernity* (Stanford University Press, Stanford, CA).

Godlewska, A., and Smith, N. (eds) (1994) *Geography and Empire* (Blackwell, Oxford).

Goodchild, P. (1996) *Deleuze and Guattari: An Introduction to the Politics of Desire* (Sage, London).

Goodchild, P. (1997) "Deleuzean ethics" *Theory, Culture & Society*, 14(2): 39–50.

Gottdiener, M. (1995) *Postmodern Semiotics: Material Culture and the Forms of Postmodern Life* (Blackwell, Oxford).

Gould, P. (1994a) "Sharing a tradition – geographies from the Enlightenment," *The Canadian Geographer*, 38(3): 194–202.

Gould, P. (1994b) "Reply," *The Canadian Geographer*, 38(3): 209–14.

Gregory, D. (1987) "Postmodernism and the politics of social theory," *Environment and Planning D: Society and Space*, 5: 245–8.

Gregory, D. (1989a) "The crisis of modernity? Human geography and critical social theory," in *New Models in Geography: The Political-Economy Perspective*, eds R. Peet, and N. Thrift (Unwin Hyman, London), pp. 348–385.

Gregory, D. (1989b) "Areal differentiation and post-modern human geography," in *Horizons in Human Geography*, eds D. Gregory, and R. Walford (Macmillan, London), pp. 67–96.

Gregory, D. (1989c) "Presence and absences: time-space relations and structuration theory," in *Social Theory of the Modern Societies: Anthony Giddens and His Critics*, eds D. Held, and J. B. Thompson (Cambridge University Press, Cambridge) pp. 235–48.

Gregory, D. (1994a) *Geographical Imaginations* (Blackwell, Oxford).

Gregory, D. (1994b) "Visions of geography: an open letter to Peter Gould," *The Canadian Geographer*, 38(3): 206–9.

Gregory, D. (1997) "Lacan and geography: the production of spae revisited," in *Space and Social Theory: Interpreting Modernity and Postmodernity*, eds G. Benko, and U. Strohmayer (Blackwell, Oxford) ,pp. 203–31.

Gregory, D., and Urry J. (eds) (1985) *Social Relations and Spatial Structures* (Macmillan, London).

Gren, M. (1994) *Earth Writing: Exploring Representation and Social Geography In-Between Meaning/Matter*, unpublished PhD thesis (School of Economics and Commercial Law, University of Gothenburg).

Grosz, E. (1994a) *Volatile Bodies: Towards a Corporeal Feminism* (Indiana University Press, Bloomington).

Grosz, E. (1994b) "Refiguring lesbian desire," in *The Lesbian Postmodern*, ed. L. Doan (Columbia University Press, New York), pp. 67–84.

Grosz, E. (1995a) *Space, Time, and Perversion: Essays on the Politics of Bodies* (Routledge, London).

Grosz, E. (1995b) "Women, *chora*, dwelling," in *Postmodern Cities and Spaces*, eds S. Watson, and K. Gibson (Blackwell, Oxford), pp. 47–58.

Guattari, F. (1992) *Chaosmosis: An Ethico-Aesthetic Paradigm*, trans. P. Bains, and J. Pefanis (Power Publications, Sydney).

Guattari, F. (1996) *The Guattari Reader*, ed. G. Genesko (Blackwell, London).

Haar, M. (1992) "The play of Nietzsche in Derrida," in *Derrida: A Critical Reader*, ed. D. Wood (Blackwell, Oxford), pp. 52–71.

Habermas, J. (1984) *The Theory of Communicative Action: Volume 1: Reason and Rationalization of Society*, trans. T. McCarthy (Beacon, Boston).

Habermas, J. (1987a) *The Theory of Communicative Action: Volume 2: Lifeworld and System: A Critique of Functionalist Reason*, trans. T. McCarthy (Beacon, Boston).

Habermas, J. (1987b) *The Philosophical Discourse of Modernity*, trans. F. Lawrence (Polity, Cambridge).

Haggett, P. (1979) *Geography: A Modern Synthesis*, third edition (Harper & Row, New York).

Hallward, P. (1997) "Gilles Deleuze and the redemption from interest," *Radical Philosophy*, 81: 6–21.

Halton, E. (1992) "The reality of dreaming," *Theory, Culture & Society*, 9(4): 119–39.

Hamnett, C. (1997) "The sleep of reason?" *Environment and Planning D: Society and Space*, 15(2): 127–8.

Hannah, M., and Strohmayer, U. (1991) "Ornamentalism: geography and the labour of language in structuration theory," *Environment and Planning D: Society and Space*, 9: 309–27.

Hannah, M., and Strohmayer, U. (1992) "Postmodernism (s)trained," *Annals of the Association of American Geographers*, 82: 308–10.

Hannah, M., and Strohmayer, U. (1993) "The obsolescence of labor: reference and finitude in Barnett and Sayer," *Antipode*, 25(4): 359–64.

Haraway, D. (1991) *Simians, Cyborgs and Women: The Reinvention of Nature* (Routledge, London).

Hardt, M. (1993) *Gilles Deleuze: An Apprenticeship in Philosophy* (University of Minnesota Press, Minneapolis).

Harvey, D. (1973) *Social Justice and the City* (Edward Arnold, London).

Harvey, D. (1982) *The Limits to Capital* (Blackwell, Oxford).

Harvey, D. (1985a) *Consciousness and the Urban Experience: Studies in the History and Theory of Capitalist Urbanization. Volume 1* (Blackwell, Oxford).

Harvey, D. (1985b) *The Urbanization of Capital: Studies in the History and Theory of Capitalist Urbanization. Volume 2* (Blackwell, Oxford).

Harvey, D. (1987) "Three myths in search of a reality in urban studies," *Environment and Planning D: Society and Space*, 5: 367–376.

Harvey, D. (1989) *The Condition of Postmodernity* (Blackwell, Oxford).

Harvey, D. (1995) "A geographer's guide to dialectical thinking," in *Diffusing Geography: Essays for Peter Haggett*, eds A. D. Cliff, P. R. Gould, A. G. Hoare, and N. J. Thrift (Blackwell, Oxford), pp. 3–21.

Harvey, D. (1996) *Justice, Nature and the Geography of Difference* (Blackwell, Oxford).

Harvey, D., et al. (1987) "Reconsidering social theory: a debate," *Environment and Planning D: Society and Space*, 5: 367–433.

Heidegger, M. (1982) *The Basic Problems of Phenomenology* (University of Indiana Press, Bloomington).

Hollier, D. (1989) *Against Architecture: The Writings of George Bataille* (MIT Press, Cambridge, MA).

Horkheimer, M., and Adorno T. W. (1993) *Dialectic of Enlightenment*, trans. J. Cumming (Continuum, New York).

Hulme, P., and Jordanova L. (eds) (1990) *The Enlightenment and its Shadows* (Routledge, London).

Imprimatur (1996) "Derrida applied," *Imprimatur*, 1(2 & 3), special issue.

Irigaray, L. (1984) *Ethique de la Différence Sexuelle* (Minuit, Paris).

Irigaray, L. (1985) *This Sex Which is Not One*, trans. C. Porter with R. Burke (Cornell University Press, Ithaca, NY).

Irigaray, L. (1991) *The Irigaray Reader*, ed. M. Whitford (Blackwell, Oxford).

Irigaray, L. (1993) *Je, Tous, Nous: Toward a Culture of Difference*, trans. A. Martin (Routledge, London).

Jameson, F. (1984) "Postmodernism, or, the cultural logic of late capitalism," *New Left Review*, 146: 53–92.

Jameson, F. (1995) "Marx's purloined letter," *New Left Review*, 209: 75–109.

Jardine, A. (1984) "Woman in limbo: Deleuze and his (br)others," *SubStance*, 44/45: 46–60.

Jardine, A. (1985) *Gynesis: Configurations of Woman and Modernity* (Cornell University Press, Ithaca).

Jay, M. (1993) *Downcast Eyes: The Denigration of Vision in in 20th-century French Thought* (Routledge, London).

Jencks, C. (1986) *What is Postmodernism?* (Academy Editions, London).

Johnston, R. J. (1991) *Geography and Geographers: Anglo-American Human Geography since 1945*, 4th edn (Arnold, London).

Jung, H. Y. (1996) "Phenomenology and body politics," *Body & Society*, 2(2): 1–22.

Kafka, F. (1992) "The trial," in *Kafka: The Complete Novels* (Minerva, London), pp. 11–128.

Kamuf, P. (1991) "Introduction: reading between the blinds," in *A Derrida Reader: Between the Blinds*, ed. P. Kamuf (Harvester Wheatsheaf, Hemel Hempstead), pp. xiii–xlii.

Kearney, R. (1988) *The Wake of Imagination: Ideas of Creativity in Western Culture* (Hutchinson, London).

Kobayashi, A., and Mackenzie, S. (eds) (1989) *Remaking Human Geography* (Unwin Hyman, London).

Krell, D. F. (1997) *Archeticture: Ecstasies of Space, Time, and the Human Body* (State University of New York Press, Albany).

Kroker, A., and Cook, D. (1988) *The Postmodern Scene: Excremental Culture and Hyper-aesthetics* (Macmillan, London).

Kundera, M. (1996) *The Book of Laughter and Forgetting*, trans. A. Asher (Faber and Faber, London).

Kuspit, D. (1990) "The contradictory character of postmodernism," in *Postmodernism–Philosophy and the Arts*, ed. H. J. Silverman (Routledge, Chapman & Hall, Andover) pp. 53–68.

Lacan, J. (1977) *Écrits: A Selection*, trans. A. Sheridan (Tavistock, London).

Laclau, E., and Mouffe, C. (1987) "Post-Marxism without apologies" *New Left Review*, 166: 79–106.

Lacoue-Labarthe, P. (1989) *Typography: Mimesis, Philosophy, Politics*, ed. C. Fynsk (Harvard University Press, Cambridge).

Laplanche, J. (1992) *La Révolution Copernicienne Inachevée* (Aubier, Paris).

Laplanche, J. (1996) "Psychoanalysis as anti-hermeneutics," *Radical Philosophy*, 79: 7–12.

Latour, B. (1992) "Where are the missing masses? The sociology of a few mundane artifacts," in *Shaping Technology/Building Society: Studies in Sociotechnical Change*, eds W. E. Bijker, and J. Law (MIT Press, London) pp. 225–258.

Latour, B. (1993) *We Have Never Been Modern* (Harvard University Press, Cambridge, MA).

Latour, B., and Woolgar, S. (1986) *Laboratory Life: The Social Construction of Scientific Facts* (Princeton University Press, Princeton).

Lawson, H. (1985) *Reflexivity: The Postmodern Predicament* (Hutchinson, London).

Leavey, J. P. (1986) *Glassary* (University of Nebraska Press, Lincoln).

Lecercle, J.-J. (1985) *Philosophy through the Looking-Glass: Language, Nonsense, Desire* (Open Court, La Salle).

Lechte, J. (1994) *Fifty Key Contemporary Thinkers: From Structuralism to Postmodernity* (Routledge, London).

Lechte, J. (1995) "(Not) belonging in postmodern space," in *Postmodern Cities and Spaces*, eds S. Watson, and K. Gibson (Blackwell, Oxford) pp. 99–111.

Lefebvre, H. (1991) *The Production of Space*, trans. D. Nicholson-Smith (Blackwell, Oxford).

Lefebvre, H. (1996) *Writings on Cities*, trans and eds E. Kofman, and E. Lebas (Blackwell, Oxford).

Leslie, E. (1996) "Wrapping the Reichstag: re-visioning German history," *Radical Philosophy*, 77: 6–16.

Levin, C. (1996) *Jean Baudrillard: A Study in Cultural Metaphysics* (Prentice Hall, Hemel Hempstead).

Levin, D. (ed.) (1993) *Modernity and the Hegemony of Vision* (University of California Press, Berkeley).

Levinas, E. (1981) *Otherwise than Being or Beyond Essence* (Martinus Nijhoff, The Hague).

Ley, D., and Samuels, M. (eds) (1978) *Humanistic Geography: Prospects and Problems* (Croom Helm, London).

Leyshon, A. (1995) "Annihilating space?: the speed-up of communications," in *A Shrinking World? Global Unevenness and Inequality*, eds J. Allen, and C. Hamnett (Oxford University Press, Oxford), pp. 11–54.

Lingis, A. (1994) *Foreign Bodies* (Routledge, London).

Livingstone, D. (1992a) *The Geographical Tradition: Episodes in a Contested Enterprise* (Blackwell, Oxford).

Livingstone, D. (1992b) "A brief history of geography," in *The Student's Companion to Geography*, eds A. Rogers, H. Viles, and A. Goudie (Blackwell, Oxford), pp. 27–35.

Livingstone, D. (1994) "Science and religion: foreword to the historical geography of an encounter," *Journal of Historical Geography*, 20: 367–83.

Livingstone, D. (1995) "Geographical traditions," *Transactions of the Institute of British Geographers*, 20(4): 420–2.

Llewelyn, J. (1986) *Derrida on the Threshold of Sense* (Macmillan, London).

Löwy, M. (1996) "Walter Benjamin and surrealism," *Radical Philosophy*, 80: 17–23.

Löwy, M. (1998) "Consumed by night's fire: the dark romanticism of Guy Debord," *Radical Philosophy*, 87: 31–4.

Lucie-Smith, E. (1996) *Visual Arts in the Twentieth Century* (Laurence King, London).

Lyotard, J.-F. (1971) *Discours, Figure* (Klincksieck, Paris).

Lyotard, J.-F. (1977) *Rudiments Païens: Genre Dissertatif* (Union Générale d'Editions, Paris).

Lyotard, J.-F. (1984a) *The Postmodern Condition: A Report on Knowledge*, trans. G. Bennington, and B. Massumi (University of Manchester, Manchester).

Lyotard, J.-F. (1984b) *Driftworks*, trans. R. McKeon et al. (Semiotext(e), New York).

Lyotard, J.-F. (1986/7) "Rules and paradoxes and svelte appendix," *Cultural Critique*, 5: 209–19.

Lyotard, J.-F. (1987) *Que Peindre? Adami Arakawa Buren* (Editions de la Différence, Paris).

Lyotard, J.-F. (1988a) *The Differend: Phrases in Dispute*, trans. G. Van Den Abbeele (University of Manchester, Manchester).

Lyotard, J.-F. (1988b) *Peregrinations: Law, Form, Event* (University of Columbia Press, New York).

Lyotard, J.-F. (1989a) *The Lyotard Reader*, ed. A. Benjamin (Blackwell, Oxford).

Lyotard, J.-F. (1989b) "Defining the postmodern," in *Postmodernism: ICA Documents*, 4 & 5 ed. L. Appignanesi (Free Association, London), pp. 7–10.

Lyotard, J.-F. (1990a) *Heidegger and "the jews"*, trans. A. Michel, and M. Roberts (University of Minnesota, Minneapolis).

Lyotard, J.-F. (1990b) *Duchamp's TRANS/formers*, trans. I. McLeod (Lapis, Venice).

Lyotard, J.-F. (1990c) *Pacific Wall*, trans. B. Boone (Lapis, Venice).

Lyotard, J.-F. (1992) *The Postmodern Explained to Children: Correspondence 1982–1985*, ed. J. Pefanis, and M. Thomas (Turnaround, London).

Lyotard, J.-F. (1993) *Libidinal Economy*, trans. I. H. Grant (Indiana University Press, Bloomington).

Lyotard, J.-F. (1997) *Postmodern Fables*, trans. G. Van Den Abbeele (University of Minnesota Press, Minneapolis).

Lyotard, J.-F., and Thébaud, J.-L. (1985) *Just Gaming*, trans. W. Godzich (University of Minnesota Press, Minneapolis).

McDonald, C. V. (1988) "Rereading deconstruction (today?)," in *Postmodernism and Continental Philosophy*, eds H. J. Silverman, and D. Welton (SUNY, Albany, NY) pp. 180–92.

Macherey, P. (1996) "The encounter with Spinoza," in *Deleuze: A Critical Reader*, ed. P. Patton (Blackwell, Oxford) pp. 139–61.

McHale, B. (1989) *Postmodernist Fiction* (Routledge, Chapman and Hall, Andover).

McLuhan, M. (1967) *The Medium is the Message* (Penguin, Harmondsworth).

McNay, L. (1992) *Foucault and Feminism: Power, Gender and the Self* (Polity, Cambridge).

Malabou, C. (1996) "Who's afraid of Hegelian wolves?" in *Deleuze: A Critical Reader*, ed. P. Patton (Blackwell, Oxford) pp. 114–38.

Malik, S. (1996) "Différantial technics" *Imprimatur*, 1(2 & 3): 200–3.

Marcus, G. E. (1992) "More (critically) reflexive than thou," *Environment and Planning D: Society and Space*, 10(5): 489–93.

Marden, P. (1992) "The deconstructionist tendencies of postmodern geographies: a compelling logic?" *Progress in Human Geography*, 16(1): 41–57.

Marks, J. (1995) "A new image of thought," *New Formations*, 25: 66–76.

Martin, J.-C. (1996) "The eye of the outside," in *Deleuze: A Critical Reader*, ed. P. Patton (Blackwell, Oxford), pp. 18–28.

Massey, D. (1978) "Regionalism: some current issues," *Capital and Class*, 6: 106–25.

Massey, D. (1984) *Spatial Divisions of Labour: Social Structures and the Geography of Production* (Methuen, London).

Massey, D. (1991) "A global sense of place," *Marxism Today* (June): 24–9.

Massey, D. (1992) "Politics and space/time," *New Left Review*, 196: 65–84.

Massey, D. (1993) "Power-geometry and a progressive sense of place," in *Mapping the Futures: Local Cultures, Global Change*, eds J. Bird, B. Curtis, T. Putnam, G. Robertson, and L. Tickner (Routledge, London), pp. 58–68.

Massey, D. (1995) "Reflections on debates over a decade," in *Spatial Divisions of Labour: Social Structure and the Geography of Production*, 2nd edn (Macmillan, London), pp. 296–354.

Massumi, B. (1988) "Translator's foreword: pleasures of philosophy," in G. Deleuze, F. Guattari *A Thousand Plateaus: Capitalism and Schizophrenia* (Athlone, London), pp. ix–xv.

Massumi, B. (1992a) *A User's Guide to Capitalism and Schizophrenia: Deviations from Deleuze and Guattari* (MIT Press, London).

Massumi, B. (1992b) "Everywhere you want to be: introduction to fear," *Pli: Warwick Journal of Philosophy*, 4(1 & 2): 175–215.

Massumi, B. (1996a) "Becoming-deleuzian," *Environment and Planning D: Society and Space*, 14(4): 395–406.

Massumi, B. (1996b) "The evolutionary alchemy of reason," http://www.telefonica.es/fat/emassumi.html.

Matless, D. (1990) "Nature, the modern and the mystic: tales from early twentieth century geography," *Transactions of the Institute of British Geographers*, 16: 272–86.

Matless, D. (1992) "A modern stream: water, landscape, modernism, and geography," *Environment and Planning D: Society and Space*, 10: 569–88.

Matless, D. (1995) "Effects of history," *Transactions of the Institute of British Geographers*, 20(4): 405–9.

May, T. (1993) "The system and its fractures: Gilles Deleuze on otherness," *Journal of the British Society for Phenomenology*, 24(1): 3–14.

Megill, A. (1985) *Prophets of Extremity: Nietzsche, Heidegger, Foucault, Derrida* (University of California, Berkeley).

Merquior, J. G. (1986) *From Prague to Paris: A Critique of Structuralist and Post-Structuralist Thought* (Verso, London).

Michaux, H. (1992) *Spaced, Displaced: Déplacements Dégagements* (Bloodaxe, Newcastle upon Tyne).

Mikkonen, K. (1996) "Theories of metamorphosis: from metatrope to textual revision," *Style*, 30(2): 309–340.

Miller, C. L. (1993) "The postidentitarian predicament in the footnotes of *A Thousand Plateaus*: nomadology, anthropology, and authority," *Diacritics*, 23(3): 6–35.

Millett, N. (1997) "The trick of singularity," *Theory, Culture & Society*, 14(2): 51–66.

Mohan, G. (1994) "Destruction of the con: geography and the commodification of knowledge," *Area*, 26(4): 387–90.

Morris, M. (1996) "Crazy talk is not enough," *Environment and Planning D: Society and Space*, 14(4): 384–94.

Moss, P. (1993) "Focus: feminism as method," *The Canadian Geographer*, 37(1): 48–9.

Mouffe, C. (1992) "Democratic politics today," in *Dimensions of Radical Democracy: Pluralism, Citizenship, and Community*, ed. C. Mouffe (Verso, London), pp. 1–15.

Mugerauer, R. (1994) *Interpretations on Behalf of Place: Environmental Displacements and Alternative Responses* (SUNY, New York).

Mugerauer, R. (1995) *Interpreting Environments: Tradition, Deconstruction, Hermeneutics* (University of Texas Press, Austin).

Nancy, J.-L. (1992) "Elliptical sense," in *Derrida: A Critical Reader*, ed. D. Wood (Blackwell, Oxford), pp. 36–51.

Nancy, J.-L. (1996) "The Deleuzian fold of thought," in *Deleuze: A Critical Reader*, ed. P. Patton (Blackwell, Oxford), pp. 107–13.

Natter, W., and Jones III, J. P. (1993) "Signposts towards a poststructuralist geography," in *Post-

modern Contnetions: Epochs, Plitics, Space eds J. P. Jones, W. Natter, and T. R. Schatzki (Guilford, New York), pp. 165–203.

Natter, W., and Jones III, J. P. (1997) "Identity, space, and other uncertainties," in *Space and Social Theory: Interpreting Modernity and Postmodernity*, eds G. Benko, and U. Strohmayer (Blackwell, Oxford), pp. 141–61.

Nietzsche, F. (1968) *The Will to Power*, trans. T. Kaufman (Vintage, New York).

Norris, C. (1987) *Jacques Derrida* (Fontana, London).

Nottingham, P. (1983) *Bobbin Lace Making* (Batsford, London).

Oates, C. (1989) "Metamorphosis and lycanthropy in Franche-Comté, 1521–1643," in *Fragments for a History of the Human Body. Part One*, eds M. Feher, with R. Naddaff, and N. Tazi (Zone, New York), pp. 305–63.

Ollman, B. (1993) *Dialectical Investigations* (Routledge, London).

Olsson, G. (1980) *Birds in Egg/Eggs in Bird* (Pion, London).

Olsson, G. (1984) "Toward a sermon of modernity," in *Recollections of a Revolution: Geography as Spatial Science*, eds M. Billinge, D. Gregory, and R. Martin (Macmillan, London), pp. 73–85.

Olsson, G. (1991) *Lines of Power/Limits of Language* (University of Minnesota Press, Minneapolis).

Olsson, G. (1993) "Chiasm of thought-and-action," *Environment and Planning D: Society and Space*, 11(3): 279–94.

Olsson, G. (1994) "Heretic cartography," *Ecumene*, 1(3): 215–34.

Openshaw, S. (1996) "Fuzzy logic as a new scientific paradigm for doing geography," *Environment and Planning A*, 28(5): 761–68.

Outhwaite, W. (1987) *New Philosophies of Social Science: Realism, Hermeneutics and Critical Theory* (Macmillan, London).

Papadakis, A., Cooke C., and Benjamin A. (eds) (1989) *Deconstruction: Omnibus Volume* (Academy Editions, London).

Peat, F. D. (1991) *Superstrings: and the Search for The Theory of Everything* (Scribners, London).

Peet, R. (1998) *Modern Geographical Thought* (Blackwell, Oxford).

Pefanis, J. (1991) *Heterology and the Postmodern: Bataille, Baudrillard, and Lyotard* (Duke University Press, Durham, NC).

Perez, R. (1990) *On An(archy) and Schizoanalysis* (Autonomedia, New York).

Peters, G. (1997) "The rhythm of alterity: Levinas and aesthetics," *Radical Philosophy*, 82: 9–16.

Philo, C. (1984) "Reflections on Gunnar Olsson's contribution to the discourse of contemporary human geography," *Environment and Planning D: Society and Space*, 2: 217–40.

Philo, C. (1992) "Foucault's geography," *Environment and Planning D: Society and Space*, 10: 137–61.

Philo, C. (1994) "Escaping Flatland: a book review essay inspired by Gunnar Olsson's Lines of Power/Limits of Language," *Environment and Planning D: Society and Space*, 12: 229–52.

Pile, S. (1994a) "Echo, desire, and the grounds of knowledge: a mytho-poetic assessment of Buttimer's *Geography and the Human Spirit*," *Environment and Planning D: Society and Space*, 12: 495–507.

Pile, S. (1994b) "Masculinism, the use of dualistic epistemologies and third spaces," *Antipode*, 26: 255–77.

Pile, S. (1996) *The Body and the City: Psychoanalysis, Space and Subjectivity* (Routledge, London).

Pile, S. (1997) "Space and the politics of sleep," *Environment and Planning D: Society and Space*, 15(2): 128–34.

Pile, S., and Rose, G. (1992) "All or nothing? Politics and critique in the modernism–postmodernism debate," *Environment and Planning D: Society and Space*, 10(2): 123–36.

Plotnitsky, A. (1994) *Complementarity: Anti-Epistemology after Bohr and Derrida* (Duke University Press, Durham, NC).

Plotnitsky, A. (1997) "But it is above all not true: Derrida, relativity, and the 'Science Wars,'" *Postmodern Culture*, 7(2). http://muse.jhu.edu/journals/postmodern_culture/.

Porter, R., and Teich, M. (eds) (1979) *The Enlightenment in National Context* (Cambridge University Press, Cambridge).

Pred, A. (1983) "Structuration and place: on the becoming of sense of place and structure of feeling," *Journal for the Theory of Social Behavior*, 13: 45–68.

Pred, A. (1984) "Place as historically contingent process: structuration and the time-geography of becoming places," *Annals of the Association of American Geographers*, 74: 279–297.

Pred, A. (1986) *Place, Practice and Structure: Social and Spatial Transformation in Southern Sweden, 1750–1850* (Cambridge University Press, Cambridge).

Probyn, E. (1994) "The ampersand returns," *Environment and Planning D: Society and Space*, 12: 509–12.

Probyn, E. (1996) *Outside Belongings* (Routledge, London).

Pynchon, T. (1975a) *V* (Picador, London).

Pynchon, T. (1975b) *Gravity's Rainbow* (Picador, London).

Readings, B. (1991) *Introducing Lyotard: Art and Politics* (Routledge, London).

Relph, E. (1976) *Place and Placelessness* (Pion, London).

Revill, G. (1993) "Reading *Rosehill*: community, identity and inner-city Derby," in *Place and the Politics of Identity*, eds M. Keith, and S. Pile (Routledge, London) pp. 117–40.

Rodowick, D. N. (1997) *Gilles Deleuze's Time Machine* (Duke University Press, London).

Rojek, C., and Urry, J. (eds) (1997) *Touring Cultures: Transformations of Travel and Theory* (Routledge, London).

Ropars-Wuilleumier, M.-C. (1994) "The cinema, reader of Gilles Deleuze," in *Gilles Deleuze and the Theatre of Philosophy*, eds C. V. Boundas, and D. Olkowski (Routledge, London), pp. 255–61.

Rorty, R. (1989) *Contingency, Irony, and Solidarity* (Cambridge University Press, Cambridge).

Rose, G. (1993a) *Feminism and Geography: The Limits of Geographical Knowledge* (Polity, Cambridge).

Rose, G. (1993b) "Some notes towards thinking about the spaces of the future," in *Mapping the Futures: Local Cultures, Global Change*, eds J. Bird, B. Curtis, T. Putnam, G. Robertson, and L. Tickner (Routledge, London), pp. 70–83.

Rose, G. (1994) "The cultural politics of place: local representation and oppositional discourses in two films," *Transactions of the Institute of British Geographers*, 19(1): 46–60.

Rose, G. (1995a) "Distance, surface, elsewhere: a feminist critique of the space of phallocentric self/knowledge," *Environment and Planning D: Society and Space*, 13: 761–81.

Rose, G. (1995b) "Tradition and paternity: same difference?" *Transactions of the Institute of British Geographers*, 20(4): 414–16.

Rose, G. (1995c) "Making space for the female subject of feminism: the spatial subversions of Holzer, Kruger and Sherman," in *Mapping the Subject: Geographies of Cultural Transformation*, eds S. Pile, and N. Thrift (Routledge, London) pp. 332–54.

Rose, G. (1997) "Situating knowledges: positionality, reflexivities and other tactics," *Progress in Human Geography*, 21(3): 305–20.

Rosen, S. (1987) *Hermeneutics as Politics* (Oxford University Press, Oxford).

Rotman, B. (1987) *Signifying Nothing: The Semiotics of Zero* (Macmillan, London).

Sack, R. D. (1997) *Homo Geographicus: A Framework for Action, Awareness, and Moral Concern* (Johns Hopkins University Press, Baltimore, MD).

Saussure, F. (1974) *Course in General Linguistics* (Fontana, London).

Sayer, A. (1981) "Abstraction: a realist interpretation," *Radical Philosophy*, 28: 6–15.

Sayer, A. (1985) "The difference that space makes," in *Social Relations and Spatial Structures*, eds D. Gregory, and J. Urry (Macmillan, London), pp. 49–66.

Sayer, A. (1991) "Behind the locality debate: deconstructing geography's dualisms," *Environment and planning A*, 23: 283–308.

Sayer, A. (1992) *Method in Social Science: A Realist Approach*, 2nd edn (Routledge, London).

Sayer, A. (1993) "Postmodernist thought in geography: a realist view," *Antipode*, 25(4): 320–44.

Schrift, A. D. (1990a) *Nietzsche and the Question of Interpretation: Between Hermeneutics and Deconstruction* (Routledge, London).

Schrift, A. D. (1990b) "The becoming-postmodern of philosophy," in *After the Future: Postmodern Times and Places*, ed. G. Shapiro (SUNY, Albany, NY), pp. 99–113.

Schroeder, M. (1991) *Fractals, Chaos, Power Lines: Minutes from an Infinite Paradise* (W. H. Freeman, New York).

Schwartz, H. (1992) "Torque: the new kinaesthetic of the twentieth century," in *Zone 6: Incorporations*, eds J. Crary, and S. Kwinter (Zone, New York), pp. 70–126.

Scott, J. S., and Simpson-Housley, P. (1988) "Relativizing the relativizers: on the postmodern challenge to human geography," *Transactions of the Institute of British Geographers*, 14: 231–36.

Seem, M. (1984) "Introduction," in G. Deleuze, and F. Guattari, *Anti-Oedipus: Capitalism and Schizophrenia*, trans. R. Hurley, M. Seem and H. R. Lane (Athlone, London), pp. xv–xxiv.

Sennett, R. (1994) *Flesh and Stone: The Body and the City in Western Civilization* (Faber & Faber, London).

Shamdasani, S., and Münchow, M. (eds) (1994) *Speculations After Freud: Psychoanalysis, Philosophy and Culture* (Routledge, London).

Shapin, S., and Schaffer, S. (1985) *Leviathan and the Air-Pump: Hobbes, Boyle, and the Exoperimental Life* (Princeton University Press, Princeton, NJ).

Shaviro, S. (1993) *The Cinematic Body* (University of Minnesota Press, Minneapolis).

Shepherdson, C. (1995) "History and the real: Foucault with Lacan," http://muse.jhu. edu/journals/postmodern_culture/.

Shotter, J. (1993) *Cultural Politics of Everyday Life* (Open University Press, Milton Keynes).

Sibley, D. (1988) "Survey 13: the purification of space," *Environment and Planning D: Society and Space*, 6: 409–21.

Sim, S. (1992) *Beyond Aesthetics: Confrontations with Poststructuralism and Postmodernism* (Harvester Wheatsheaf, Hemel Hempstead).

Sim, S. (1996) *Jean-François Lyotard* (Harvester Wheatsheaf, Hemel Hempstead).

Simms, K. (1996) "The time of deconstruction and the deconstruction of time" *Imprimatur*, 1(2 & 3): 194–199.

Smart, B. (1993) *Postmodernity* (Routledge, London).

Smith, D. W. (1997) "Introduction: 'a life of pure immanence': Deleuze's 'Critique et Clinique' project," in G. Deleuze, *Essays Critical and Clinical*, trans. D. W. Smith, and M. A. Greco (University of Minnesota Press, Minneapolis), pp. xi–Lvi.

Smith, N. (1992) "Geography, difference and the politics of scale," in *Postmodernism and the Social Sciences*, eds J. Doherty, E. Graham, and M. Malek (Macmillan, New York), pp. 57–79.

Smith, N. (1996) "Rethinking sleep," *Environment and Planning D: Society and Space*, 14: 505–6.

Smith, N. (1997) "Beyond sleep," *Environment and Planning D: Society and Space*, 15(2): 134–5.

Soja, E. W. (1980) "The socio-spatial dialectic," *Annals of the Association of American Geographers*, 70: 207–25.

Soja, E. W. (1989a) *Postmodern Geographies: The Reassertion of Space in Critical Social Theory* (Verso, London).

Soja, E. W. (1989b) "Modern geography, Western Marxism, and the restructuring of critical social theory," in *New Models in Geography: The Political-Economy Perspective*, eds R. Peet, and N. Thrift (Unwin Hyman, London), pp. 318–47.

Soja, E. W. (1993) "Postmodern geographies and the critique of historicism," in *Postmodern Contentions: Epochs, Politics, Space*, eds J. P. Jones, W. Natter, and T. R. Schatzki (Guilford, New York), pp. 113–136.

Soja, E. W. (1996) *Thirdspace: Journeys to Los Angeles and Other Real-and-Imagined Places* (Blackwell, Oxford).

Spivak, G. C. (1988) "Can the subaltern speak?" in *Marxism and the Question of Interpretation*, eds C. Nelson, and L. Grossberg (Macmillan, London), pp. 271–313.

Spivak, G. C. (1989) "A response to 'The difference within: feminism with critical theory,'" in *The Difference Within: Feminism and Critical Theory*, eds E. Meese, and A. Parker (John Benjamins, Amsterdam), pp. 207–20.

Stoddart, D. R. (1981) "The paradigm concept and the history of geography," in *Geography, Ideology and Social Concern*, ed. D. R. Stoddart (Blackwell, Oxford), pp. 70–80.

Stoddart, D. R. (1986) *On Geography: and its History* (Blackwell, Oxford).

Strohmayer, U. (1997a) "Be*longing*: spaces of meandering desire," in *Space and Social Theory: Interpreting Modernity and Postmodernity*, eds G. Benko, and U. Strohmayer (Blackwell, Oxford), pp. 162–85.

Strohmayer, U. (1997b) "Forget the delivery, or, what *post*, are we talking about," in *Space and Social Theory: Interpreting Modernity and Postmodernity*, eds G. Benko, and U. Strohmayer (Blackwell, Oxford), pp. 383–92.

Strohmayer, U. (1998) "The event of space: geographical allusions in the phenomenological tradition," *Environment and Planning D: Society and Space*, 16(1): 105–21.

Strohmayer, U., and Hannah, M. (1992) "Domesticating postmodernism," *Antipode*, 24(1): 29–55.

Sweeney-Turner, S. (1996) "Intervals and closures: deconstruction, music theory, and the swerve from dialectics," *Imprimatur*, 1(2& 3): 226–33.

Tallis, R. (1988) *Not Saussure: A Critique of Post-Saussurean Literary Theory* (Macmillan, London).

Taylor, P. J. (1994) "The state as container: territoriality in the modern world-system," *Progress in Human Geography*, 18(2): 151–62.

Taylor, P. J. (1995) "Beyond containers: internationality, interstateness, interterritoriality," *Progress in Human Geography*, 19(1): 1–15.

Taylor, P. J. (forthcoming) "Places, spaces and Macy's: place-space tension in the political geography of modernities," *Progress in Human Geography*.

The Fall (1983) *Perverted By Language* (Rough Trade Records, London).

Thrift, N. J. (1983) "On the determination of social action in space and time," *Environment and Planning D: Society and Space*, 1: 23–57.

Thrift, N. J. (1990) "For a new regional geography 1," *Progress in Human Geography*, 14(2): 272–79.

Thrift, N. J. (1991) "For a new regional geography 2," *Progress in Human Geography*, 15(4): 456–65.

Thrift, N. J. (1993) "For a new regional geography 3," *Progress in Human Geography*, 17(1): 92–100.

Thrift, N. J. (1994) "Inhuman geographies: landscapes of speed, light and power," in P. Cloke,

M. Doel, D. Matless, M. Phillips, and N. Thrift *Writing the Rural: Five Cultural Geographies* (Paul Chapman, London), pp. 191–248.

Thrift, N. (1995) "A hyperactive world," in *Geographies of Global Change*, eds R. J. Johnston, P. J. Taylor, and M. J. Watts (Blackwell, Oxford), pp. 18–35.

Thrift, N. (1996a) "New urban eras and old technological fears: reconfiguring the goodwill of electronic things," *Urban Studies*, 33: 1463–93.

Thrift, N. (1996b) *Spatial Formations* (Sage, London).

Thrift, N. (1997) "The rise of soft capitalism," in *Globalising Worlds*, eds A. Herod, S. Roberts, and G. Toal (Routledge, London). pp. 25–71.

Thwaites, T. (1995) "Facing pages: on response, a response to Steven Helmling" *Postmodern Culture*, 6(1), http://muse.jhu.edu/journals/postmodern_culture/.

Tschumi, B. (1994) *Architecture and Disjunction* (MIT Press, London).

Tuan, Y-F. (1977) *Space and Place: The Perspective of Experience* (Minnesota University Press, Minneapolis).

Urry, J. (1985) "Social relations, space and time," in *Social Relations and Spatial Structures*, eds D. Gregory, and J. Urry (Macmillan, London), pp. 20–48.

Urry, J. (1995) *Consuming Places* (Routledge, London).

van Reijen, W. (1992) "Labyrinth and ruin: the return of the Baroque in postmodernity," *Theory, Culture & Society*, 9(4): 1–26.

Virilio, P. (1994) *The Vision Machine* (Indiana University Press, Bloomington).

Wark, M. (1994) *Virtual Geography: Living with Global Media Events* (Indiana University Press, Indianapolis).

Weber, S. (1985) "Afterword: literature – just making it," in J.-F. Lyotard, and J.-L. Thébaud, *Just Gaming*, trans. W. Godzich (University of Minnesota Press, Minneapolis), pp. 101–20.

Welchman, A. (1992) "On the matter of chaos," in *Pli: Warwick Journal of Philosophy*, 4(1 & 2): 137–57.

Whitford, M. (1991) "Introduction to section I," in *The Irigaray Reader*, ed. M. Whitford (Blackwell, Oxford) pp. 23–9.

Wigley, M. (1993) *The Architecture of Deconstruction: Derrida's Haunt* (MIT Press, London).

Wigley, M. (1994) "The domestication of the house: deconstruction after architecture," in *Deconstruction and the Visual Arts: Art, Media, Architecture*, eds P. Brunette, and D. Wills (Cambridge University Press, Cambridge), pp. 203–27.

Wood, D. (1988) "Nietzsche's transvaluation of time," in *Exceedingly Nietzsche: Aspects of Contemporary Nietzsche-Interpretation*, eds D. F. Krell, and D. Wood (Routledge, London), pp. 31–42.

Wood, D. (1990) *Philosophy at the Limit* (Unwin Hyman, London).

Woods, L. (1993) *War and Architecture/Rat I Arhitektura – Pamphlet Architecture 15* (Princeton Architectural Press, New York).

Wylie, J. (1996) "Wilderness and the paradisical: Shakespeare's *Tempest*, and the vision of Arcadia," copy available from the author, Department of Geography, University of Bristol, BS8 1SS, UK.

Yeung, W. C. H. (1997) "Critical realism and realist research in human geography: a method or a philosophy in search of a method?" *Progress in Human Geography*, 21(1): 51–74.

Žižek, S. (1991) "Why should a dialectician learn to count to four?" *Radical Philosophy*, 58: 3–9.

Žižek, S. (ed.) (1992) *Everything You Always Wanted to Know About Lacan: But Were Afraid to Ask Hitchcock* (Verso, London).

Name index

Subject index